UNENDING STRUGGLE
The Long Road
to an
Equal Education
in St. Louis

By Judge Gerald W. Heaney and Dr. Susan Uchitelle

REEDY PRESS
St. Louis, Missouri

Distributed by University of Nebraska Press

Reedy Press
PO Box 5131, St. Louis, MO 63139, USA

This book is printed on acid-free paper. ∞

Library of Congress Cataloging-in-Publication Data: On File

ISBN: 0-9753180-1-2

For all information on all Reedy Press publications
visit our Web site at http://www.reedypress.com.

Distributed by University of Nebraska Press
Designed by Nick Hoeing

Printed in Canada
04 05 06 07 08 9 8 7 6 5 4 3 2 1

Cover image: Students participate in a mathematics game at Crestwood Elementary School in the Lindbergh School District, February 1988. Photo courtesy the *St. Louis Post-Dispatch*.

Contents

We dedicate *Unending Struggle* to Minnie Liddell, who recently passed away; her late son Craton; and to the parents who worked with them to bring an end to the 160 years of discrimination against black students in St. Louis. It is further dedicated to the thousands of young black students who rode early morning buses so they could attend integrated, but not always hospitable, county schools.

We must strive to ensure that we do not lose the gains that have been made in providing a quality education to the students of the St. Louis public schools since 1983.

Foreword

The St. Louis desegregation struggle lasted for decades and produced some of the most important experiments in the nation in dealing with the problems of segregated and obviously unequal education in old cities, particularly in exploring the possibilities of very large-scale, voluntary, mutually beneficial transfer programs across city-suburban boundary lines.

What happened in St. Louis was, of course, conditioned by all the inherited and deeply institutionalized inequality so characteristic of our urban communities. St. Louis had the special problems of cities in very rapid decline—it had been a national leader in losing population and jobs for decades. Had it been a period where there was serious national attention to civil rights and urban policy, there might have been more attention to the surprisingly positive possibilities of racial desegregation and peacefully expanding access to stronger suburban schools for black students that are evident in the St. Louis story. This book makes a very valuable contribution by seriously reviewing what happened in metropolitan St. Louis, why it happened, and what effect it had over a generation.

St. Louis achieved peaceful desegregation under very difficult conditions with a plan designed by local educators, not a judge, and recognized as fulfilling the commands of the Constitution. The plan produced sudden educational change in the city and a flood of new resources for the city schools, upgraded the school district's rating in the state, and reversed a long process of racial transition in the city as the proportion of white enrollment stabilized for a generation.

More important, the plan showed a way that there could be a politically acceptable major increase in minority access to white suburban schools that gained widespread support among many educational leaders, generated a large demand for access to suburban schools among black families, and produced a significant transfer of suburban white students to the magnet schools created in the city under the plan—

schools which broke the widely held stereotypes about educational failure in the city.

The St. Louis story offers no simple answers, and its hopeful findings are severely shadowed by the resegregation decisions of the U.S. Supreme Court in the 1990s, which ultimately forced the phasing out of the plan that produced many of the gains achieved over a quarter-century. Nonetheless it represents an amazing story of transformed opportunity for many thousands of city and suburban kids in a large metropolitan community not known for positive leadership on race relations. If this could be done in St. Louis it could surely be done in many communities if the courts and local school officials provided the kind of leadership seen in St. Louis during this period.

When St. Louis was ordered to desegregate in 1980, the civil rights era had been over for more than a decade, the Executive branch enforcement apparatus for school desegregation had been pretty well dismantled by the Nixon Administration and Congress. The 1980s brought the election of the most conservative president in more than a half-century, a consistent opponent of federal civil rights enforcement. Under the Reagan Administration the officials appointed to run the major civil rights agencies would be strong opponents of school desegregation, and one of the administration's basic goals was to use the judicial appointment process to select federal judges who would favor rolling back civil rights law. President Reagan's 1986 appointment of William Rehnquist, a consistent opponent of school desegregation as Chief Justice was one step in this process. The effort by the Justice Department to persuade federal courts that desegregation should be limited and temporary had little success during Reagan's presidency but forshadowed what a changed Supreme Court would do a few years later. St. Louis was one of the last of the major urban desegregation orders and began during a period of clear national retreat on the major civil rights gains of the 1960s. So, desegregating St. Louis was a very hard problem in very difficult circumstances with very little external support or the courts.

The problem was compounded in Missouri by the role of then State Attorney General John Ashcroft (later to be governor, senator, and U.S. attorney general). Ashcroft was a fierce opponent of the St. Louis and the later Kansas City desegregation orders, seriously impeding implementation, politicizing the issues and fanning resistance, and repeatedly appealing issues to the Supreme Court, consistently failing for fifteen years until a changed Supreme Court limited desegregation in Kansas City in 1995.

One of the basic realities of public policy is that the truly important stories are usually told by outside observers who often try to impose theories of their own and have never been directly involved in the exercise of power or in the implementation of a major social change. Their ideas are often formed by their academic discipline, and they are often striving to make a contribution or challenge an idea in the discipline, not primarily to get the story right, though they certainly try to do this too. Having been involved both as a scholar and an actor in some important events, I know that what you can learn from the outside is truly important if the work is done carefully with sufficient confirmation, but there are things that you simply do not know and cannot fully understand about what actually happened without inside knowledge or the kind of sources rarely available to scholars. Since reality is a complex flow and the major actors often have many things going on at the same time and have little incentive, and sometimes little ability, to describe things as they actually occurred. One of the problems of truly complex policy issues is that the largest ones have a very long time span, sometimes decades in length, but researchers usually have a finite time to do their work and often tend to describe a short part of a long stream of policy development as if it is the whole thing.

The problem is particularly serious with the uniquely American reality of class action civil rights lawsuits under which a court that finds a history of illegal discrimination possesses vast power to impose major institutional changes in basic social and political institutions. The decision of the Supreme Court fifty years ago in *Brown v. Board of Education* began a process in which the federal courts gained the possibility and the responsibility to repair, as much as possible, the damage to black and Latino students and communities from generations of overt segregation and inequality. The reality of these cases is that they often involve not one decision (the typical framework for both legal and social science analysis) but a series of decisions and actions that stretch over decades. In a big civil rights case there is often fierce legal argument about the existence and extent of legal responsibility for the present problem, which is the necessary condition for gaining a civil rights remedy under the U.S. Constitution. That often takes years of vastly complex and costly litigation.

Once civil rights lawyers win a case, however, there is an even more complex stage of legal struggle about deciding what should be done, followed by a long and multidimensional process of trying to successfully implement a remedy. How are lawyers fighting for and against a civil rights remedy in a court and a judge, who often has little experience or interest in these issues, going to figure out what are the best policies and plans to change a history of inequality? A central problem of civil rights policy is that those ordered to implement the change are almost always the same organization that were proved to have violated rights for many years. Are they able and willing to change? Do they know how to? Should outsiders be appointed to do the work? How can the courts be sure that the orders are ever implemented and the victims of discrimination receive a real remedy?

The reason I was pleased to write a foreword to this book is that it was written by two authors with intimate knowledge of the entire history of this important case, Judge Gerald Heaney—one of the nation's most perceptive appellate judges on civil rights issues—and Susan Uchitelle, who, for a generation, created and directed the nation's largest city-suburban student exchange program in metropolitan St. Louis. Both not only have deep knowledge of the case, but they also contributed directly and personally to its resolution. It is hard to imagine a better team to describe a major civil rights case than a powerful, experienced, and eloquent federal judge and the administrator who made a major part of the St. Louis remedy viable and successful. I know of nothing like this in the literature on school desegregation. I believe readers will be deeply grateful for their work.

My own direct involvement in the St. Louis case in deep ways at some important junctions makes me particularly appreciative of this effort. Twenty-five years ago I testified as a witness for the Justice Department in the case. Missouri was one of the seventeen states which had state-mandated segregation of its schools when the Supreme Court handed down its 1954 decision in *Brown v. Board of Education*. Since St. Louis had a large black population for a long time and a high level of segregation, blacks were highly concentrated in the central city, and the school district was overwhelmingly black by the time the desegregation case went to trial. The federal courts faced a very difficult challenge in cities like St. Louis in the 1970s. There was no question that the city was guilty of intentional segregation historically since segregation had been required by state law. Under the Supreme Court's desegregation decisions of the late 1960s and early 1970s, the courts were obliged to promptly implement a remedy that would produce the highest possible level of integration, even if mandatory reassignment of students and teachers were required. But, with only one-fourth white students and a white enrollment that had been declining for decades and with many affordable nearby almost all-white suburbs, the degree of substantial and lasting desegregation that could be achieved within the city, was very doubtful.

The Supreme Court had blocked the way to the other logical possibility—inclusion of the suburbs—in its 1974 decision, *Milliken v. Bradley*, on metropolitan Detroit, which gave primary value to the independence of suburban school districts and limited desegregation orders to single districts unless the complicity of the suburbs in the segregation of the central city could be proved. So in St. Louis the courts confronted the need to take dramatic and rapid action in a situation where the remedy might actually compound the problem by creating a city where all the schools would have large black majorities and the decline in white enrollment would accelerate. In my testimony I proposed that—rather than initially reassign the students across the city so that all the schools would be three-fourths black and overwhelmingly poor—the plan for the central city be a partial plan designed to create as many 50-50 schools as possible, not only by using magnets as educational incentives for parents to transfer their children, but also by concentrating on trying to develop exchanges with the suburbs using the resources of the state government—the same government that had imposed mandatory segregation for generations. This plan was authorized by the Court of Appeals and accepted by the St. Louis School Board, which developed and submitted a new plan for the entire school district in less than two months' time, and it was promptly accepted by the courts. During this period I served as the court's expert. In my report I recommended that the state pay for the plan, since state law had mandated segregation and the state had done nothing to correct the problem. The federal courts quickly approved the city's desegregation plan, including voluntary transfers for suburban students to city magnets, which was implemented without any significant incidents just three months later. The solution was one of the most peaceful and educationally creative of any big largely minority city.

The magnet schools were successful during the next two decades and showed strong educational results. After an initial loss of white students during the first year of the plan, the previous decline in percentage of whites in the city schools actually stopped. The city also received state funds to meet the requirements of a triple A rating in the state system and special funding was made available to the schools, which could not be integrated under this system. Many surplus schools that had deteriorated and were no longer needed were closed, and a new grade structure better fitting the city's curriculum was implemented, all in a very short period of time. The federal courts praised the city school leaders and found the state government to be the primary constitutional violator, responsible for funding the solution. Author Gerald Heaney served on the Court of Appeals, which set the framework for this remedy.

As soon as this stage of the process was completed, the city school leaders began to develop an approach to a metropolitan solution to integrate the students who could not be integrated within the city. The school board sued all of the suburban districts asking for a metropolitan merger and full desegregation. Preparation for the lawsuit produced massive evidence of discrimination by suburban districts and communities. During that period I filed a report with the court recommending a full merger and desegregation of city and county schools as the remedy if the suburbs were found guilty and the court indicated that that would happen if the claims were proven. Just before the case was to go to trial the suburbs agreed to a negotiated settlement under which each suburb agreed to accept substantial numbers of transfer students from St. Louis schools and to permit their students who wished to transfer into St. Louis magnet schools.

When the framework for transfer efforts was first being put into place, I filed a report with the federal court recommending that one of the authors of this book, Susan Uchitelle, be appointed to head what became the Voluntary Interdistrict Coordinating Committee, the institution that eventually coordinated the annual enrollment of more than fourteen thousand students across district boundary lines— the largest interdistrict transfer program in U.S. history. I took the unusual step of recommending a specific appointment because my experience in the St. Louis area and with state educational officials led me to conclude that she was the only person who had the skills and the respect of all the parties to make this complex transfer arrangement work. I was very pleased when she agreed to do it in spite of a threat from Missouri's attorney general, John Ashcroft, that she would never be able to work for Missouri state government if she accepted the appointment. Her decision was crucial to the long-term success of a program that greatly improved educational opportunities for many thousands of St. Louis students for many years.

My involvement with the case was very intense but limited in time. Heaney and Uchitelle were in key positions for many years.

The St. Louis story is not the story of an ideal plan for an unblemished success. It is the story of a variety of leaders caring enough and having enough talent and dedication to make some very good things happen for a quarter-century by choosing and implementing the best available remedies among imperfect policies. Facing these constraints required leadership to select and implement the best available policies. Judged by these standards, St. Louis came out far better than other older heavily black and poor central cities facing possible desegregation orders—cities like Cleveland, Chicago, Atlanta, Detroit, and many others. In St. Louis, educators actually played a central role in designing and implementing solutions that offered both tangible benefits of added choice and a level of integration widely acceptable to both white and minority families. Unlike those other cities, there was substantial access to suburban white schools, enough to offer very different opportunities and experiences to about a fourth of the city's black students, something not equaled anywhere else. When the federal courts were considering how to end desegregation plans under the Supreme Court's three decisions in the 1990s, which authored termination of desegregation orders even if the result would be a great increase in racial separation, St. Louis's plan—unlike the above mentioned cities' plans—developed a substantial constituency in both the city and the suburbs and had defenders who pointed to the obvious educational gains connected with the plan. In the end this was not enough to block the phasing out of the plan, but it was sufficient to guarantee that thousands more students would benefit from it before it was ended.

The art of doing good public policy on very difficult issues within serious policy limits is an honorable and difficult art. It is only fair to judge what has been done in light of what was possible. By this standard the St. Louis plan was a great success and we must learn the lessons it holds. We could not have better guides on this journey than Heaney and Uchitelle.

Gary Orfield
Harvard University
July 2004

Acknowledgments

Our involvement in the St. Louis public school case over a period of eighteen years convinced us that we should, after having recused ourselves from further participation in the case, write a history of education in St. Louis. While much has been written about education during the slave years, 1820–1865, and the years of segregated schools, 1865–1983, no one has attempted to pull together the rich material written about these years. Nor has much been written about the most recent period from 1983–1999, the period of court-ordered desegregation of the St. Louis public schools, highlighted by an interdistrict transfer program between the school district in the city of St. Louis and the districts in St. Louis County. We have attempted to write a history of education of the entire period from statehood in 1820 to court-ordered desegregation ending in 1999, a period of 179 years.

We would not have been able to complete this work without the full cooperation and help of many persons and organizations. We are grateful to the librarians at the United States Court of Appeals in Minneapolis and St. Paul, Joyce Larson Schampel and Nancee Halling, who generously assisted us in obtaining books, treatises, and newspaper articles.

We acknowledge the great help we received from Gerri Ogle, coordinator of the Missouri Department of Elementary and Secondary Education, in finding data and information for us. We thank Dirk DeYong, whom we called from time to time to secure court documents and memoranda relating to the St. Louis desegregation case, and Phyllis Shapiro, former law clerk to Judge George F. Gunn, Jr., who was helpful in directing us to the record made in the district court.

We would not have been able to complete this history without the cooperation of the school principals and teachers. Not only did they help us understand the transformation taking place in the public schools in the city and county, but they also generously shared their views and recommendations. We used their comments as the basis for our plan to improve the St. Louis school system. Among those who made significant contributions were Vera Atkinson, principal, Cote Brilliante Elementary School; Emma Cannon, principal, Banneker Elementary School; Doris Carter, principal, Carver Elementary School; Juanita Doggett, principal, Sherman Elementary School; Carmel Hall, principal, Cardinal-Ritter High School; Cleveland Hammonds, superintendent, St. Louis Public Schools; George Henry, education director, St. Louis Archdiocese; Jimmy Irons, principal, Farragut Elementary School; Terre Johnson, principal, Webster Middle School; Barbara Kohn, former principal, Captain School, Clayton; Dorothy Ludgood, principal, Vashon High School; Floyd Irons, assistant principal, Vashon High School; Rosalyn Mason, principal, Wilkinson Early Childhood Center; Ann Meese, principal, Jefferson Elementary; Georgia Nikolaison, principal, Cleveland NJROTC Academy; Joyce Roberts, principal, LaClede Elementary; Ann Russek, principal, Dewey School of International Studies; A. Susan Tieber, principal, Gateway Institute of Technology; Stephen Warmack, principal, Roosevelt High School; Lloyd Washington, principal, Henry Elementary School; Betty Wheeler, former principal, Metro High School; Sandra Wilson, principal, Ashland Elementary School; Barbara Moseby, instructional coordinator, Ashland Elementary School; and Chris L. Wright, superintendent, Riverview Gardens School District.

Our history would have been less than complete had not many persons with a great concern for the education of the area's children shared their views with us, including former Mayor Freeman Bosley; LuVerne Cameron, associate director of the Desegregation Monitoring Committee; Glen Campbell, former executive director of the Desegregation Planning and Monitoring Office; Dr. William H. Danforth, settlement coordinator; James A. DeClue, local leader of the NAACP; Steven Ehlmann, Missouri legislator; Dr. George Hyram, executive vice president of Harris-Stowe College; Bruce LaPierre, special master; and Minnie Liddell.

We are also indebted to the many students who shared their views with us with respect to both the hardships and benefits of participating in the various aspects of the desegregation program, particularly the voluntary interdistrict transfer program. Talking with these students and sharing in their experiences convinced us that the St. Louis desegregation program, with all of its problems, provided a quality education to thousands of students who otherwise would have been denied the opportunities the program provided. Among these students were Charlie Bean, Derrick Brooks, Jamie Fisher, Tiffany Gant, Maureen Meyer, and Karen Swain.

We cannot complete our thanks without recognizing the dedicated help of Judge Heaney's secretaries, Mary Bibbey and Barbara Newcomer, and many of his law clerks, who assisted in the research and editing of the book. The law clerks included Ron Bailey, Thomas W. Beimers, Rozi Bhimani, Mary Pat Byrn, Miriam A. Cherry, Michael F. Cockson, Angela M. Crandall, Abigail E. Crouse, Heidi L. Johnson, Gayle E. Littleton, and Christopher Sundberg.

Finally, thanks to Cheryl Heilman and Catherine Rankovic, who made final edits of the book and whose ideas and recommendations have been incorporated therein, and to Attorney Shulamith Simon, at one time a special master who with confidence helped support this work.

UNENDING STRUGGLE

So I just simply started ringing doorbells and talking to my—because all of us up in that area were being put out of that school. And I began to walk and ring doorbells and see if other parents were as upset by this as I was.

–Minnie Liddell

On an average day, I woke up at 5:00 in the morning, got quickly prepared, and walked to the bus stop down the street. My bus time was 6:18 a.m. I had to be at the bus stop at 6:18 in the morning because I was one of the first stops. So I usually slept on the bus; or if I didn't finish my homework for some reason, I'd do homework on the bus.

–Derrick Brooks

No, you shouldn't make everybody go to city schools. Transfer either way from city to county, or county to the city, but that option should always remain there . . . because you cannot begin to put a dollar sign, to put an amount of the value that you gain, from an interracial learning experience.

–Derrick Brooks

One of the things that our study showed was that if you were a ninth-grade male in a non-magnet school in the city, in one of the city high schools . . . the chances of your graduating from the St. Louis public schools were under 15 percent. I think that is a clear example that things were not working well.

–William H. Danforth

There's something called Across City Connections, and I was invited to attend. It's when the largest urban schools in the country get together once or twice a year to share common problems and common solutions, and I went two years ago. I think the members are like New York City, L.A., Seattle, Indianapolis, St. Louis, Boston. We know what the problem is, but how—it's a national problem and the nation isn't ready to take it on.

–Anne Meese

I'm not going to be around. I tell them this all the time. I don't feel like a lot of meetings and all of that. I don't have any children in school. My fire's not as hot as it used to be. I tell that to my daughter-in-law and my son. I say, "Look, you've got kids in the school. You've got to see what's going on. So I want to see parents committed to see that the world of education is—the administration lives up to the spirit of the settlement agreement." That's the only thing that's going to work.

–Minnie Liddell

Introduction

In different capacities, the authors of this book have been involved in the seminal St. Louis school desegregation case, *Liddell v. Board of Education*, since its inception. Judge Gerald W. Heaney, as a member of the U.S. Court of Appeals for the Eighth Circuit, authored the majority of the opinions reviewing the decisions of the U.S. District Court for the Eastern District of Missouri. His connection with the lawsuit began in 1980, when he first sat on the case, and it did not end until the final settlement agreement was reached in 1999. While Judge Heaney was a member of the court that ordered the state and local school districts to put various programs in place, Dr. Susan Uchitelle established some of these programs. As the director of the Voluntary Interdistrict Coordinating Council, she was responsible for monitoring and implementing the program that allowed black students from the city of St. Louis to transfer to county schools and white students from the county to transfer to city schools.

Our involvement in the *Liddell* case and its aftermath convinced us that a comprehensive study of education in Missouri from the slave years to the present—with an emphasis on the St. Louis metropolitan area—would enrich the current national debate about how poor African American students in major metropolitan areas can obtain a quality education. We supplement our personal experiences and historical research with personal interviews with students, teachers, administrators, and public officials who participated in the St. Louis metropolitan area desegregation programs. It is our hope that the complete history and the views of the interviewees will add an important, and until now, largely missing, element to the national debate.

Various proposals to improve the academic achievement of poor African American students in metropolitan areas consume scholarly and political discussions across the nation. These proposals include standardized high-stakes tests, particularly in reading, math, and science; the creation of more charter schools; and vouchers available for use at private and parochial schools. Absent in most proposals, however, is any notion of meaningful integration as an element of reform. Additionally, very little has been done to provide the resources necessary to improve the quality of education for these students. Unfortunately, many of them will remain in their racially segregated, economically segregated, and underfunded neighborhood schools. This book will emphasize that better management, integration, and additional resources are essential for improving the quality of education for students in large metropolitan school districts.

Before we examine the history of education in Missouri, we introduce a central character to the fight for an integrated education in Missouri: Minnie Liddell, who spearheaded *Liddell v. Missouri Board of Education*, beginning in 1973. This court case was a determining factor in the integration of the St. Louis public school system.

The history of education in Missouri begins during the slavery years, with the state's refusal to allow African Americans to be educated. Missouri entered into the Union as a slave state in 1821 as a result of the Missouri Compromise of 1820. By 1847, the Missouri General Assembly made it illegal to educate African Americans. Following the Civil War, Missouri organized a separate-but-equal educational system, which theoretically ended in 1954 with *Brown v. Board of Education*.

With an overview of the history of African American education in Missouri, Minnie Liddell's struggle for an equal education for her children becomes clear. After evaluating the impact of *Brown v. Board of Education* on the St. Louis school system from 1954–1971, we follow Liddell's case to its conclusion, including a discussion of the numerous court orders and the final settlement agreement that ended the litigation. We assess the impact of these court orders and the settlement agreement on the quality of education for poor African American students in St. Louis. Finally, we recognize that the struggle did not end with Minnie Liddell's case. In order to truly change the course of Missouri's history of providing an inferior education to African American children, school districts must take steps to improve the quality of education. We end the book by outlining those steps.

[T]he superintendent] finally . . . said, "I'm going to tell you something. I've been working in this school system for 27 years. You can't change a thing." He said, "You can't change anything in this system." And of course that made me angry. . . . And that's the day we set about to change things in the St. Louis schools.

–Minnie Liddell[1]

{Chapter One}

Minnie Liddell Goes to Federal Court

Minnie Liddell, an African American mother, went to court seeking better schools for her children.

More than any other person, Mrs. Liddell was responsible for the integration of the St. Louis City and St. Louis County public schools. Mrs. Liddell led Concerned Parents, a group that sued to desegregate the schools and pursued the litigation from 1972 until 1983, when a plan to desegregate the city and county schools was agreed to and approved by the United States District Court and the United States Court of Appeals for the Eighth Circuit. She remained involved until a final settlement agreement was reached in 1999.

The story of school desegregation in St. Louis reaches back to the 1820s, when the state of Missouri legally denied all African Americans, slaves and free, the opportunity for a public education. This inspired a few individuals to open small private schools in defiance of the law; however, most such schools were quickly shut down. After the Civil War and the passage of the Fourteenth Amendment to the U.S. Constitution, public education had to be opened to African Americans, but in 1865 Missouri specified in its constitution that black children and white children were to be educated separately, a law not officially removed from the state constitution until 1976.

In 1954, public school segregation in all U.S. schools had been declared unconstitutional by the U.S. Supreme Court in *Brown v. Board of Education*.[2] Colleges, universities, and Catholic schools in the St. Louis area had been integrated in the 1940s and early 1950s, but in 1954 the St. Louis Board of Education continued to operate the second-largest segregated public school system in the nation.[3] It had seven all-white high schools, two all-black high schools, and two technical schools, one for blacks and one for whites.[4] Of its 121 grade schools, 36 were for black students.[5] White students were assigned to the public schools nearest to their homes, while the district's thirty-one thousand black students—about a third of the total number[6]—were bused to schools in the inner city.[7] Then, as now, 25 percent of the city's children attended private and parochial schools; few of those students were black.[8]

St. Louis's black community rejoiced over *Brown v. Board of Education*. The black-owned weekly *St. Louis American* ran a celebratory headline: "The 'Big Wheels' of Justice Have Spoken: May 17—Unanimous! Segregation Unconstitutional."[9] In the black-owned *St. Louis Argus*, Howard B. Woods declared in his column: "Classroom segregation for your child and mine is over. Within a short period it will be but a memory."[10] Rumors circulated that the St. Louis Board of Education's superintendent had a desegregation plan ready. Joseph Carpenter of the *St. Louis American* wrote:

> If, as Superintendent Philip Hickey says, machinery is already
> set up here to implement integration, I see no reason why it should
> not begin to mesh gears next fall . . . . St. Louis need not wait for
> our Attorney General to tell us what to do: the Supreme Court of
> the United States has already spoken with clarion clarity.[11]

Irving Dillard, chief editorial writer for the *St. Louis Post-Dispatch*, wrote enthusiastically that the St. Louis Board of Education "has in hand plans for developing a single school system. It can be hoped that this program is already far enough along on paper that it can be completely worked out and put into effect next September."[12]

The Board did have a plan in hand. On June 22, 1954, it announced and approved a three-step desegregation plan created by Superintendent Hickey, who had anticipated the *Brown* decision. However, Hickey's plan was neither as aggressive nor as comprehensive as many St. Louisans wished. Under the plan, school desegregation would be undertaken in three steps and would take more than a year to complete. In support of the plan, Daniel Schlafly, secretary of the Board of Education, presented the following resolution:

> It is the general policy of the Board of Education of the City
> of St. Louis to begin the integration process in September, 1954,
> and to complete it by the opening day of school in September,
> 1955. . . .
> It would, of course, be possible to end segregation in the St.
> Louis Public Schools by next September. Although it would be
> possible, it would, in our judgement, be educationally undesirable
> for many children to undertake the complete change so precipi-
> tately.[13]

The plan was implemented in three phases from 1954 to 1956.[14] First, in September 1954, the Stowe Teachers and Junior College for Negroes and the Harris

Teachers and Junior College for whites were combined into one institution. All "special needs" students were integrated. All physically handicapped students were assigned to the Elias Michael School. All deaf students were assigned to the Gallaudet School, and mentally handicapped children were assigned to schools within existing school-district boundaries, without regard for race.

The second step integrated the high schools in February 1955, excluding the technical high schools. Also, the Adult Education Program was integrated at that time.

The third and final step went into effect in September 1955 when the technical high schools and regular elementary schools were integrated. The new elementary school district boundary lines were published in February 1955.

The plan abolished all reference to race or color in the St. Louis public schools' records.[15] "IBM cards" were made for every student. The cards identified only the city block where each child lived without any indication of his or her race.[16] New attendance boundaries were drawn for each school, and students were assigned to the school nearest their homes, provided it could handle the number of students.[17]

Students or their parents who wanted desperately to escape integration could, however, take advantage of some of the "general principles" the Board had decided would govern the integration process,[18] which offered certain loopholes. Although students were to attend the school in their neighborhood, exceptions could be made. Authorities could transfer students from one district to another to relieve overcrowding,[19] and white students newly assigned to majority black schools could stay in the white school until they graduated.[20] William Russell, who later served as a lawyer for the black plaintiffs in Minnie Liddell's lawsuit against the St. Louis School District, said that the Board's policy meant that "blacks who wanted to transfer had a difficult time doing it, but there was no problem for white families to transfer their children into schools that were practically all-white."[21]

There is no question that, for black children, the segregated public schools, supposedly "separate but equal" under both Missouri and federal law, had always been inferior. Black schools were more crowded, inconveniently located, less well equipped, and housed in aging buildings. However, not all black St. Louisans had a bad experience attending, or teaching in, the segregated schools during the pre-*Brown* years. Some St. Louis teachers and school administrators interviewed for this book remembered their schooling in the 1940s and early 1950s as adequate or better. Dr. George Hyram, executive vice president of Harris-Stowe State College, attended Simmons Elementary School. He remembered "remarkably fine teachers" and his class gathering around a Philco radio each week to listen to a classical music broadcast. "We never felt any shortage of books or supplies," he said. "As a matter of fact, in Simmons School there was a shower that all the kids once a week went to, and we had a shower matron, and we just had all kinds of wonderful things."[22] Doris Carter, principal of Carver Elementary School, attended the same school Minnie Liddell attended, Lincoln Elementary School, located on Twenty-third and Spruce Streets, from 1945 until her eighth-grade graduation in 1954.[23] "[W]e never had any deficits in books and supplies," said Ms. Carter. "I really do not remember any problems like that. My memory of Lincoln School is happy. First of all, I had a wonderful principal that would often come to the home. We walked to school right across the street. There was nothing unusual for teachers and principals to come to your home and visit. Had good teachers. It's because of my teachers in elementary school that I wanted to become a teacher."[24]

Others look back with mixed feelings. Juanita Doggett, principal of Sherman Elementary School, went to Sumner High School from 1944 to 1946. She not only remembered the overcrowding and shortages of supplies—her high school class had nearly four hundred students—but also the dedication shown by her teachers, who were all black. "I had a solid education by teachers who were dedicated to educating students in the separate or inequitable schools that existed at that time," she said.[25] Interviewee James DeClue, former president of the St. Louis chapter of the NAACP, said the St. Louis School District had a system for obtaining exceptional black educators from the ranks of its own students. "[The school district] didn't call it tracking back in the '30s and '40s, but they certainly were doing it," DeClue said. "They were selecting a few students out of each class and were going to see to it that they got well educated. They had to do it, and the city of St. Louis had to do it; they had to see to it that there were some black students who came through those schools that were well educated, because they needed them to maintain a system of segregation. That's the reason why Stowe Teachers' College was absolutely free; it didn't cost a dime to go."[26]

Juanita Doggett attended Stowe and herself became a public school teacher. She remembered that during the early years of her career, "We had different funds [and] textbooks; and we might have gotten leftover books. Supplies were somewhat limited. There were no additional funds to do anything different. The funds came from fundraisers—you had to do that to get anything additional."[27] But, she added, "We had strong support from families and you knew every child you taught. We knew the neighborhood and families. We made family calls, and many children lived in alleys, in what was called garages, and you had to get them to come. You did it because of community spirit. Everything was focused on the community and churches."[28]

George Hyram also remembers "community spirit" in the segregated world of the 1940s and 1950s. He said, "[B]efore . . . the '54 desegregation ordered by the court took place, there was something that we all had in mind. That is, we had to struggle and strive to be very good in order to win a place in society. And the whole thrust was: 'Do the very best you can; you can succeed.' Show everybody that being black had no bearing on whether or not you could be a high achiever."[29]

Sandra Wilson, principal of Ashland Elementary School, however, cautioned against comparing the past with the realities faced by city school children in the twenty-first century. She said, "[W]e have to let go of what we said was so great and wonderful, because back in those days also a whole lot of kids walked out of school and they went right to the Philco factory with their fathers, or their uncles, or somebody, or to Magnavox, whatever factory there was, and they hired them and they stayed on there for thirty years and had a nice life and retired. That stuff doesn't exist anymore. You can't walk in that easily now, or go to the corner grocery store and work for somebody. There are no corner grocery stores."[30]

"Enough is Enough"

The Supreme Court in 1954 had not outlined when and how the nation's public school districts should integrate their schools. A year later, in *Brown II*, the Court said only that segregated school systems should be dismantled with "all deliberate speed"[31] and allowed district courts to rule on local cases.[32]

Some school districts immediately began to conform to the Supreme Court's ruling. But because the *Brown II* ruling permitted authorities to take more time if "necessary in the public interest,"[33] other districts interpreted the time allowance as a license to take all the time they could to integrate, and in St. Louis significant school desegregation moved forward very slowly—and it did not always move forward. According to Minnie Liddell, whose older children were in the school system, "[The St. Louis Board of Education] would change the boundary lines in the school district to contain black folks in North St. Louis and white folks in South St. Louis. They went through a lot of changes between '54 and '72, but they all were to maintain separation. . . . [T]here was a lot of transportation of children because of overcrowding, but it was—by the time we came along, it was from one black school to another black school. They said it wasn't their policy to do any transportation of children to integrated schools. So they guaranteed they were going to keep things the way they was."[34]

Minnie Liddell had been brought to St. Louis from Mississippi by her mother, Eddie May Thompson, in 1940. Thompson and nine-month-old Minnie settled in Mill Creek Valley, a neighborhood near present-day Union Station, where the only whites were the mailman and the owners of a mom-and-pop corner store.[35] Growing up, Minnie attended Lincoln, an all-black elementary school. There she was encouraged by her eighth-grade teacher, Earl Cook, who told her, "Minnie, you have got a brain. Don't you get carried away."[36] Years later, Liddell said, "Cook opened up a world for us that we didn't even know existed. For me it was a lifesaver. I have to be honest; I wasn't getting a lot of that at home. Schools can be that safe place. They can be that place that will help a child."[37]

Also attending school with Minnie were black children from the Carondelet neighborhood. They told her that they went to school with her because there was no black high school in their area. As Liddell said, "There was a working agreement between the Board of Education and all of those school districts" to send black high school students who lived in surrounding county districts to the three black high schools in St. Louis: Sumner, Vashon, and Washington Tech.[38]

As a student, Liddell said, she did not expect a great deal. She knew that the

Minnie Liddell spearheaded the fight against segregated schools in St. Louis. Photo courtesy the *St. Louis Post-Dispatch*.

white schools were better equipped, better maintained, and received new textbooks, while the black students were often housed in inferior, overcrowded schools and had to make do with books previously used by white students. She also knew that this had been the case for many years. However, she was not bitter and felt fortunate to have received the education that she did.

Minnie completed eighth grade and enrolled in Washington Tech, but when her mother became ill she had to quit school to support herself and her mother.[39] Nevertheless, she loved learning and continued to read. At age twenty-seven, she passed her high school equivalency test on her first try. It was this love of learning that led Mrs. Liddell to insist on a high-quality education for her children and ultimately for all children in St. Louis.

When she was sixteen, Minnie married Charles Liddell. In 1971, they were living on the north side of St. Louis with their five children: Craton, Donna, Charles, Jr., Brian, and Michael.[40]

Due to overcrowding in the neighborhood schools, Craton was assigned to a school across town, in largely white South St. Louis.[41] He and his entire class, and a black teacher, were bused to a school where there was a room set aside for them, apart from white students. Black and white students had separate recess and lunch periods.[42]

The St. Louis Board of Education had promised to build new schools in North St. Louis with proceeds from a school bond issue passed in 1962 with the support of the Liddells and other black parents.[43] One of the new schools was Yeatman—within walking distance of the Liddells' home. All of the Liddell school-aged children had been assigned to the new school. It was overcrowded from the day it opened, but even so, Mrs. Liddell was pleased. Because it was nearby, she had a chance to participate in her children's schooling. She said, "We had an outstanding principal, George Fisher. . . . He was a white man, but he knew those kids. He encouraged involvement . . . of parents. We supported him and he supported us. So I got real busy working in school and enjoying it."[44]

After a year, the Liddells were notified that their children would be assigned to Bates, a nineteenth-century school that had been closed because of its poor condition. "The plumbing and furnace and everything was terrible in that school," Mrs. Liddell remembered. "But they wanted to open it back up and start sending the overflow from various neighborhood schools into Bates."[45] Worst of all, it was far from the Liddells' home. As Mrs. Liddell told it, "Not only the one child [Craton] was moved around a lot, but all of my children were going to have to go to Bates, and I said, 'Enough is enough.'

"So I just simply started ringing doorbells and talking to my [neighbors]—because all of us up in that area were being put out of that school. And I began to walk and ring doorbells and see if other parents were as upset by this as I was."[46]

Obstacles to Desegregation

The demographics and city planning strategies of St. Louis help to explain the slowness and ineffectiveness of the integration process. Local, state, and federal governments all played a part in perpetuating segregation after 1954.[47] The city of St. Louis failed to enforce building codes in predominantly black neighborhoods, insurance companies and lenders "redlined" certain neighborhoods, and newspapers continued to print "colored" housing ads separately from ads for whites.[48]

From 1950 to 1970, approximately four hundred thousand white residents left the city for the suburbs, while more than one hundred thousand African Americans moved into the city.[49] Within the city, black residents moved out of the inner-city area into the Central West End neighborhood, and later to the northwest areas of the city and into the county.[50] Census data shows that in 1950, 17.9 percent of the city was black.[51] In 1960 and 1970, the percentage increased to 28.6 percent and 40.9 percent, respectively.[52] As the black population in St. Louis increased and spread throughout the city, housing opportunities decreased.

For example, between 1960 and 1965 several "slum areas" in the inner city were razed to make room for new housing developments, displacing thousands of black residents.[53] Although approximately six thousand new housing units were built in St. Louis during those years, more than twelve thousand units were destroyed by urban renewal and highway construction projects.[54] In this way, the federal government contributed to housing discrimination against blacks.[55] Urban black families generally had few opportunities to live in private housing. In 1958, less than 1 percent of private housing was open to blacks.[56] As white families and upper-middle-class black families moved to the suburbs, their homes in the city typically became rental properties and were occupied by less stable and often unemployed people, resulting in the neighborhoods' decline in market value.[57] As Lorenzo Greene wrote, "Racial discrimination and poverty limited affordable housing for blacks, forcing many into dilapidated, poorly managed public housing projects. Inflation and rising costs also compounded the tenants' problems."[58] A series of rent hikes in St. Louis's public housing projects forced many tenants to pay more than half of their income for rent.[59]

The Pruitt-Igoe Housing Project represents the worst of St. Louis's housing crises. Designed to provide affordable housing in a minimally integrated environment and praised for its innovative design, it proved to be a disastrous social experiment. Built in the early 1950s, it consisted of 33 buildings 11 stories tall, containing a total of 2,762 apartments.[60] Researcher Amy Wells depicted the horrible conditions within which its residents, primarily black, lived:

> Pruitt-Igoe was built on fifty-seven acres of land set off from the rest of the city; there were no social service organizations, grocery stores, or shopping centers nearby. According to a St. Louis University report on Pruitt-Igoe, the area was "isolated from the

main business district and major centers of industrial employment and devoid of commercial activities except the marginal corner-store type of operation." With no job opportunities in the vicinity and no public transportation to jobs in other parts of the city, the project became a mecca for organized crime. And despite their architectural awards, the Pruitt-Igoe buildings were poorly designed: the elevators stopped only on the fourth, seventh, and tenth floors; there were no restrooms on the ground floor; there was little recreational space for the thousands of children who lived there.[61]

It seemed that only people desperate for housing were willing to live in the project. Wells wrote, "[T]enants complained of broken glass and trash everywhere, problems that led to infestations of mice and cockroaches; there were numerous fights, thefts, and attacks."[62] Pruitt-Igoe was finally razed in 1976. In 1971, the city council had adopted an ordinance to restrict the concentration of low-income housing in any one neighborhood in response to the Pruitt-Igoe disaster, but the ordinance was largely ignored.[63] Most of St. Louis's black residents remained confined to segregated, dilapidated neighborhoods. The Board of Education's "neighborhood schools" plan guaranteed that desegregation of the city's public schools would be impossible.

At the beginning of the school year in 1965, at a meeting with the NAACP, the Board lamented that the housing pattern in the city frustrated efforts at complete integration of most schools.[64] High concentrations of black students in many urban schools were the result of the neighborhood school policy.[65]

Researchers have concluded that integration efforts were also hindered by the attitudes of some parents, teachers, and administrators. White teachers remained reluctant to teach at predominantly black schools. In 1966, "thirty-five of the district's 41 all-black elementary schools had no white teachers, and in 1973, more than 90 percent of the black teachers were still teaching in all-black schools."[66] Moreover, according to research by LaNoue and Smith,

> A 1969 Survey Research Center analysis of racial attitudes in large cities found St. Louisans among the least liberal. . . . St. Louis, then, has a school system that seemed to many incapable of overcoming the pathologies of the inner city. Its schools appeared not very integrated, not very academically successful, and dominated by socially elite whites in a city that was increasingly lower-class black.[67]

For these reasons, while the St. Louis Board of Education had announced its intention to comply with *Brown* shortly after the Supreme Court handed down that decision in 1954, as of 1972 no real progress had been made toward integration of the St. Louis public schools. Neither the St. Louis Board of Education nor the state of Missouri had the courage or resolve necessary to overcome the long and torturous history of slavery and segregation without being required to do so by the federal courts. The opportunity to integrate all the St. Louis city schools was lost when the Board of Education and the state of Missouri failed to integrate the schools in 1954, when two-thirds of St. Louis's public school students were white and one-third were black. Only through the tireless efforts of Minnie Liddell, the black mother with five children in the St. Louis public schools, would the goal of integration of the city schools begin to be met.

In an interview for this book, Minnie Liddell described in detail how the lawsuit known as *Liddell v. Board of Education of St. Louis* got started in the fall of 1971, when the Liddells received a letter from the City School Board saying that on account of the overcrowding at Yeatman, the neighborhood school, her children were being assigned to the distant and decrepit Bates School. Her oldest son, Craton, was twelve. She said:

> We got this letter in late August. School, at that time, always started the day after Labor Day. So we didn't have a lot of time. . . .
>
> So our district superintendent was Benjamin Price. So I attempted to have a meeting with him, I and another group of parents. He wouldn't meet with us. He said the Board had spoken, and that was that. So again we tried to meet with the Board downtown. We—I was having a meeting in the church right across from the school, and we asked them to come out so we could state our case. And of course they ignored us. They didn't show up.
>
> So basically the only one that we were kind of talking to—Ben would see me, Ben Price would see me at the district caucus, but he wouldn't come to a meeting with the group. So that was where we were stopped at. That was a brick wall. And when school started, we decided—a bunch of us, all of us, in fact, whose children were in the cutout from Yeatman to Bates—we decided we were not going to send our kids to school. And so we did what we seen them doing all over the country. We demonstrated and had our signs and they just ignored us. That's how they had resolved their problems; they just waited you out. But we kept the kids out of school and we home-schooled them.
>
> After about six weeks, the Board said, 'Pick any school in St. Louis you want to put them in. They don't have to go to Bates.' So after a lot of discussion, we decided to put the kids back in school and continue to fight. They wouldn't let none of them go to Yeatman, but they said you could pick any school in St. Louis. Craton was twelve, Donna was eleven, and Chuckie was ten, and Brian was eight. I put them in Simmons, which was the elementary school my husband had attended. A lot of the teachers there

taught him. And—oh, yes, no transportation was included in this deal. Wherever you went to, you had to get there yourself." [68]

Charles Liddell drove the children to and from school.

Finally, said Mrs. Liddell, Acting School Superintendent Ernest Jones "agreed to meet with two of us, just two. So we went down and we met with him. . . .

> So then Ernest finally said, I'm going to tell you something.
> I've been working in this school system for twenty-seven years.
> You can't change a thing. He said, You can't change anything in
> this system. And of course that made me angry. So you tell me the
> taxpayers, the parents of the children who are your clients, can't
> change anything? And he says, No, you can't change anything in
> this school. And that's the day we set about to change things in the
> St. Louis schools. [69]

Mrs. Liddell and Concerned Parents had to decide what to do. As Mrs. Liddell recalls, "We were just out there, the blind leading the blind. No money." [70] A pastor at St. Peter's Church recommended two lawyers, William Russell and Joseph McDuffy. Mrs. Liddell said that the lawyers asked the parents to "look at your school system and see if you're upset at a principle thing rather than at what's really going on in your schools. They told us that we couldn't change things for just our children without changing things for other children." [71] Even though the group had no money, Russell agreed to take the case but told the parents they would have to be involved in research. The parents collected data on student assignments, the physical conditions of the schools, distribution of resources, and student achievement. They "began to see a pattern of the Board treating black students like pawns on a chessboard." [72] They learned the full details about the Board's repeated redrawing of attendance lines and the constant opening and closing of black schools. The Concerned Parents held barbecues, dances, and raffles to raise money to pay the filing fees necessary to file their court case. [73]

On February 18, 1972, the Concerned Parents filed a class-action lawsuit against the St. Louis Board of Education, individual board members, the school superintendent, and district superintendents in the United States District Court for the Eastern District of Missouri. [74] They asked the court to

> require the defendants to prepare and submit for approval of this
> court a plan for the operation of all the public schools within
> the defendant Board of Education school system in conformity
> with the requirements of the Fourteenth Amendment, including,
> but not limited to, the nondiscriminatory allocation of financial
> and physical resources; the establishment of school geographical
> boundaries and district geographical boundaries which are not

racially identifiable; the location, construction and utilization
of new buildings and the utilization of existing school buildings
in a manner which [is] not racially identifiable; the assignment
of pupil populations, staffs, faculties, transportation routes and
activities which are not racially identifiable; and that the plan be
effective at the earliest possible date.[75]

Two months later, the defendants filed an answer in which they admitted that
prior to 1954, the state of Missouri, by its constitution and laws, required separate
schools for black children. The defendants denied, however, that they had actively or
passively administered the schools in a manner that had the effect of denying equal
educational opportunities to black citizens and students. The case was assigned to
Chief Judge James H. Meredith.

A giant step had been taken to fulfill the promise in *Brown v. Board of Education.*

"We hold these truths to be self-evident: that all men are created equal; that they are endowed by their Creator with certain unalienable rights; that among them is life, liberty, and the pursuit of happiness . . . ." The general words above quoted would seem to embrace the whole human family. . . . But it is too clear for dispute, that the enslaved African race were not intended to be included, and formed no part of the people who framed and adopted this declaration. . . .

–Chief Justice Roger B. Taney, 1857 [1]

{Chapter Two}

The Establishment of Education in Missouri:
Pre-Statehood and Slave State Years

Minnie Liddell's lawsuit to desegregate the St. Louis public schools was a challenge to the state of Missouri's policies regarding the education of black children—policies rooted in the history of the state and the nation. Long before the Civil War, when the French and Spanish ruled the territory now known as Missouri, their laws promoted slavery, restricted the movement of slaves, and permitted blacks only limited education in the Catholic religion. Little changed when Missouri entered the Union, as a slave state, in 1821. Although the new state's constitution provided for the creation of public schools, public education was clearly a low priority and exclusively for white children.

The only opportunities for black children, slave or free, to learn even basic knowledge of reading and writing were provided by private individuals and churches, both Catholic and Protestant. Even these efforts were curtailed in 1847, when the Missouri General Assembly outlawed "any school for the instruction of negroes or mulattoes." Excluding black children from public and private education may have saved pre–Civil War Missouri and its local units of government millions of dollars, but these policies imposed enormous short- and long-term social, cultural, and economic costs on the state and its individual citizens.

Missouri was originally a part of the Louisiana Territory and subject to the laws of France. Under the *Code Noir*, issued by Louis XV of France in 1724, blacks could not leave the master's plantation without a pass, carry arms, assault their masters, own property, engage in business, or marry.[2] Although the *Code Noir* entitled slaves to be educated and baptized in the Catholic religion, this limited right to education was offset by a law preventing slaves of different masters from gathering together by night or day.[3]

In 1769, Spain assumed control of the Louisiana Territory, and Spanish law superseded the French *Code Noir*.[4] The Spanish code, *Las Siete Partidas*, contained

23

elaborate provisions concerning the economic enfranchisement of slaves but otherwise gave the master full power over his slaves, with certain limits on appropriate
punishments.[5] For example, if a slave was suing for freedom in court, the master
had to give security to ensure that the slave would not be harmed while the lawsuit
was pending. The burden of proof in such a lawsuit rested on the petitioning slave.[6]
Occasional decrees from the governors of the Louisiana Colony supplemented the
Spanish Code.[7] In response to reports of unruliness among slaves in St. Louis, in
1781 a decree was issued prohibiting slaves from assembling at night, leaving their
cabins at night except with the consent of their master, or receiving guests in their
cabins other than slaves of the same master.[8] Under Spanish rule, educational opportunities for blacks continued to be limited to religious instruction.

The United States purchased the Louisiana Territory in 1804, and its administration was entrusted to William Henry Harrison, governor of the Indiana Territory.[9] Governor Harrison, who later became president of the United States, devised
a Black Code for the territory based on the laws of Virginia and Kentucky.[10] The
Black Code prohibited slaves from leaving home or visiting other plantations without a pass.[11] Additionally, a vague provision made "unlawful assemblies" punishable
by "strips" (whippings) at the discretion of the local justice of the peace.[12] These
rules against assembly also applied to free blacks.[13] These laws continued unchanged
from 1804 until Missouri's application for statehood in 1818. The U.S. Congress
in 1820 authorized the people of Missouri to form a state government and draft a
constitution. With regard to education, Congress directed that "Religion, morality
and knowledge being necessary to good government and the happiness of mankind,
school, and the means of education, shall be encouraged and provided for."[14]

Missouri's application for statehood created a fervent debate in the U.S. Congress. At that time, the United States had an equal number of free states and slave
states, resulting in an equal number of U.S. Senators holding views on slavery in
accordance with the laws of their states. Although the balance between slave and free
states had been upset a number of times, an entering state's status had always been
determined by reference to the Mason-Dixon Line and the Ohio River.[15] Because no
such line existed west of the Mississippi, the question of Missouri's status took on
meaning beyond the state itself.

A series of compromises initiated by Representative James Tallmadge of New
York attempted to resolve the issue of whether Missouri should be admitted as a
free state or a slave state. Tallmadge's proposal prohibited any further importation
of slaves into Missouri and granted freedom to the children of slaves born within
the state after its admission. Although passed by the House, this original version of
the Missouri Compromise was defeated in the Senate because Southern states were
concerned about national intrusion into the law of slavery.[16] The prospects for a
workable compromise improved when Maine applied for statehood in 1820. Admitting a slave state and a free state at the same time would maintain equilibrium on
the slavery issue in the Senate.

On March 1, 1820, Congress authorized the voters of the Missouri Territory to draft a state constitution. The constitution contained a clause "prohibiting the Missouri General Assembly from intermeddling with the subject of slavery except to provide a proper police for its defense."[17] Approved by the constitutional convention in July 1820, the constitution was submitted to Missouri voters and promptly ratified. The U.S. Congress debated "long and furiously before recognition was granted."[18]

As part of the final Missouri Compromise, several agreements were reached: slavery would be banned from the territories of the Louisiana Purchase north of the line marking Missouri's southern border, except for Missouri,[19] and the Missouri General Assembly could not pass any legislation denying the constitutional rights of free black citizens.[20]

This second stipulation, known as the "Clay Formula" after Henry Clay, became necessary because the state constitution allowed the General Assembly to enact "such laws as may be necessary to prevent free negroes and mulattoes from coming to, and settling in this state, under any pretext whatsoever."[21] The compromise language limited the effect of this clause, stating that it should "never be construed to authorize the passage of any law . . . by which any citizen of either of the States of this Union shall be excluded from the enjoyment of any of the privileges and immunities to which such citizen is entitled under the Constitution of the United States."[22] With these understandings in place, Missouri was admitted as a slave state in 1821.[23]

The act of Congress admitting Missouri into the Union generously set aside every sixteenth section of land throughout the state, together with seventy-two sections of congressionally dedicated land, for school purposes.[24] This made a grand total of 1,254,200 acres of land.[25] The act further provided that "Schools and the means of education shall forever be encouraged in this State and the General Assembly shall take measures to preserve from waste or damage such lands as have been, or shall hereafter be granted, by the states, for the use of schools, within each township in this state. . . . One school, or more, shall be established in each township, as soon as practicable and necessary, where the poor shall be taught gratis."[26]

Missouri began organizing a school system in 1825. The assembly passed a law requiring that the townships operate as school districts under the county court's control. To manage school lands, three "householders" from each district were elected as commissioners. Commissioners could petition to incorporate their district. This allowed the district to lease school lands, manage school funds, and hold property for the schools' benefit.[27]

Also, a five-person board of trustees was elected, but only white men over the age of twenty-one and householders could vote for the trustees. The board of trustees built and managed schoolhouses and appointed teachers. The trustees appointed nine "visitors" to inspect and certify schoolhouses within the district. Only certified schoolhouses could be operated.[28]

Chronic funding problems plagued the public schools. In 1831, the General Assembly permitted the counties to sell school lands. The proceeds were supposed to be used for public education. Many counties either sold or leased their lands, but many of the mortgages and leases were defaulted on, or otherwise proved to be worthless. A year later the assembly passed a law requiring that the proceeds from the land be turned over to the newly formed Missouri State Bank, which would invest the money in the bank's capital stock and pay dividends to the public schools. Unfortunately, the dividend declared by the Missouri State Bank gradually diminished until the annual dividend amounted to less than 1 percent of the value of the bank's capital stock. T. A. Parker, then state superintendent of schools, observed, "It was evident that the bank was enacting the role of Saturn, and devouring all its own progeny."[29]

In 1835, the assembly gave the county courts the power to administer the school lands. The next year, the newly installed governor, Lilburn Boggs, admitted that some proceeds from the sale of school lands had been used to reduce the state debt rather than to support public schools. Thus, the public schools were permanently deprived of the revenues from the lands that had been sold.

Meanwhile, in 1833, the assembly had created a statewide system of education. Governor Daniel Dunklin appointed a committee to plan a common and primary school system.[30] In the fall of 1834, this three-member committee met in Jefferson City and drafted a proposal. It asked for the creation of a state board of education made up of five commissioners: the governor, secretary of state, treasurer, attorney general, and auditor.[31] On the local level, boards of trustees would be elected in each district. These boards would have the power to hire teachers, appoint the visitors who would inspect the schools, and manage the schools within the district.[32] The committee's report was submitted to the assembly, which passed it into law in 1835. No funding was appropriated for the State Board of Education.

On February 6, 1837, the Missouri General Assembly established a permanent fund to support common schools. Under the act, the governor was required to invest the principal and interest of the fund, together with money received from the United States Revenue Fund, in Missouri Bank stock. The return on the investment was to be used to fund schools within the state. However, by law, the interest could be appropriated for schools only after the funds totaled $500,000, which did not occur until 1840, and even then the allocation was only sixty cents per pupil in the thirteen counties that had attempted to organize public schools.[33]

The most comprehensive school legislation was passed in 1839, when the assembly created a common school fund, a county school fund, and a township school fund, and granted the school districts permission to sell some remaining school lands. The legislation also established the office of the state superintendent of common schools. This office would distribute school funds based on the number of white children six to eighteen years of age in each county. The superintendent, chosen by a joint vote of the assembly, was to serve a two-year term.[34]

In the early 1840s, approximately 60 percent of the white children between the ages of six and eighteen were enrolled in public schools in Missouri, and common schools had been organized in forty-two of the state's seventy-seven counties. The superintendent of Missouri's public schools, James L. Miner, wrote that despite general public agreement about the "blessings of education," "popular education moved forward with discouraging slowness."[35]

Secretary of State F. H. Martin reported in 1846 that the schools were slow to organize because they lacked money. He added, "The people were not yet willing to pay the necessary tax for the maintenance of schools, and the sagacious Bank doled out a mere pittance of dividends on the school fund, just sufficient to keep the whole system in a state of starvation."[36]

In January 1853, Missouri Governor Sterling Price appointed John W. Henry as superintendent of common schools. Henry described vividly the decrepit condition of the schools he visited:

> With regard to our district school houses, they are the old kind, ten by twelve log cabins, with one door in the middle, and one oblong window extending from the door casing to the corner of the house. Who has seen one, has seen the counterpart of nine-tenths of the school houses in the State; low, dismal, dreary things, in an open space to themselves, with missiles of every description scattered around them, even the view cause enough for the fever and ague to the whole neighborhood. No humane master would cabin his negroes in such noisome dens, and yet, with an inexplicable infatuation, affectionate parents send their children there to sit and sweat a whole summer day, to acquire habits of neatness and order, and a love of knowledge.[37]

The Missouri Constitution had ensured that the poor could obtain a public education for free.[38] Wealthy landowners sent their sons and daughters to private schools in the East. To attract wealthy students, the first high school in Missouri was built in St. Louis in 1854. The board provided ample funds for the few hundred scholars who studied at its high school. In 1857, the state superintendent reported improvement "in the spirit and effect of education. . . . Unorganized portions of the country were brought under the operation of the law. Cities and towns . . . were building school houses [and] St. Louis . . . had fostered a separate system of public schools."[39] More money, more teachers, and more students poured into the system. By 1860, it was asserted that the public schools were equal to many colleges.[40]

The following table[41] indicates the status of public education in the state immediately prior to the beginning of the Civil War.

Year	No. of dists.	No. of children between 5 & 20	No. taught during year	No. of schools	No. of teachers	$ paid to teachers	$ raised to build & repair schools
1856	3,858	302,126	97,907	2.671	2,889	379,815	32,571
1857	4,640	341,121	141,328	3,392	4,397	497,810	130,236
1858	4,916	367,248	159,941	3,878	5,053	580,767	107,599
1859	5,277	385,639	171,378	4,272	5,720	691,421	192,423

By the outbreak of the Civil War, "the taint of charity" had been removed from the public schools.[42] The schools suffered a devastating blow, however, when in 1861 the General Assembly, controlled by Confederate sympathizers, forbade the superintendent of common schools from apportioning state school monies and instead gave the funds to the state's Confederate militia. Schoolhouses were inevitably closed. Although in 1862 supporters of the Union took over the Missouri General Assembly, they too failed to provide for the support of the public schools.[43]

The struggles over funding for public education suggest that public education in pre–Civil War Missouri was a low priority. It appears that there was not much more interest in educating poor white children than there was in educating poor black children, whether slave or free.

As difficult as it was for white children to receive an education in the public schools during this time, educational opportunities for Missouri's black children were even more limited. Despite Congress's condition that a free education be provided to poor students in the state of Missouri, before the Civil War this public education was effectively open only to white children. Until 1847, no legislation explicitly prohibited blacks from being educated.[44] However, school funding was allocated based on the number of white students within each county. Thus, as a practical matter, black children were denied the opportunity to attend public schools.[45]

A few black students were able to learn through private means. Before 1825, Missouri's apprenticeship system required that masters teach their apprentices—slaves, free blacks, and whites—reading, writing, and arithmetic.[46] Others volunteered to educate black children. John Mason Peck, a white Baptist missionary, arrived in St. Louis in 1817 and opened a Sunday school for blacks. Nearly one hundred pupils enrolled. Most of them were slaves permitted by their masters to attend. Peck forcefully advocated education for both blacks and whites.[47] Timothy Flint, a white minister in St. Charles, held Sunday school classes for slaves from 1816 to 1826.

The Catholic Church played a significant role in educating blacks during the early nineteenth century as well. In 1835, the Notre Dame Night School for blacks opened under the leadership of Bishop Joseph Rosati.[48] Black teachers taught the black students under the supervision of white Jesuit priests. However, in response to opposition from whites, Bishop Rosati closed the school.[49]

In 1845, Catholics in St. Louis again attempted to educate blacks, this time opening a school for black girls. The school was operated by Father Augustin Paris. The Sisters of St. Joseph taught approximately one hundred girls, most of them daughters of free blacks. Slave girls were instructed in the Catechism on Sundays and after school. Pressure from whites forced the school to close the following year.

In 1827, the First African Baptist Church opened, under the guidance of the Reverend John Berry Meachum.[50] Meachum was born a slave in Virginia, but through his industry as a craftsman he earned enough money to buy his freedom. In St. Louis he opened a cooperage plant and earned enough to buy freedom for his family. Meachum became a Baptist minister in 1826 when he was ordained by the Reverend Peck. Meachum was strongly committed to black education and at the time was probably one of the most outspoken advocates in Missouri for black education.[51] Through his church, Meachum educated numerous blacks. He saw education as the means of participating in economic life and of understanding the "universal principles of proper conduct."[52] "Ignorance," according to Meachum, was "slavery for a man's mind."[53]

Blacks also were educated in other private efforts outside of churches. Marion College, an academic institution with a strong antislavery student body, supported a black education program in the 1830s. White college students taught blacks reading and writing. At first, the college students taught all blacks, without restrictions, but in 1835, the college required that no slave could be taught to read without the written consent of his owner.[54]

Missouri sought to curtail these private efforts by placing restrictions on slaves, slave masters, and free blacks. In 1825, the assembly relieved masters of the duty of having to educate their black apprentices. The assembly stated that "when the said apprentice is a negro or mulatto child, it shall not be the duty of the master or mistress to cause such apprentice to be taught to read or write or a knowledge of arithmetic." Further, "if such apprentice or servant be a free negro or mulatto, he/she shall be allowed, at the expiration of his or her term of service, a sum of money in lieu of education, to be assessed by the probate court."[55]

The same year, the assembly prohibited slaves from assembling and traveling within the state. To enforce the law, the assembly authorized the county courts to appoint local patrols of no more than five men, called "patter rollers," to police "negro quarters and other places of suspected unlawful assemblies."[56] If the "patter rollers" found slaves unlawfully assembling, they were authorized to give each slave up to ten lashes—and more if the slave's owner permitted it.[57] The justice of the peace also was authorized to administer up to thirty-nine lashes to violators. Masters were fined if they allowed the slaves of others to remain on their plantations without

In 1846, John Berry Meachum, in defiance of state law, educated African American St. Louisans onboard a steamship on the Mississippi River. The river fell under federal jurisdiction. Image courtesy the St. Louis Public Schools Archives.

the permission of their owners, allowed their slaves to go in public without passes, or permitted or attended unlawful assemblies of slaves.[58]

In the 1820 constitution, the state proclaimed its hostility towards free blacks with Article III, which became known as the Free Negro Code. The General Assembly was required to pass laws preventing free blacks from entering and settling in Missouri, no matter the reason.[59] Few free blacks lived in Missouri; in 1830, out of a total population of 66,437, only 347 were free blacks.[60]

From 1820 to 1835, the Free Negro Code remained unchanged. During this period, however, the South experienced a number of slave insurrections. One such insurrection occurred in 1831 when Nat Turner and sixty to seventy other slaves in Virginia revolted against their master. The uprising resulted in the death of Turner's owner and approximately sixty other whites.[61] The "Nat Turner Uprising" heightened fears of mutiny among slave owners. Also, the fact that Turner was an educated preacher caused whites to fear educated blacks.

Concerned that the institution of slavery might be in jeopardy, the assembly amended the Free Negro Code in 1835. Under this code, free blacks had to obtain a residence license from the county court.[62] To obtain a license, they were required to post a large bond and prove their good character and employability. When a free black person wished to move from one county in the state to another, he/she was required to re-license and pay an additional bond.[63] The license could be revoked if the free black committed a felony or other infamous crime.[64] The penalty for being found in the state without a license was a ten- to one hundred–dollar fine, with jail time until the fine was paid, and upon payment, a free black could be ordered to leave the state.[65] If a free black failed to pay the fine, he or she could be whipped, or hired out until the fine and costs of imprisonment had been paid.[66]

In 1843, the Missouri General Assembly passed an even more drastic law.[67] All free blacks were prohibited from entering the state, unless they were Missouri natives or had resided in the state since 1840.[68] A person caught bringing a free black into St. Louis was fined two hundred dollars for the first violation and imprisoned for six months for the second violation. A third violation resulted in a one thousand–dollar fine. In 1847, however, the assembly went further and specifically prevented free blacks from coming to anyplace in Missouri, stating that "no free negro or mulatto shall, under any pretext, emigrate to this State, from any other State or territory."[69] Vessels trading in the state were strictly regulated to ensure compliance with the law. Captains were required to report the free blacks on board and to pay a bond ensuring that they would take them back out of the state. Furthermore, free blacks were confined on board the vessels while at port.[70] As one historian notes, this law clearly violated the Clay Amendment to the Missouri Compromise, which guaranteed free black citizens their constitutional rights.[71]

By prohibiting and restricting free blacks who lived in or passed through the state, the assembly minimized the opportunity for education. Furthermore, the assembly went beyond prior legislation and explicitly cut back the already limited opportunity for black children to pursue an education.

Anti-education sentiment reached a climax in 1847 when the assembly passed a law stating, "No person shall keep any school for the instruction of negroes or mulattoes, reading or writing, in this State."[72] Violators were fined or imprisoned for six months or both.[73] Although the law was aimed at those who wanted to educate blacks, the practical effect was to prohibit education for blacks altogether. Knowing that blacks were being privately educated in some churches, the assembly also outlawed meetings where black religious services were being held, unless a white law enforcement officer was present.[74]

These anti-education laws did not deter many of the advocates of black education, particularly those in St. Louis. All evidence indicates that the basic knowledge of reading and writing continued to spread among blacks in Missouri.[75] John Meachum, whose Sunday school attendance at his African Baptist Church in St. Louis ranged from 153 to 300 in 1846, continued to provide educational services. When opposition to even his limited instruction arose, Meachum held classes on a steamship anchored in the Mississippi River. Because the river was subject to federal rather than state jurisdiction, by transporting students to the steamship via skiff, Meachum legally educated blacks in defiance of state law.[76] The leading study on black education in antebellum Missouri noted that "countless unknowns" learned under his instruction.[77]

Black churches in St. Louis also continued their education efforts under the cover of Sunday schools.[78] Whites sympathetic to the need for black education provided money for books and other materials in these schools, while wealthier free blacks in St. Louis circumvented the law by sending their children to schools in eastern cities such as Philadelphia.[79]

The Catholic Church also was undeterred by the anti-education laws. The Catholic Sisters of St. Louis and free black women educated both enslaved and free blacks under the guise of sewing classes. In 1856, the Sisters of Mercy in St. Louis opened a school for blacks, and in 1858, Father Peter Konung of St. Xavier's Catholic Church taught a small, exclusively black congregation.[80]

Hiram K. Revels,[81] who later became the first black U.S. Senator, opened a school in St. Louis in 1856 that enrolled around 150 free and enslaved blacks.[82] In 1860, Revels left Missouri to accept a pastorate in Baltimore, but he returned to Missouri in 1863 to start a school for freedmen. At the end of the war, he was elected to the U.S. Senate from Mississippi to fill the unexpired term of Jefferson Davis, who had given up his seat to become president of the Confederacy.

Just before the Civil War, Tom Henderson, a free black Methodist minister, opened a school to educate blacks in Hannibal, Missouri. Classes were held in the Second Baptist Church in Hannibal, and Henderson taught there until the beginning of the Civil War. After Henderson left, Blanche K. Bruce, who had been a slave and who later became the first black to serve a full term in the U.S. Senate,[83] took over the school.

Despite these many efforts to defy the 1846 anti-education law,[84] by 1860, "hardly more than 5 percent (1,925) of the Negro population [of 118,503] possessed the simplest tools of learning."[85] This percentage was probably a good deal lower in rural Missouri, where a black person who had even a limited ability to read was considered a great novelty.[86] The mosaic of laws built up over forty years had succeeded in severely limiting blacks' access to education.

The U.S. Census and Annual Reports published by the Missouri Department of Education indicate that between 1820 and 1860 the state saved nearly $121 million in current dollars by refusing to educate black children.[87] Thereafter, the state saved approximately $5 million per year. However, the policy of excluding black children from public education imposed enormous and continuing costs to the state as a whole.

O Captain! My Captain! our fearful trip is done,
The ship has weather'd every rack, the prize we sought is
won.

–Walt Whitman[1]

{Chapter Three}

Education During the Civil War
and Reconstruction Years: 1860–1878

Rural Missouri school superintendents gave grim reports about the state of their schools following the Civil War:

> [T]here are no school-houses in the county worthy of the name, most of them having been destroyed during the rebellion.[2]

–H. W. G. Koontz, Newton County Superintendent

> This county has been without schools from the year 1862 until the present time. The school-houses, libraries, and all apparatus pertaining to school purposes were nearly all destroyed during the war.[3]

–A. M. Tatum, McDonald County Superintendent

Many of the schoolhouses had been burned or were beyond repair. Teachers had sometimes been threatened and had fled the area.[4]

> [O]ur county is not unlike many of our adjacent counties in southwest Missouri, which had suffered a general demolition of our public school organizations, from the rebellion, whose withering and desolating scourge for the past few years seemed to have held the moral energies of the people, and the interest of popular education spell-bound during the reign of terror.[5]

–Dr. S. W. Tyree, Pulaski County Superintendent

35

> Our school houses in this county shared the same fate that
> the dwellings and churches did during the late rebellion and were
> almost entirely destroyed by fire; the few that survived are almost
> worthless. The doors, windows and flooring were generally taken
> away.[6]

–David McGaughey, Bates County Superintendent

> During the war schools were scarce in this county; many of
> the sub-districts did not have any while the war lasted. In some
> places school-houses were burned; in others they became worthless
> from neglect.[7]

–A. Y. Carlton, Camden County Superintendent

During the Civil War and Reconstruction, Missouri's public education system
saw both setbacks and modest improvements. The devastation of rural schools by
force or neglect during the war years reduced the educational opportunities for
white children outside of the city of St. Louis, and after the war matters improved
only slightly. Black children, whether children of freedmen or slaves, had no opportunity to learn during the war. Afterward, laws prohibiting the education of
black children were repealed, but their educational opportunities remained limited.
The school superintendent of Osage County described the social climate in his 1867
report to the state superintendent of schools:

> It is not to be imagined that a community of people, who are
> uninterested in the education of their own children will take any
> interest in the education of the poor, neglected, despised negro.[8]

During the war, Missouri became a battleground between pro- and antislavery
forces. In 1860, Missouri elected as its governor Claiborne Jackson, a proslav-
ery Democrat who leaned toward secession. Shortly after Jackson's inauguration,
however, voters called for a state convention to meet and make a recommendation
on the issue of secession. When the convention met in March 1861, the delegates
rejected secession but continued to support the right of Missouri's citizens to hold
slaves. Before adjourning, the convention appointed a special committee that could
reconvene the convention in the event of an emergency.[9]

On April 12, 1861, rebel forces fired upon Fort Sumter and the Civil War
began. In Missouri, tensions escalated between the Unionists, who were especially
concentrated in St. Louis among the city's abolitionist German immigrants, and the
Southern sympathizers loyal to Governor Jackson. Each side began to recruit and
organize troops anticipating a confrontation. The Unionist Home Guards received
support from the federal government, and the secessionist militias covertly received

arms that Confederates had stolen from a federal arsenal at Baton Rouge. Martial law was declared in August 1861 due to escalating concerns over violence.

The tensions came to a head in May 1862 when the Home Guards, command-ed by abolitionist Captain Nathaniel Lyon, moved to seize the stolen arms from a Confederate militia encampment—named Camp Jackson, located on the present site of Saint Louis University's east campus—in St. Louis. The militia was outnumbered, and its members arrested without resistance. As the militia was marched through St. Louis to the federal arsenal, a melee erupted between local secessionists and Union-ists who had gathered to watch the procession. In June 1862, Lyon's Union forces, aided by troops from Iowa, forced the Jackson government out of Jefferson City. The exiled government eventually fled to the southwest corner of the state.[10]

The state convention then reconvened in July to consider what to do about the sudden power vacuum. The convention elected officers to form a provisional state government until popular elections could be held in November. The exiled Jackson government struggled to regain control of the state with the aid of Confederate funds and supplies and declared in November 1862 that the state had joined the Confederacy. Meanwhile, the state convention met again, postponing elections until August 1862, and declared that all civil officials must take a test oath of allegiance to the state and federal constitutions or forfeit their positions. The Union military command attempted to squelch the remaining secessionist citizenry with harsh sanctions for those supporting the rebel cause. The command later required the test oath for all those in leadership positions and declared that voters must take the oath before being allowed to vote.[11]

During the war years, Unionists were comprised of both a conservative faction, who resisted emancipation of the slaves and favored preserving the status quo, and a more liberal, progressive wing, whose members for a variety of ethical, practical, and economic reasons advocated an end to slavery. Although the emancipation ques-tion emerged as the major issue in Missouri's 1862 elections, because voters had to take the test oath the question was decided by those willing to declare loyalty to the Unionist cause. The results of the 1862 election favored candidates who supported some form of emancipation, but no plan for emancipation emerged from that legis-lative session.[12]

In response to mounting pressure for action, generated in a large measure by President Lincoln's January 1, 1863, proclamation freeing the slaves in the Confed-erate states, politically moderate Governor Hamilton Gamble called a fifth meeting of the state convention in June 1863. It produced an ordinance calling for the end of slavery in Missouri by July 1870. However, liberal Unionists began a campaign for immediate emancipation. A group of adamant abolitionists, called the Radi-cal Unionists, launched their campaign at a mass convention in Jefferson City on September 1, 1863.

By February 1864, the Radicals had gained sufficient strength in the Gen-eral Assembly to demand a referendum on calling yet another state convention to consider emancipation, suffrage, and the revision of the Missouri Constitution. The proposal passed with strong support, and three-fourths of the delegates to the convention—elected at the same time as the referendum vote—were Radicals.[13]

On January 11, 1865, two years after President Lincoln's Emancipation Proclamation, the convention passed a measure providing for the immediate and unconditional emancipation of all Missouri slaves. "On Sunday, January 14," said a report, "thousands took to the streets of St. Louis . . . with flags and banners proclaiming their joy at finally having achieved their most sought-after dream."[14] Of sixty-six convention delegates, only four voted against the measure.

However, by this time, many of Missouri's slaves had for all practical purposes been free for more than a year. The federal Confiscation Acts, which liberated any slaves held by Confederate sympathizers,[15] and the active recruitment of black troops into the Union Army, had left few slaves in the custody of their masters.[16]

During the war years, no efforts were made to educate black children in rural Missouri, but as of 1863 private interests had established four subscription schools for black children in the city of St. Louis. These four schools had a combined enrollment of 187 students; each student typically paid a monthly tuition of one dollar. Other organizations also sought to operate free schools for black students. A white charitable organization, the New York–based American Missionary Association, attempted to open a free school for blacks in the Missouri Hotel, but the school was destroyed by arson three days after it opened. The Western Sanitary Commission—a private organization founded by William Greenleaf Eliot and James E. Yeatman originally concerned with medical care for wounded Civil War soldiers—was able to successfully organize classes for black students at Benton Barracks in St. Louis.[17]

In the winter of 1863, concerned St. Louisans, both black and white, established the privately sponsored Board of Education for Colored Schools, which planned to take over the existing subscription schools. It subsequently established free schools, awaiting a change in the law that would allow it to merge with the St. Louis Public School System. By February 1864, the Board oversaw the operations of four free schools, with a total of four hundred students. The schools were located in rented facilities that were financed by organizations such as the Western Sanitation Commission, which donated one hundred dollars a month. A year later, enrollment had risen to six hundred students, taught by eight teachers. In addition, fifty to sixty black students attended high school in Eliot's Unitarian Church basement at Eighth and Locust Streets.[18]

However, the Board had trouble obtaining qualified black teachers for its free schools. It could not hire teachers away from subscription schools, because it could not afford to pay them as much. Relatively well-off black families preferred to keep their children in the subscription schools, away from the poorer black children in the free schools. Additionally, some black Catholic parents joined the parents of white students and sent their children to parochial schools. These schools enrolled 25 percent of all of the students attending school in St. Louis in 1863. For a time, the American Missionary Association supplied and paid white teachers for the parochial school system.[19]

During the 1864–65 school year, there were five free black schools in St. Louis with a combined attendance of fifteen hundred students.[20] In February 1865, the Missouri General Assembly officially rescinded the earlier law forbidding the education of blacks.[21] That same month, the Board of Education for Colored Schools requested financial assistance from the St. Louis School Board, saying that it had thus far survived on a few thousand dollars in contributions from the Western Sanitary Commission, two prominent white citizens, and the black community. The St. Louis School Board offered to contribute five hundred dollars to the "colored" schools. This was the first appropriation from Missouri public funds for the education of black children, although black taxpayers had been contributing to the public education system all along. In his 1865 report to the Board of Directors, St. Louis Superintendent Ira Drivoll observed, "It is a well known fact that the colored people of this city pay taxes on two or three million dollars of property; they should, therefore, as a matter of right and justice, as a matter of principle . . . receive in educational facilities the benefit of their taxation."[22]

The five hundred–dollar allocation (.2 percent of the School Board's budget), however, proved to be insufficient and the black free schools were forced to close in the early spring of 1865.[23]

A Constitutional Convention, controlled by antislavery Unionists, met in the summer of 1865 and adopted a constitution that forbade slavery and established public education as a responsibility of the state. In response to the Act of Congress admitting Missouri as a state, the Constitution that was adopted in 1865 required "free schools for the gratuitous instruction of all persons in this state between the ages of five and twenty-one years."[24]

The schools mandated by the constitution were to be funded in part by federal land grants. School funds were to be "appropriated in proportion to the number of children, without regard to color."[25] But the Reconstruction-era Constitution hedged on the issue of fully integrated public education, saying that "[s]eparate schools may be established for children of African descent."[26] The 1865 Constitution was ratified in the summer by a slim majority.

The General Assembly, controlled by a more conservative element, required local boards of education to "establish within their respective jurisdictions one or more separate schools for colored children."[27] However, such schools were required only when there were more than twenty colored children within a district. If the average attendance at the school fell below twenty for a month, local officials had to close the school for up to six months. In all other respects, schools for colored children were to be "equal to others of the same grade in their respective townships, cities and villages," and afford their students "the advantages and privileges of a common school education."[28]

Opposition, fraud, and indifference at the local level thwarted the state laws mandating the public education of blacks. Under the 1865 statutes, apportionment of the state school fund was to be made according to a count of students conducted by the local school director or town clerk, with white and black children to be counted separately.[29] An accurate count would have ensured that black schools received all the state funds due them. But local officials evaded the law by failing to count black children, and then, in turn, pleading a lack of funds or teachers.[30] Missouri's superintendent of schools would later point out that the law did not include sanctions against local officials who failed to perform the duties required.[31] Outside of St. Louis, black schools tended to be maintained by white benevolent societies, such as the American Missionary Association and the Northwestern Freedmen's Aid Commission.[32]

In 1866, the St. Louis School Board absorbed the subscription schools run by the Board of Education for Colored Schools, which enrolled 437 black students in 3 black schools.[33] Despite increasing attacks on black public education from local Democratic Party elements,[34] the superintendent of schools for St. Louis reported that between twelve and fifteen "colored" schools were operating, with a total enrollment estimated between two and three thousand.[35] The small student population scattered throughout the large metropolitan area meant that black schools could not be as conveniently located as white schools; an 1867 report of the St. Louis Board of Education noted that attendance and punctuality were problems in the black schools.[36] Moreover, the Board found it difficult to rent or purchase suitable buildings for schools. The general condition of black schools was so bad that they were continually closed and moved to new locations. At best, blacks might inherit old white schoolhouses that had been abandoned for more modern facilities. More often, however, blacks were educated in inferior, inadequate, and inconveniently located buildings, sometimes pursuing instruction at a different location each year.[37] For instance, in 1869, teaching in Colored School No. 3 became impossible due to dampness and generally unhealthy conditions, and the school was forced to move to scattered, ill-equipped, unused rooms in another building.[38]

Such disruptions made it difficult to maintain stable district boundaries for black students and to maintain a standardized, graded curriculum. Some black students walked more than two miles to attend school, often passing multiple white schools. The black community tried to raise money for new facilities through dinners, festivals, fairs, and picnics.[39] However, even these efforts were met with resistance from some members of the white community.

The county superintendents' reports from the postwar years also reflect the limited educational opportunities available for white, rural, Missouri students during the Civil War. In 1861, short on funds, the State Board of Education recommended that all administrators and teachers accept a 27 percent pay cut. The committee also recommended that families pay tuition of $1.50 per quarter in the elementary schools, and $7 per quarter in the high school.[40] Attendance dropped radically, from 8,000 in the 1861–62 school year to 3,700 in the 1862–63 school year.[41] Most affected by the tuition requirements were the children of blue-collar workers and skilled and unskilled laborers. Records show that about two-thirds of the students from these families stopped attending the public elementary schools. Enrollment in the high school continued at the existing levels.[42]

Top: Rock Spring Colored School No. 7, ca. 1873.
Bottom: Colored School No. 6 was located on Fifth Street Between Filmore and Market. In 1890, the school was renamed Delany School. This photograph was taken ca. 1885. Photos courtesy the St. Louis Public Schools Archives.

At a meeting in July 1863, the directors voted to reinstate free education in the elementary schools while maintaining the tuition of seven dollars per quarter at the high schools. This action had the desired result: The children came back and filled the schools.[43] In 1864, tuition was also eliminated for the high schools, and the board once again adopted the principle that "schools should be free and ample for all who wish to attend."[44]

By 1867, fifty-six schools for blacks—most still privately run—had been established in thirty counties in Missouri.[45] Two years later, the Freedman's Bureau reported that the number of black schools in Missouri had doubled and that public schools had begun to predominate.[46] Despite these increasing numbers, public education for all races in Missouri was still hobbled by the lingering hostilities that followed the Civil War.

As T. A. Parker, the state superintendent of schools, pointed out in his annual report to the assembly in 1867:

> The encouragement given to the free school is in exact ratio to the prevalence of liberal ideas. Where there has been much treason there is little public school sentiment; where there has been much loyalty there is much public school sentiment. The one moves parallel to the other and is co-ordinate in its extent and effects.[47]

Parker continued:

> There are certain portions of our State where there has been no school-house for years. The inhabitants are either under the influence of strong political prejudices against all legislation emanating from your honorable body, and willfully refuse to organize under the revised school law, or are wretchedly ignorant of its beneficence.[48]

County superintendents decried the poor condition of the public schools attended by white children in their districts:

> It is, in my opinion, useless to expect much improvement in the character of our schools until the old and unsightly schoolhouses, which now disgrace so many of our districts are torn down and replaced by others worthy of the name and of the high and almost sacred uses for which they are designed. If the parents, instead of the children, could be sent for a season to those dreary and prison-like houses, with their bare and dingy walls and comfortless seats, we would not have to wait long for the needed reform.[49]

–Edward B. Neely, Buchanan County Superintendent

We have not one decent school-house in the county. . . .
About one-fourth of our schools are held in skeleton churches,
where there is not a desk, and often not a back to the seats on
which from forty to a hundred children are compelled, for seven
or eight hours per day, five days in the week, to sit and weary out
their blessed little natures. O, God, is there mercy for the drunk-
ard, the outcast and the negro, and none for the innocent loves of
our own household?[50]

–James H. Kerr, Cape Girardeau County Superintendent

During the war nearly all the public schools of Jefferson
County were suspended, and it is only during the past six months
that any general effort has been made to re-open them. The difficulties we encounter are these: 1st. Want of competent teachers; 2d. Poor school-houses; 3d. Want of definiteness in many of
the provisions of the new law; 4th. The impossibility of raising a
school fund by taxation prior to the fall of 1867.[51]

–C. A. Clark, Jefferson County Superintendent

State Superintendent Parker noted that Missouri's black students faced the
additional obstacles of indifference and outright hostility, and urged action on the
matter:

[The school law] gives authority to all Boards of Education
to establish colored schools within their jurisdiction, and requires
them so to do. It also requires these schools to be separate from
those designed for white children, but the enumeration of the
colored children must amount to twenty. . . . What if the local directors (as is the case frequently) refuse to employ the teachers for
these colored schools, even where there may be the requisite number? Even where there may be no evident hostility to this statute
and to the education of the colored people, there has been a failure
to make the requisite enumeration of the colored children in many
townships, and, consequently, they will be deprived by the very
law itself, from any participation in the State School Fund. . . .

Unless, therefore, there be made a special order of the legislature directing the proper officer to take another and a correct
enumeration of the colored youth, the supreme will of the people
will be thwarted. If this may be deemed impracticable by you, I
yet urge upon you the necessity of meeting in some efficient man-

ner the demands of justice toward the youth of this unfortunate
people; for I regard it but as compliance with the cruel spirit of
our once common crime to deprive them of two years education
in our public schools.[52]

County superintendents also remarked on the barriers black students faced in
rural areas of Missouri and, in some cases, the ways that the barriers were circumvented:

> There are not a sufficient number of colored children in most
> of the rural districts of the county to make schools of any size,
> and I am clearly of the opinion that under the existing opposition
> colored schools could not be conducted in and of the country
> districts of the county.[53]

–W. H. Thomas, Callaway County Superintendent

> There is no public school for the colored children, as there is
> no district with a sufficient number for the support of a school.
> The colored people of the county, both old and young, meet every
> Sabbath at the county seat, and are instructed by the citizens of
> the place.[54]

–John H. Williams, Caldwell County Superintendent

> I am sorry to say that there is so little interest manifested in
> behalf of educating the colored people. The directors . . . of this
> township have provided them with a school house, and they are
> now carrying on a good school with their own private means.[55]

–F. J. R. Seller, Cooper County Superintendent

Other county superintendents gave opinions reflecting their own racial and
political prejudices:

> There seems to be a general desire to give the colored people
> all the advantages offered them in the new school law; and noth-
> ing but their own impudence will hereafter prevent them from
> enjoying every civil right.[56]

–James H. Kerr, Cape Girardeau County Superintendent

In regard to the interest manifested in the education of colored people, I must state that it has been, so far, of little account; but the leaders of the Radical party in our county intend to try to organize a school for the negro children, and I hope that they will succeed.[57]

–Chas Moeller, Carroll County Superintendent

Never knew but one darkey in the county, and he learned all manner of mischief very readily.[58]

–A. J. Bader, Schuyler County Superintendent

Comments made by county superintendents in the 1870 Report of the State Superintendent of Public Schools identified financing as the primary obstacle to the expansion of public education statewide. Thomas G. Deartherage of Howard County wrote, "One of the greatest difficulties to be overcome is a reluctance to be taxed for school purposes. . . . Another difficulty is the willingness of the people to employ the poorest teachers in our most backward schools. This is often done for the reason that this class of teachers can be obtained cheaper than others."[59]

Other superintendents wrote that because public education was thought generally to be for poor children, taxation to assist public schools lacked support among those best able to provide it:

The feeling, so common in some parts of our country, that public schools are for the education of the children of poor people, and that select schools should be established for the children of the wealthy, is prevalent in a part of the county, and will no doubt continue until it shall have been demonstrated that public schools are the best. This would be comparatively easy, but for the fact that a large part of the best influence is withdrawn from, if not actually arrayed against them.[60]

–J. Markham, Iron County Superintendent

If the wealthy parents of children would expend one-fourth the money wasted in boarding their children abroad, in an increase of the salaries of the teachers in the primary schools at home, so as to get better teachers, they would be enable to give them a sound, practical English education, on which they could then build a good classical, or any other education calculated to make them practical business men and ornaments of society.[61]

–S. F. Murray, Pike County Superintendent

Lingering political differences among the populace in the wake of the Civil War served as an additional barrier to securing adequate funds for public schools:

> [T]he greatest of all obstacles is the "oath of loyalty," and the infamous manner in which the registration has been carried out in this county. Schools never can flourish until relieved of their blighting influence. They cause quarrels in the districts, thus destroying that harmony of feeling which is essential to the prosperity of schools.[62]

–Lincoln County Superintendent

> A great many men are disfranchised, so they are not eligible to vote for directors, nor to act in that capacity. And there are many townships in the county which do not contain more than one, two or three men who are allowed to vote, and sometimes none, and it is difficult to get men to take an interest in their own township, much less in another.[63]

–Texas County Superintendent

Inequities in school funding between rich and poor districts were worsened by a system in which a set amount of state funding was supplemented locally with monies raised in part through the sale of public lands. The saleable lands varied tremendously in quality and quantity. One superintendent observed:

> These rich citizens do not need [funds raised by land sales], because they are all abundantly able to educate their children without it. But still they get it; yes, they get all the [proceeds from land sales], and the poor, needy children . . . get none. . . . No wonder [the poor] are constrained to pronounce the whole common school system a humbug. . . . No wonder the teachers of the proper calibre turn away, and leave the business of teaching in the hands of ignorant, old fogies and young idling loafers. . . .[64]

–Madison County Superintendent

Despite shortfalls in operating funds, new school construction in Missouri increased rapidly between 1865 and 1870, helped by Republican legislation allowing school boards to tax their districts to cover new school construction costs without a vote of the people.[65] Black students, however, did not benefit from the construction boom. In 1867, the state superintendent of schools reported that just twelve counties had at least one school for black students. Sixty-one counties either reported that they had no schools for black students or failed to report on the subject; twenty-nine counties failed to file a report at all.

In the city of St. Louis, there were six "colored" schools, providing free public education for a limited number of students. By 1870, a total of approximately 20,000 school-age children attended public schools in St. Louis.[66] Of the 20,000 only 1,275 were black.[67] Sixteen thousand white children in St. Louis City attended private or parochial schools, but no data is available regarding the number of black students who attended private or parochial schools. The cost of educating a white student in the public schools was $18.70 per year while the cost of educating a black student was $12.76.[68] The tuition in private schools was three to six times this amount.

According to the 1870 census, a total of 9,080 black students throughout Missouri were then attending school "in churches and cabins with walls admirably adapted for ventilation and for admission of copious shower baths of rain."[69] According to these figures, only about 21 percent of the state's 42,000 school-age black children were being educated in either private or public schools. Although this was a significant increase over the 1867 figures, there remained 2,984 black children living in the 55 counties without schools. By comparison, about 59 percent of white children were attending school.[70] The 1870 Report of the State Superintendent of Public Schools stated that there were no black schools in eleven counties, at least one black school in thirty-five counties (an improvement over only twelve counties in 1867), and that sixty-six counties had failed to report.

The Missouri Legislature attempted to cope with the sparse number of black students in rural areas by allowing, and then mandating, the consolidation of two or more districts if such a consolidation would support the creation of a black school.[71] The legislature also decreased to fifteen the number of students required to establish a black school,[72] and it granted the state's superintendent of schools the authority to establish and maintain a black school if local officials failed to do so,[73] a power frequently exercised by the superintendent in the early 1870s.[74] Yet in 1871, thirty-nine counties still lacked black schools.[75] Some districts with black populations too small to establish separate black schools permitted black students to enroll in white schools.[76]

The problem of securing teachers for black schools persisted, in part because both races objected to having white teachers in black schools.[77] Before the establishment of black public schools, the Reverend George Caudee of the American Missionary Association noticed that the Board of Education for Colored Schools preferred to staff its classrooms with inadequately trained black teachers before hiring a qualified white teacher.[78] After the St. Louis Board of Education assumed control of the black schools, the Board initially staffed them with white teachers. However, in 1874, and again in 1877, black citizens petitioned the Board to replace the white teachers with qualified black teachers. These citizens argued that well-trained white teachers would not consider teaching in black schools because of a stigma associated with teaching in those schools. They contended that white teachers would also be prejudiced. They argued that black teachers, on the other hand, were zealous, unbiased, better equipped to meet the needs of their students, and would be powerful role models. They also recognized that black teaching positions represented a rare opportunity for blacks to advance beyond unskilled or service jobs. During the 1877–78 school year, the first year after the introduction of black teachers in the St. Louis schools, black student enrollment increased 35 percent.[79]

Teacher pay rates in St. Louis were based upon the size of the school in which the teacher worked, and most black schools were relatively small.[80] Statewide, in 1873, the average teacher salary at a white school was $87.12 per month for men and $46.64 for women; the average salary at a black school was $46.70 for men and $40.00 for women.[81] A partial solution to the teacher shortage came from contributions from veterans of the Sixty-Second and Sixty-Fifth Colored Infantries, who helped to support a black teachers' college called the Lincoln Institute, founded in Jefferson City in 1866.[82] Although Lincoln struggled in its first four years without help from the state, it managed to produce a few qualified black teachers.[83] In 1870, the Lincoln Institute secured an annual appropriation from the state of five thousand dollars. The General Assembly had probably acted on the suggestion of the state superintendent of schools, who had stated, "The most important suggestion I have to make for the further improvement of colored schools is that a normal school for training of colored teachers be established."[84] Noting that highly qualified white teachers could "usually do better in white schools," and that highly qualified black teachers "cannot yet be found in any large number," the superintendent concluded,

> In not many avocations do colored people have an equal opportunity with whites. Teaching is one of the most useful and respectable. They should be encouraged to engage in it. . . . Justice demands no less. A large part of the wealth of Missouri has been produced by the unrequited labor of slaves. It is but a small return that we should give to their children, now free, the largest privileges of education.[85]

In 1875, the city of St. Louis had twelve black public schools, all of which were identified by numbers rather than by names, as white schools were.[86] In 1875, the General Assembly authorized the establishment of a black high school.[87] This school was named Sumner High School. It became the only black high school west of the Mississippi River in the United States.[88] Simultaneously, however, the board eliminated three smaller black schools, prompting protests from the black community.[89] In addition, the operation of Sumner High School was hampered by inadequate facilities and a lack of funds. Sumner was housed in a building that had formerly housed a white elementary school, a building that the St. Louis School Board had been unable to sell. Three times as much money was spent on the education of a typical white high school student as on a black student who attended Sumner.[90] Moreover, even though designated as a high school, Sumner remained mostly an elementary school.

Statewide, the progress of public education was complicated by Reconstruction-era politics. Deep fissures had formed among the ranks of the Missouri Republicans over the questions of the enfranchisement of black men and the reinfranchisement of former rebels. Although the former question was resolved when the Fifteenth Amendment was ratified in 1870, Liberal Republicans split with Radical Republicans on the issue of the rights of former Confederate sympathizers. By 1874, the Republicans had lost control of the state to the Democrats, who favored decentralizing education in the state and returning it to local control. They eliminated the office of county school superintendent, along with the power of the district school boards unilaterally to levy taxes for new buildings. Decentralization reduced the uniformity of education throughout the state and made it more difficult to collect educational statistics, thereby reintroducing corruption.[91] As a result, both school census and enrollment figures briefly dropped despite steady increases in population. In 1875, of 41,916 black children eligible for school, only 14,832 were enrolled. However, by 1877 the reported black school-age population had dropped to 32,411 with an enrollment of 14,505. Despite the decrease in reported eligible children, enrollment surged above 21,000 in 1878, indicating that even if the eligible population had

Sumner High School's first location was at Eleventh and Spruce Streets. This portrait of Sumner's teachers was taken ca. 1882. Photo courtesy the St. Louis Public Schools Archives.

been underreported, an increasing percentage of black children were enrolling in public schools.[92]

At the end of Radical rule in Missouri in 1874, education had become firmly established as a responsibility of the state and local governments, but school segregation and inferior treatment of black students were just as entrenched. The Democrats who gained control of the General Assembly promptly called for a Constitutional Convention. Although segregation had been mandated by legislative command since 1865, Missouri's 1875 Constitution gave segregation constitutional status, abandoning the earlier Constitution's permissive language regarding separate schools ("separate schools may be established") for a new provision that clearly stated: "Separate free public schools shall be established for the education of children of African descent."[93]

Not only did African American children have to contend with deteriorating school buildings, funding shortages, and teacher shortages, but the General Assembly had further raised the legal barriers to obtaining an integrated and equal education, barriers that remained for more than one hundred years.

Together with German instruction, the most explosive issue in the 19th century was how blacks would benefit from the city's commitment to public education. Since blacks suffered from white widespread hostility and did not command significant weight in community politics, they were relegated to separate and substandard facilities. The fundamental reason for this policy was a pervasive unwillingness to transcend the distinction of race while pursuing the ideal of the common school.

–Selwyn K. Troen[1]

{Chapter Four}

Separate-But-Unequal Education: 1875–1954

Although Missouri permitted the segregated education of blacks following the Civil War, the history of public education in the state from 1875 to 1954 is a chronicle of many struggles on the part of black families and students to obtain elementary and higher education. Many of the progressive changes made during Reconstruction were undone by politicians and the courts in the 1880s and 1890s. Local school districts evaded and violated the laws mandating schools for black children. The available educational opportunities were often in crowded, dilapidated, and segregated schools.

Although education for black children improved remarkably between 1875 and 1954, the city of St. Louis, St. Louis County, and the state of Missouri maintained a segregated educational system. Educational opportunities in St. Louis were further affected by demographic changes that left most blacks confined in urban ghettoes. By the time the Supreme Court decided *Brown v. Board of Education* in 1954, black and white children in Missouri had for many years received separate and unequal educations.

In 1875, what there was of the postwar civil rights movement had ended. Conservative Democrats returned to power in Missouri as they did throughout the South and began to overturn Reconstruction-era policies. All but a few ex-Confederates were granted amnesty and the right to vote while blacks were increasingly disenfranchised through intimidation, poll taxes, and strict requirements for voting, including literacy and property ownership. In 1876, the responsibility for the enforcement of civil rights laws was transferred to the states, and prosecutions for federal civil rights violations decreased sharply.

The economic depression of the 1870s and 1880s reinforced racist reactions to Reconstruction. Whites everywhere were unwilling to share social, economic, or educational equality with blacks.[2] Professor E. F. Frazier describes this reaction as the "rise of the poor whites." Emerging industrialists appealed to the racial prejudice of poor whites, who could then be encouraged to vote against their own interests.[3] Similarly, Professor Horace Mann Bond notes how the poor quality of white schools was blamed on the existence of black schools, rather than on inadequate funding for both.[4]

A series of Supreme Court decisions further weakened the Reconstruction-era constitutional amendments and overturned several sections of the civil rights laws. Beginning in 1872 in the *Slaughterhouse Cases*,[5] the Court severely limited the Fourteenth Amendment.[6] In *United States v. Cruikshank*,[7] the Court invalidated an indictment under section six of the Civil Rights Act of 1870[8] and held that the Fourteenth Amendment did not forbid private acts of discrimination.[9] In *United States v. Harris*, the Court declared the criminal conspiracy section of the Ku Klux Klan Act of 1871[10] unconstitutional, thus making it more difficult to deter violence by the Klan.[11]

In the *Civil Rights Cases*[12] (1883), one of its most far-reaching decisions, the Supreme Court struck down two provisions of the Civil Rights Act of 1875 that prohibited segregation in public places.[13] Although the Thirteenth Amendment gave Congress the power to abolish "all badges and incidents of slavery,"[14] the Court held that "social" discrimination and segregation did not constitute such "badges of slavery."[15] Justice Bradley, writing for the Court, said:

> Can the act of a mere individual, the owner of the inn, the public conveyance, or place of amusement, refusing the accommodation, be justly regarded as imposing any badge of slavery or servitude upon the applicant. . . ?
>
> [W]e are forced to the conclusion that such an act of refusal has nothing to do with slavery or involuntary servitude. . . . It would be running the slavery argument into the ground to make it apply to every act of discrimination which a person may see fit to make as to the guests he will entertain, or as to the people he will take into his coach or cab or car, or admit to his concert or theater, or deal with other matters of intercourse or business.[16]

Justice John Marshall Harlan vigorously dissented:

> The thirteenth amendment . . . did something more than to prohibit slavery as an *institution*, resting upon distinctions of race, and upheld by positive law. . . . [I]t established and decreed universal *civil freedom* throughout the United States. But did the freedom thus established involve nothing more intended than to forbid one man from owning another as property? Were the states, against whose solemn protest the institution was destroyed, to be left perfectly free, so far as national interference was concerned,

to make or allow discriminations against that race, as such, in the enjoyment of those fundamental rights that inhere in a state of freedom?. . . .

> I am of the opinion that . . . discrimination practiced by cor-
> porations and individuals in the exercise of their public or quasi-
> public functions is a badge of servitude, the imposition of which
> congress may prevent under its power. . . .
>
> Today it is the colored race which is denied, by corporations
> and individuals wielding public authority, rights fundamental
> in their freedom and citizenship. At some future time it may be
> some other race that will fall under the ban. If the constitutional
> amendments be enforced, according to the intent with which, as I
> conceive, they were adopted, there cannot be, in this republic, any
> class of human beings in practical subjection to another class, with
> power in the latter to dole out to the former just such privileges as
> they may choose to grant.[17]

In *Younger v. Judah*,[18] the Missouri Supreme Court relied on the *Civil Rights Cases* and held that the Fourteenth Amendment did not prohibit a theater owner from reserving the better seats exclusively for whites.[19] Preferential treatment of whites, the court said, "accords with the custom and usage prevailing in this state. Such custom has the force and effect of law. . . ."[20]

The United States Supreme Court renewed its blessing on segregation in May 1889 with its decision in *Plessy v. Ferguson*.[21] *Plessy* was a challenge to a Louisiana statute requiring separate but equal railway accommodations for whites and blacks, prohibiting passengers from sitting in the coaches designated for use by the other race and providing for a fine of up to twenty-five dollars or up to twenty days in jail for those who used the wrong coach. Plessy was "of mixed descent, in the propor-tion of seven-eighths Caucasian and one-eighth African blood,"[22] who took a seat in the white coach. Justice Brown, writing for the Court, held that the Louisiana law did not violate the Fourteenth Amendment and was a reasonable exercise of the state's police power.

Justice Brown refused to acknowledge that segregation constituted a "badge of inferiority" upon either race and insisted that any such perception by blacks such as Plessy was "solely because the colored race chooses to put that construction upon it."[23] At the most basic level, Justice Brown insisted that the law could not eradicate racial prejudice: "If the two races are to meet upon terms of social equality, it must be the result of natural affinities, a mutual appreciation of each other's merits, and a voluntary consent of individuals. . . ."[24]

Justice John Marshall Harlan, the lone dissenter in the *Civil Rights Cases*, again dissented. He insisted that "[t]he law regards man as man, and takes no account of his surroundings or of his color when his civil rights as guarantied [*sic*] by the supreme law of the land are involved."[25] Justice Harlan recognized that segregation was unmistakably a badge of inferiority, and it would only feed America's seething racial tensions:

> What can more certainly arouse race hate, what [can] more certainly create and perpetuate a feeling of distrust between these races, than state enactments which, in fact, proceed on the ground that colored citizens are so inferior and degraded that they cannot be allowed to sit in public coaches occupied by white citizens? That, as all will admit, is the real meaning of such legislation as was enacted in Louisiana.[26]

Within three years of *Plessy*, the Supreme Court applied the separate-but-equal doctrine to a pair of school cases. In *Cumming v. Richmond County Board of Education*[27] (1899) a Georgia county board of education had terminated funding for a black public high school for "economic reasons,"[28] while taxing the county to subsidize a white high school for boys.[29] Nonetheless, the Court held that this was not a constitutional violation. Writing for a unanimous Court, Justice Harlan emphasized that the federal government should not interfere with state systems of education and taxation "except in the case of a clear and unmistakable disregard of rights secured by the supreme law of the land."[30]

Similarly, in *Berea College v. Kentucky*[31] (1908) a divided Supreme Court[32] upheld a Kentucky statute that made it a crime to maintain an integrated college. Berea College, a private institution, was willing to allow blacks and whites to attend college together, but Kentucky and the Supreme Court would not allow it.[33] Justices Harlan and Day dissented. In his dissent, Justice Harlan stated:

> The capacity to impart instruction to others is given by the Almighty for beneficent purposes; and its use may not be forbidden or interfered with by government,—certainly not, unless such instruction is, in its nature, harmful to the public morals or imperils the public safety. . . . If pupils, of whatever race,—certainly if they be citizens,—choose, with the consent of their parents, or voluntarily, to sit together in a private institution of learning while receiving instruction which is not in its nature harmful or dangerous to the public, no government, whether Federal or state, can legally forbid their coming together, or being together temporarily, for such an innocent purpose.[34]

The impact of the *Plessy* doctrine on black education is well documented.[35] By 1900, segregated schools for blacks were required by law in Missouri and eighteen other states.[36] In 1916, the United States Department of the Interior published a comprehensive study of black education in sixteen Southern states, the District of

Columbia, and Missouri.[37] The study found that "the Negro schoolhouses are miserable beyond all description"[38] and that separate schools fostered misunderstanding and stigmatized blacks as inferior.[39]

Backed by precedents from the nation's highest court, Missouri courts condoned segregated state schools of disparate quality through the early 1950s. In *State ex rel. Hobby v. Disman*[40] (1952), the Missouri Supreme Court considered a request to compel the transfer of black students to a white school because the appearance, construction, and arrangement of the black school were deficient.[41] Although the court determined that the black school lacked an auditorium and a cafeteria steam table and had a small playground and separate buildings,[42] it decided that these shortcomings were either insignificant or not racially motivated and concluded that the plaintiffs had not demonstrated that "substantially the same conditions as to physical facilities do not generally exist" in the white district.[43] To the court, "equality" in separate schools meant "substantial" equality.[44]

Litigation over Missouri's system of higher education had the same result. In *State ex rel. Toliver v. Board of Education of St. Louis*[45] (1950), the Missouri Supreme Court reversed a black plaintiff's successful attempt to transfer from a black teacher's college to the state's white counterpart. Although the court noted some differences in the facilities, library, and curriculum, it minimized these differences and concluded that the facilities were substantially equal.[46]

Moreover, Missouri, like other former slave states, subsequently passed numerous laws to require segregation in places where social custom had not already established it as the norm: on streetcars, buses, and railroads, and in waiting rooms, prisons, mental health institutions, and entertainment facilities.[47] By 1948, segregation by custom in Missouri was so pervasive that a court took judicial notice of the fact.[48]

The *Missouri Republican*, the leading newspaper of the Democratic Party, had embarked on an anti-"colored" school campaign as early as 1866. The *Republican* denounced the St. Louis School Board for frivolously spending public money to build extravagant schoolhouses for blacks, saying, "If they like to associate with the niggerdom, as would seem to be the case, let them go, but not at the expense of the white men."[49] This campaign continued for several years.

The state superintendent of education reported in 1878 that the laws requiring schools for black children had been repeatedly evaded and violated during the previous two years, particularly in rural areas.[50] He told local officials that all funds for their school district would be withheld unless they complied with the law and established schools for Negroes within their district.[51]

In order to reduce the burden on the superintendent of creating black schools in a district that failed to do so, the Missouri Legislature in 1879 released the superintendent from that duty. Instead, a district that failed to provide black schools would not get state school funds for the following year. This moved the school districts to act, and by 1885, the black school population had increased substantially.

Meanwhile, the *St. Louis Globe-Democrat* had reported in 1875 that St. Louis's

Board of Education had failed, for several years, to balance its budget. An economic depression that affected the country in the 1870s had reduced school revenues at the same time that enrollment and expenses were increasing.[52] A study of St. Louis students in 1880 reveals that despite the inferiority of the black schools black students were attending elementary school in numbers as large as, or greater than, whites from similar economic classes. This enthusiasm for school is particularly striking considering that black students were likely to either come from families that were fatherless and headed by a working mother[53] or from families with origins in the Deep South with no tradition of education.[54] Also, the St. Louis schools made no efforts to recruit black students, unlike their effort to recruit white students from the city's immigrant population, particularly the Germans, for whom the schools provided German-language instruction as an inducement to enroll.[55]

Among high school students, however, class origins made a marked difference. Those who dropped out of school took either semi-skilled or unskilled jobs.[56] The earnings of the father, then as now, was an important indicator of who continued to attend school. Eighty percent of the children of professionals were in school, but only 3 percent of the children of unskilled workers were in school.[57] Very few, if any, of the black students fell into the first category. After age twelve, most children, particularly black children, returned home or graduated into the working world.[58] The president of the St. Louis Board of Education, commenting on the dropout rate, stated:

> This is a sad state of things, yet it should be known to every citizen of St. Louis, that every year a vast army of public school boys and girls, who are thirteen and fourteen and fifteen years old, in the middle of the district school course, for one reason or another, stop going to school. These facts have much the nature of a public calamity, and it is the solemn duty of those in responsible charge of the schools to point out as clearly as possible the probable causes and the most practicable remedies.[59]

The provision in Missouri's 1875 Constitution mandating that separate schools for colored children "shall" be established had not been uniformly followed, and some schools admitted both black and white students. In 1881, St. Louis established its first black kindergarten. That same year, black leaders met with Missouri's governor and encouraged him to support integrated schools. He refused, although some schools continued to admit both blacks and whites.[60] In 1887, however, a white teacher in Grundy County refused to admit black students to a white school that had previously been open to them. Parents sued the teacher on the grounds that the students were being denied rights guaranteed to them by the Fourteenth Amendment.[61]

Before the court decided that issue, the Missouri General Assembly in 1889 passed a law that went a step further and declared, "It shall hereafter be unlaw-

ful in the public schools of the state for any colored child to attend a whi\
or any white child to attend a colored school."[62] In 1891, the Missouri Su\
Court held that requiring black children to attend a "colored" school outsi\
county, instead of the public school in their county, did not violate the Fourteenth
Amendment. Although this case was not related to the 1889 school-segregation law,
the court's opinion, in effect, gave a stamp of approval to the position held by the
Missouri General Assembly and prohibited black children from attending a white
school even if the district had no school for black students. The black students in
the case traveled three and one-half miles to an adjoining district. No white student
in the district traveled more than two miles. The court noted:

> There are differences in races . . . some of which can never
> be eradicated. . . . If we cast aside chimerical theories and look to
> practical results, it seems to us it must be conceded that separate
> schools for colored children is a regulation to their great advan-
> tage. . . . The fact that the two races are separated for the purpose
> of receiving instruction deprives neither of any rights. It is but a
> reasonable regulation of the exercise of the right.[63]

Unfortunately, the decisions of the assembly and the Missouri Supreme Court
left behind as many as five to six thousand black children who lived in communities that did not have to establish black schools because the black population was
sparse.[64] Under the 1889 law, districts without a black school had to pay tuition to
have their black students schooled in another district. This law, however, was not
observed for two reasons: "The Negro knew nothing of the law and made no attempt to benefit by it, and the school authorities did not enforce it."[65]

In the early part of the twentieth century, St. Louis's public schools continued
to grow, as did the city's black population. In 1907, the city appropriated almost
$300,000 for the construction of a new Sumner High School building. The three-
story building, containing a large auditorium, laboratories, facilities for industrial
education, and a swimming pool, [66] was considered to be the finest black high
school in the country.[67]

A 1919 study by the Sage Foundation ranked Missouri's school system, for
both black and white students, thirty-fourth among the forty-eight states.[68] Missouri spent more on education per black child than any former slave state, but even
its best black schools were not equal to white schools. Per-pupil expenditures were
lower, teachers were paid an average of 25 percent less and many were uncertified,[69]
and the facilities suffered from faulty construction, lack of maintenance, and overcrowding. Some black schools were so poor that "black paint was applied to wooden
walls as a substitute for black boards."[70] In 1924, out of 829 high schools in the
state, only 37 were open to black students, and nearly one-third of the state's black
children lived in districts without high schools.[71]

To alleviate the shortage of schools for black students, the legislature passed a law in 1921 requiring counties that had black children as residents and a population greater than one hundred thousand to establish a "colored" consolidated school. The law also required school districts with more than eight black children to either establish a black school or pay students' transportation and tuition costs if they had to be schooled in another district in the county.

Although this law strengthened the segregated educational system, it improved blacks' educational opportunities. In 1922, the state successfully sued the Boone County School District, which had refused to update its list of black children. The court ordered the district to add three names to its list, making a total that required the district to establish a black school.[72] In 1925, a black student from St. Louis County, who attended high school in the city because there was no black school in her district, won her lawsuit against the county. Because the county had not paid her tuition, she had been suspended from the city school. The court ruled that she had a right to attend the city school, and her home school district was required to pay her tuition.[73]

To improve overall conditions in black schools, the state also appointed an Inspector of Negro Schools; however, this position carried little authority and its holder was unable to do more than document the state of education for black students.[74] In 1924, Inspector Nathaniel C. Bruce reported:

> Six Missouri counties have no Negro persons at all, sixteen other counties have less than ten. . . . Neither, in many counties do the boards of education feel financially able to run two public schools. Missouri's poor school districts cannot maintain separate race schools except at great disparity and inequality.[75]

The Sumner January Class of 1922.

The statistics Bruce gathered demonstrated that in almost every county the number of black students enrolled in school was substantially less than the number of black children in the county who were eligible for schooling. Bruce attributed the poor attendance to the sparsity of the black population in rural Missouri. "Still," he noted:

> In many places where schools for colored children are opened, the location, sanitation, equipment, and bare chances for play-grounds, the small pay and inefficiency of such teachers as can be obtained are such that the conditions must be improved, if these people are to be encouraged to remain where they can do Missouri and themselves the most good—out in the country.[76]

In the 1927–28 school year, N. B. Young, the new Inspector of Negro Schools, announced that "Missouri makes adequate provision for the elementary and second-ary training for about fifty per cent of her Negro children. For the remaining fifty per cent she makes provisions ranging from fair to none at all."[77]

Compared with other school districts around the state, the St. Louis school system was one of the strongest. In 1921–22, it spent $104.12 per student, sub-stantially more than Missouri's rural school districts could afford.[78] But even in St. Louis, black students faced inadequate facilities and overcrowding. In 1922, the Saint Louis Patrons Association, a group including several influential St. Louisians, began a campaign to improve the black schools. In 1927, this group enjoyed a major victory with the creation of Vashon High School, St. Louis's second high school for black students.[79] Vashon opened just in time to accommodate a new surge of black students.

Total black enrollment in the school district was rising, from 10,547 in the school year 1920–21 to 15,554 in 1929–30.[80] Between 1920 and 1927, the number of black students attending high school in St. Louis had grown from 970 to 1,755. A 1929 survey of public schools in the state reported that "in St. Louis and Kansas City, educational opportunities for Negro children are relatively adequate."[81]

Other opportunities in higher education in Missouri became available during the 1920s. In 1921, the legislature reorganized Lincoln School in Jefferson City into Lincoln University.[82] The Board of Curators was responsible for offering to blacks an education similar to that offered to white students at the University of Missouri. By 1928, Lincoln had 192 students. Although Lincoln University opened higher educa-tion to black students, its creation was motivated by a desire to keep the University of Missouri all white.[83] Lincoln was supposed to satisfy *Plessy's* "separate but equal" rule, but the facilities and opportunities there paled in comparison to those available to white students. The buildings were inadequate, very few professors had extensive training, and many teachers carried very heavy workloads for extremely low salaries. One commentator observed that the institution was "'neither equipped, organized, nor financed on a basis which permits real college work' and that the institution was 'a University in name only.'"[84] Because of Lincoln's deficiencies, the state legislature passed a law requiring Missouri to pay the tuition for any black student who wanted to take a course that was offered at the University of Missouri but was unavailable at Lincoln—as long as the student took the course at an accredited institution outside of the state.[85]

Although the Inspector of Negro Schools reported in 1933 that "in 1929 Missouri began her first intensive educational program for Negroes," black education received far less attention after the Great Depression struck.[86] Expenditures in the St. Louis school system dropped from $123 per pupil in 1923 to $95 per pupil in 1935 as a result of lost tax revenue.[87] In 1938, there remained thirty-six Missouri counties with no schools for blacks. Twenty-nine counties provided a grammar-school education to blacks but had no black high schools.[88] Salary disparities between white and black teachers continued, although salaries for black teachers had increased since the 1920s. Black teachers could earn a much higher salary in St. Louis or Kansas City than in rural parts of the state.[89] Blacks with advanced degrees and limited employment opportunities could and did make careers of teaching in the public schools. Dr. George Hyram, who graduated from Sumner High School in 1938, remembered that some of the teachers at Sumner had been among the first black Ph.D.s.[90]

During the 1930s and early 1940s, the black elementary school population in St. Louis grew by about five thousand students and black high school enrollments

Vashon High School's first graduating class, 1928. Photo courtesy the St. Louis Public School Archives.

by approximately twenty-three hundred students.[91] The city created seven new black elementary schools between 1929 and 1945 but offered just two high schools: Sumner and Vashon.[92] Mrs. James Mowrey, a black activist in St. Louis, encouraged a number of black Catholic boys to enroll in one of the city's white Catholic high schools. They were denied admission, but Mrs. Mowrey persevered and forced the establishment in 1937 of St. Joseph's, a black Catholic high school.[93]

Blacks also made strides in the realm of college education but met with many obstacles. In 1935, Lloyd Gaines, a successful graduate of Lincoln University, sought to break down the color barriers at the University of Missouri. He and three other Lincoln graduates applied to the schools of law, engineering, medicine, and journalism. The registrar refused to enroll them because the state constitution prohibited integrated education. The state told the students that it would help them pay to attend graduate schools outside of Missouri. Gaines, represented by the NAACP, challenged the university. The Missouri Supreme Court ruled against him, but the United States Supreme Court found in Gaines's favor in 1938, holding that Missouri had violated the equal protection clause by breaching *Plessy v. Ferguson's* "separate but equal" principle:

> By the operation of the laws of Missouri a privilege has been created for white law students which is denied to negroes by reason of their race. The white resident is afforded legal education within the State; the negro resident having the same qualifications is refused it there and must go outside the State to obtain it. That is a denial of the equality of legal right to the enjoyment of the privilege which the State has set up, and the provision for the payment of tuition fees in another State does not remove the discrimination.[94]

Although the *Gaines* decision was a legal victory for black students, Missouri's governor and rural Democrats then passed a law that required Lincoln to establish new departments, schools, and courses at Lincoln if students asked for them. Black students could still be sent out of state, but such transfers were limited to the time it took Lincoln University to create the department or program. Although Missouri refused to integrate the University of Missouri's law school, it appropriated $1 million to Lincoln, designating $200,000 for the creation of a black law school. The University of Missouri finally admitted black students in 1950, after a state court found that Lincoln did not and could not offer programs in engineering and graduate economics comparable to the programs offered at the University of Missouri.[95]

Into the 1940s and early 1950s, the city of St. Louis, St. Louis County, and the state of Missouri continued to maintain a segregated educational system. By popular vote, Missourians approved the 1945 Constitution, which retained the mandate of segregated schools.[96] Between the school years of 1936 and 1955, St. Louis County suburban districts paid tuition to send 2,632 black students to segregated schools in the city. Minnie Liddell, at that time a city student, met some of these students who had been sent into the city by their home districts. "I went to school in Mill Creek . . . it's down near where Union Station is," she remembered. "I went to school with kids who came from Carondelet. . . . They came all the way over there. . . . There was a working agreement between the Board of Education and all of those school districts. . . . They had been guilty of sending their black high school students into the St. Louis school system for years so they could attend the three black high schools that we had: Vashon, Sumner, and Washington Tech. . . . I said, 'Why do you all come into the city to go to school?' They had segregated elementary schools for them, but they did not have a high school for the black kids."[97]

Although more black students were attending school in St. Louis, the majority of students in the district, by more than a two-to-one margin, continued to be white.[98] In the 1949–50 school year, the average daily enrollment was 12,856 in white high schools and 4,853 in black high schools. At the elementary level, the average daily enrollment was 41,565 whites and 19,457 blacks.[99] Black students' classes were larger than white classes. In 1939, the average kindergarten class size was 27.5 students in white schools and 34.8 students in black schools. In elementary schools, the average white class consisted of 41.4 students while the average black class had 45.4 students. Class size began to equalize at the high school level with average sizes of 29.4 students in white schools and 30.9 students in black schools.[100]

In every category of expenditures except transportation, St. Louis spent more on its white schools than on its black schools, partly because there were more white students.[101] However, even though the number of white students attending elementary schools was more than double the number of blacks, the district spent one-and-a-half times more for the transportation of black elementary students than it spent on whites,[102] an expense generated by the state's segregation mandate.

Until 1954, the state of Missouri clung to the segregated system of education, which was expensive for the state and school districts and kept black students at a disadvantage. In fact, the city of St. Louis, at the time of the *Brown* decision, had the second-largest segregated public school district in the United States.

As the system of legal or "de jure" segregation prospered in Missouri, the stage was being set for a system of "de facto" segregation that would continue to divide the races long after segregationist policies were outlawed. Although it was an unintentional result, the first such change to entrench segregated education in St. Louis took place in 1876 when the city of St. Louis separated from St. Louis County. At that time, Unionist Republicans held political power in the city, but Conservative Democrats controlled the state government. The Republican city leaders feared state and county interference.[103] City residents were concerned about the county siphoning away city tax money to pay for projects in the predominantly rural county.[104] City residents resented paying county taxes on top of city taxes when county residents received most of the benefits.[105]

A provision in Missouri's 1875 Constitution made "home rule" available to any city with a population greater than one hundred thousand. St. Louis City and

St. Louis County appointed a board of freeholders to propose a plan for separation. Their plan gave the city 61 square miles, three times its size at the time, and gave the county 506.[106] An election was held, and because of mass election fraud, many returns were thrown out. But the mayor and a presiding judge certified to the secretary of state that the measure had passed.[107]

In 1876, sixty-one square miles appeared to give the city ample room for growth, and for forty-five years, the boundaries were sufficient as St. Louis grew into the fourth-largest city in the United States. However, one keen citizen predicted during the ratification campaign that St. Louis would someday outgrow its boundaries and "there will be established in the new county and along our borders suburban villages which will grow into cities."[108] By the 1920s, the city limits could not contain the population growth, and it would later become clear that the city/county division had the unintended effect of advancing racial and economic segregation in the metropolitan area.

In the 1920s, business leaders, realizing the harm caused by the 1876 vote to separate the city from St. Louis County, sought unsuccessfully to undo the 1876 "divorce." A 1924 consolidation measure was approved by a majority of city voters but rejected in the county.[109] St. Louis County's population doubled between 1920 and 1930, remaining less than 5 percent black, and in the five years between 1935 and 1940, 80 percent of construction in the metropolitan area occurred outside the city limits.[110] The 1940 census revealed that for the first time in 120 years the city's population had actually declined slightly, while the county's population continued its strong growth.[111]

Several waves of black migration changed the demographics in the city of St. Louis. Former slaves came to St. Louis from the area along the Missouri River known as Little Dixie. Ex-slaves and rural blacks also tried to come to St. Louis from farther south, prompting threats from then-mayor Henry Overstolz to fine any steamboat companies carrying blacks to the city. Nevertheless, St. Louis's black population more than quintupled between 1860 and 1880, growing from less than four thousand to more than twenty-two thousand, creating the country's third-largest concentration of urban blacks after Baltimore and Philadelphia.[112]

The city's black population continued growing at a rate comparable to that of the city's population at-large between 1890 and 1910, rising from nearly twenty-seven thousand to almost forty-four thousand. In the decade between 1910 and 1920, however, the city's black population grew faster than the city as a whole, evidencing a second wave of black migration.[113] Racial tensions in American cities increasingly boiled over into full-scale race riots. In July 1917, in East St. Louis, Illinois, just across the Mississippi River from St. Louis, white workers striking an aluminum processing plant attacked black strikebreakers. Thirty-nine blacks were killed, and the East St. Louis police and Illinois National Guard did nothing to stop the massacre.

In 1920, St. Louis was home to approximately seventy thousand blacks. But despite its surging black population, the city's growth had slowed, and the city had fallen to sixth place in a list of America's largest cities.[114] A pattern of racially segregated housing had emerged. In 1870, the city was divided into twelve wards, three of them housing 55 percent of black St. Louisans and only 30 percent of the white population. In 1900, the city had more than thirty wards, but 49 percent of the city's black population lived in six of them. Four of those six wards were crowded areas with poor housing conditions.[115]

Landlord discrimination, high rents, hostility by white residents, racial steering, and restrictive covenants all kept blacks confined to the emerging ghetto. In February 1916, the desire to maintain racial segregation in St. Louis resulted in passage by a 3-to-1 margin of a racial zoning ordinance. Although such ordinances had long been an essential component of the Jim Crow–type segregation found farther south, St. Louis had the dubious distinction of being the first community to enact such an ordinance by popular vote.[116]

The ordinance was short-lived, however. In 1917, in *Buchanan v. Warley*,[117] the United States Supreme Court struck down a similar Louisville, Kentucky, ordinance. In a unanimous opinion authored by Justice William R. Day, the Court held that racial zoning laws violated the Fourteenth Amendment. While the Court unfortunately still permitted segregation in public places, it concluded that the city could not interfere with the rights of individuals—in this case, a white man—to sell property without regard to the race of the purchaser. The Court acknowledged that there was a problem with racial hostility, "but its solution cannot be promoted by depriving citizens of their constitutional rights and privileges."[118]

White St. Louisans excluded blacks from their neighborhoods by entering into private contractual agreements not to sell or rent their property to blacks. Such agreements, binding for a set period of time on the property owners and their heirs, were often the product of neighborhood "improvement associations" ostensibly formed for the purpose of protecting property values and promoting security.[119] Neighborhood associations also maintained the color line by lobbying for the closing of hotels and rooming houses for blacks; threatening boycotts of real estate agents who sold property to blacks; boycotting white businesses that catered to blacks; agitating for public investments that would inflate neighborhood property values beyond the reach of black buyers; and organizing efforts to purchase vacant properties or properties occupied by black residents. However, private actions were not the only reason residential segregation was growing. The City Planning Commission restricted the growth of black neighborhoods by designating the areas around them as commercial or industrial zones. Local governments passed zoning ordinances that inflated housing prices in certain areas. For example, by requiring that all homes be a certain minimum size, poor blacks were kept out of white residential neighborhoods.[120]

The largest wave of the Great Migration began in the early 1940s. Agricultural innovations, such as the mechanized cotton picker, and New Deal policies forcing farm owners to pay farm hands minimum wage, meant that black agricultural workers were no longer needed or wanted in rural areas. Furthermore, the country's entry into World War II created a shortage of factory workers in the Northern cities that attracted huge numbers of black migrants from the South. The new factory jobs and lack of rural work led to the urbanization of the country's black population. In 1940, almost two-thirds of the country's black population lived in rural areas, but by 1970, 81 percent lived in cities.[121] Ninety-five thousand blacks migrated into St. Louis during this period, increasing the proportion of St. Louisians who were black from 13 percent in 1945, to 18 percent black in 1950, to 30 percent in 1957.[122]

As this huge influx occurred, migrating blacks faced dire housing shortages in the city, and the density of black areas increased dramatically. This increase was partly due to the in-migration of new black residents and in part to the growing outmigration of white residents. By the late 1940s, new home construction in the suburbs was soaring, and a large-scale suburbanization of the metropolitan region began. Between 1940 and 1960, the population of the city decreased by 66,000 residents, while the population of the county increased by 429,000.[123] This trend mirrored suburbanization of metropolitan areas throughout the country. In 1940, only one-third of residents living in metropolitan areas lived in the suburbs; by 1970, suburbanites constituted the majority of metropolitan residents.[124]

Efforts to maintain residential racial separation continued, but they encountered one legal setback. In the mid-1940s, a white property owner who lived on the edge of a black neighborhood decided to sell his home to a black family, the Shelleys. The sale was restricted, however, by a covenant entered into by the homeowner and thirty-seven nearby property owners that prohibited their houses from being occupied by "any person not of the Caucasian race."

A number of the parties to the covenant sued the Shelleys, seeking to prevent them from taking possession of the property and to divest them of the title to it. The Missouri Supreme Court concluded that enforcement of the covenant was neither contrary to public policy nor unconstitutional.[125] It held that "to sustain such a claim would be to deny the parties to the agreement one of the fundamental privileges of citizenship, access to the courts."[126] It stated:

> The chancellor found the negro population in St. Louis has greatly increased in recent years, and now numbers in excess of 100,000; and that some of the sections in which negroes live are overcrowded, which is detrimental to their moral and physical well being.
>
> Such living conditions bring deep concern to everyone, and present a grave and acute problem to the entire community. Their correction should strikingly challenge both governmental and private leadership. It is tragic that such conditions seem to have worsened although much has been written and said on the subject from coast to coast. But their correction is beyond the authority of the courts generally, and in particular in a case involving the determination of contractual rights between parties to a lawsuit. If their

correction is sought in the field of government, the appeal must be addressed to its branches other than the judicial.[127]

The United States Supreme Court in 1948 overruled the Missouri Supreme Court, holding that it was a violation of the Fourteenth Amendment for state courts to enforce restrictive covenants: "The Constitution confers upon no individual the right to demand action by the state which results in the denial of equal protection of the laws to other individuals."[128]

Shelley v. Kraemer and other court decisions, such as *Missouri ex rel. Gaines*, provided minor legal victories for blacks and called into question the longevity of the "separate but equal" doctrine. However, even as legal segregation began to weaken, the isolation of blacks in the inner city was setting the stage for *de facto* segregation. This segregation would prove to be one of the most difficult factors to overcome in efforts to provide an equal, integrated education to the children of St. Louis. Even after the landmark decision in *Brown v. Board of Education*, it took Minnie Liddell's federal court case to bring about a change for the better.

In the field of public education the doctrine of "separate but equal" has no place. Separate educational facilities are inherently unequal.

–Brown v. Board of Education

{Chapter Five}

Segregated Education Continues: 1954–1971

In *Brown v. Board of Education*, the U.S. Supreme Court unanimously held that the "segregation of children in public schools solely on the basis of race, even though the physical facilities and other 'tangible' factors may be equal, deprive the children of the minority group of equal educational opportunities,"[1] in violation of the Constitution's Fourteenth Amendment. The Court stated:

> Today, education is perhaps the most important function of state and local governments. . . . It is the very foundation of good citizenship. . . . It is a principal instrument in awakening the child to cultural values, in preparing him for later professional training, and in helping him to adjust normally to his environment.[2]

The Court did not immediately decide how schools should go about the process of desegregation but requested additional argument on that issue.[3] A year later, in *Brown II*, the Court unanimously declared that school authorities should dismantle segregated school systems with "all deliberate speed."[4] As school districts began to conform to the Supreme Court's mandate, school authorities were allowed additional time to comply if "necessary in the public interest" and "consistent with good faith compliance at the earliest practicable date."[5]

St. Louis had greeted the *Brown I* decision with enthusiasm and hope. The month after the decision, in June 1954, the St. Louis Board of Education presented a plan to integrate its schools in three distinct steps. Under this plan, integration would be achieved in two years. But some St. Louisans objected, saying the schools could be and should be integrated immediately. The Citizen's Protest Committee, a grassroots organization concerned about the overcrowding of black students in black schools, petitioned the Board "in the name of decency, fair-play and Democratic Practice" to "integrate the St. Louis schools in September, 1954. You will do the thing that your conscience bids you do, you will save hundreds of children from the inconvenience of hazard travel, you will give opportunities to many others, your actions will put St. Louis in front with leaders in desegregation."[6]

The *St. Louis Post-Dispatch*, in an editorial, also criticized the integration plan's timetable, asserting that "the only question that arises is whether it is necessary to wait [two years] to achieve fully this most desirable end. In our opinion the answer is no."[7] The editorial continued, "Segregation does violence to the democratic concept and the sooner it is eliminated, the better."[8] The weekly *St. Louis Argus* editorial page had expressed impatience and asserted that "St. Louis should integrate its schools right now. . . . The Board of Education has announced it will take action June 22. It will be good if it doesn't put it off any longer."[9]

Some St. Louisans thought the Board's caution was appropriate. A member of the community wrote to the *Post-Dispatch*, "With all the problems involved and the desire to get the job done peaceably and with the least possible amount of friction, if the School Board gets the job completed by September of 1955 it will have done a man-sized job in record time."[10] Another St. Louisan disagreed, labeling the Board's cautious plan "callous and stupid" and asserting that "the assignment of teachers, the re-zoning of districts, and all other matters can be done by September."[11]

On June 30, 1954, a month after the *Brown* decision, Missouri Attorney General John M. Dalton announced that the Missouri segregation laws were superseded by *Brown* and were unenforceable.[12] However, the state of Missouri had no plans to address the problems that were sure to arise during the process of integration. Dalton, who later became the governor of Missouri, stated blandly, "We do not rule herein as to whether school districts must integrate immediately or as to the method of which or by what date such integration must be completed."[13]

At the first regular session of the Missouri General Assembly following the *Brown* decision, the state cut off funding for separate black and white schools.[14] Other changes took longer. In 1957, the *St. Louis American* reported that the Missouri Assembly voted to remove the term "colored" from school census laws.[15] "The only part left in the Missouri law that has a racial discrimination," the *American* reported, "is the part of Sect. 3361 which forbids 'the intermarriage between white persons and negroes or white persons and Mongolians.'" The same article noted, however, that "[t]he provision in the Missouri Constitution providing for separate schools for 'children of African descent' is still in the Constitution."[16] In the late 1950s and early 1960s, laws were enacted to prohibit discrimination in housing, employment, and public accommodations.[17] But Missourians would have to wait over twenty years, until 1976, for the state to revise its constitution to abolish segregation officially, and even longer before many of its schools were desegregated by federal court order.[18]

The St. Louis Board of Education was not swayed by criticism and kept to its desegregation plan. By the autumn of 1954, there were minor achievements in the process of preparing the St. Louis schools for the initial stage of integration. There were also mounting concerns. One concern was black teachers' employment prospects under the desegregation plan. The *St. Louis Argus* reported that "Negro school teachers in the City of St. Louis are assured of their jobs if the Board of Education follows its announced plan to employ teachers on the basis of qualifications. . . . The average Negro teacher in the elementary and high schools has more college semester hours than the average white teacher."[19] Yet, under the plan, teachers were allowed to stay in the schools to which they had been assigned before 1954.[20] No one would be forced to take a teaching position in a newly integrated school. Meanwhile, out in the St. Louis suburbs, Clayton and Riverview High Schools enthusiastically reported that they were fully integrated: each had enrolled five black students.[21] The State Commissioner of Education announced in October 1954 that "[i]n 52 of 114 counties some form of integration has been undertaken. In 54 school districts with an enrollment of 15,992, a total of 449 Negro pupils have been integrated into white schools."[22]

On September 9, 1954, Superintendent Hickey addressed the combined faculties of St. Louis's high schools, saying, "The people of this city, for the most part, have accepted the fact that segregation is at an end with a wise calmness and sincere intent to accept it gracefully. Our local people have always had a deep respect for the laws of our land." He admonished the teachers, saying, "If you assume an apprehensive, defeatist attitude in your home or among your closest friends, that attitude will reflect itself, perhaps unconsciously, in your classroom teaching. The attitudes of you, the teachers in the classrooms, will determine the general trend of conduct in the entire school system."[23]

At Harris Teachers College, the news was all good. Dr. Charles Naylor, Harris College president, reported that the first few weeks of racial integration at Harris was "a satisfying success."[24] In his address to the newly integrated student body, he said, "Harris Teachers College must prove to other educational units in the St. Louis Public School System that integration is easy. No incidents must arise at any time to mar the fine record that has been achieved during the first five weeks. . . . [O]n behalf of our faculty and administration may I extend a most cordial welcome to all of our students. Together we shall move forward toward a better Harris."[25]

In 1956, the St. Louis County branch of the NAACP surveyed the suburban schools to chart their desegregation efforts. The *St. Louis School News* reported that "[w]ith desegregation an accomplished and all but forgotten fact in St. Louis, Kansas City and other Missouri cities, the [NAACP] took a look at suburban St. Louis this month and found the view generally to its liking."[26] The article continued, "Every school district in the county—whose school population is now almost as large as that of the city proper—has either completed the integration process successfully or has begun it at some level."[27] At that time there were approximately 1,650 black students in the county schools and 32,000 in the city.[28] The relatively small number of black students in the suburban schools allowed districts such as Clayton to report: "Integration complete at all levels, Negro enrollment 2 per cent."[29] The suburban Eureka R-6 district reported: "Integration begun September, 1955, Negro enrollment less than 2 per cent. Supt. Morgan Selvidge reports no difficulty." However, the district's report added that segregated housing in the area, plus a new school in a black neighborhood, meant that there were still all-white and all-black Eureka elementary schools.[30]

According to the three-step plan, elementary schools were among the last city schools to be integrated. In a September 1957 open letter to the "children of Dixie," a columnist for the *St. Louis American* expressed her fears about the psychological impact desegregation would have on African American students:

> Dear Boys and Girls,
>   Did you really want school integration, or are you pawns in this great and final struggle for civil rights—a struggle about which you know little and care even less? . . . We saw the hate-filled faces of white students as they taunted you. . . . In most cases you looked resigned and very miserable but once we saw you fighting back at your tormenters and then we knew the answer. You do want to walk in the sunlight of equality, but everything happened so quickly that you haven't quite been able to get your bearings. . . . Just as "Rome wasn't built in a day," neither will the South be desegregated in a year or maybe not even in a decade, but the walls of its traditions have been cracked and in time they will crumble, burying bigotry and hatred beneath their ruins.[31]

Despite the turmoil, as the plan was put into place St. Louis received national praise. In 1957, St. Louis was awarded "All-America City" status by the National Municipal League and *Look* magazine for its "progress achieved through intelligent citizen action" from September 1954 through September 1956.[32] In reality, the desegregation program had little effect on the segregated school structure that had been in place for nearly one hundred years. Amy Wells, who conducted extensive research on the St. Louis school desegregation effort, found that the Board had "made only minor adjustments to the attendance boundaries of 16 of its 84 white elementary schools to include a small number of black students."[33]

Meanwhile, the continued migration of blacks into St. Louis caused overcrowding in the black schools, and migration of whites out of South St. Louis left vacancies in the predominantly white schools in that area. The Board's reaction to the overcrowding was to begin busing nearly five thousand black students to predominantly white schools in South St. Louis in 1961. Amy Wells wrote, "The process, known as intact busing, ensured that the black students would arrive at school after the white students were in class. The black students were kept in self-contained classrooms, given lunch and recess at different times from the white students, and loaded onto their buses for home after the white students had departed."[34]

Intact busing was severely criticized. Later that year, Superintendent Hickey appointed a three-member committee within the Board to study the district's racial problems, particularly intact busing.[35] The local chapter of the NAACP was immediately skeptical of the committee's ability to assess the program in an unbiased manner. Superintendent Hickey and other school officials reportedly had turned down proposals to transport white students to predominantly black schools because such a plan would be "artificial and nothing could be accomplished."[36]

Sandra Wilson, later the principal of Ashland Elementary School, remembered the overcrowding in black schools during the early 1960s. "I had my first year of teaching in January [1962]," she said. "I inherited a classroom of forty-eight kids and they were first-graders."[37] Temporary structures housed the overflow at some schools, such as Sherman Elementary, where Juanita Doggett taught. She remembered, "The Branch building was aluminum, and it was built as a temporary building. It was uncomfortable in the winter and summer. It was an eight-room building."[38] Minnie Liddell also described "a lot of overcrowding in the '60s and '70s," and said that because of overcrowding her son Craton, who was then in grade school, was bused out of his neighborhood—not to a white school, but to another all-black school in North St. Louis.[39]

By the end of 1962, eight years after *Brown I*, the rosy predictions that school desegregation had lessened were shown to be false. The *St. Louis American* reported, "School Integration Here Worse Than Seven Years Ago: Housing Bias, Distribution of Teachers Are Blamed."[40] This view was also reflected in a 1962 United States Civil Rights Commission report:

> St. Louis did not move far between 1955 and 1962. In some ways the pattern has been retrogressive. Not a little "resegregation" has developed; that is, some schools which were predominantly white or substantially interracial schools, just after desegregation, have since become all-Negro schools or virtually so. This is notably true in the city's West End and an extended Negro residential section toward the northwest. Such resegregation is traceable in the main to a conjunction of population flux and the school administration's fundamental commitment to a neighborhood school concept. . . .
>
> Classroom teachers, although not extensively reassigned in transition stages, have subsequently moved, or have failed to move, in such a fashion as generally to aggravate Negro-white contrasts among the schools. . . .
>
> On balance, de facto segregation in St. Louis public schools has patently worsened during the last 7 years.[41]

The 1962 Civil Rights Commission staff report predicted that the Board's neighborhood-school policy, if continued, would increase segregation.[42] The report added that the St. Louis black community seemed to be exerting no pressure to reform the neighborhood school plan, possibly because many black parents "consciously prefer uniracial but uncrowded neighborhood schools, if the only feasible alternative were the daily transportation of their children to remote parts of the city."[43] The staff also speculated that "[d]eeply ingrained feelings of racial and individual inferiority would undoubtedly shape the reluctance of some Negro parents to have their children compete with culturally advantaged white children."[44]

The report to the Civil Rights Commission concluded:

> [M]uch greater freedom of choice in school attendance
> could be allowed and even encouraged in St. Louis. Large Negro
> concentrations pose special transfer problems, but in 1961–62,
> 3,000 Negro children were bused daily, to distant and for the most
> part, white schools to relieve overcrowding in their neighborhood
> schools. Several thousand more could escape from segregated
> schools in like fashion if the St. Louis "transportables" were moved
> to other locations.[45]

Concerns about teacher assignments and retaining black teachers were also voiced in 1962. On November 8, 1962, the *St. Louis American* headline read: "Teachers Fear Loss of Jobs at Harris College."[46] The junior-college division of Harris Teachers College would close that winter because a new St. Louis/St. Louis County Junior College (later known as St. Louis Community College), was slated to open in February 1963.[47] Black teachers feared that the new junior college district plan would establish schools only in the county, leaving "a jim crow school in the city."[48] Few black students lived in the county, and few black teachers expected to be hired in the new county schools.[49] Much to their frustration, several black junior-college teachers at Harris received letters asking them to teach in the city grade schools.[50]

Early in 1963, the West End Community Conference, a group of civil rights activists, brought 137 allegations of race discrimination against the St. Louis Board of Education.[51] The group charged that "through deliberate policies the Board allowed white children to transfer from the area's increasingly black classrooms to all-white schools in South St. Louis, thereby accelerating the rise in the proportion of black students in the rapidly changing West End."[52] The West End Conference's report, filed with the Board, asserted:

> In 1960 when the U.S. Census showed a racial proportion
> of 60 per cent Negro and 40 per cent white in the neighborhood,
> parents reported that west end schools were over 90 per cent
> Negro, which is defined by educational authorities as segregated.
> Negro children were crowded into west end schools while white
> children were transferred out of the district. Busing was not
> instituted to relieve the crowding until these schools were over 90
> per cent Negro. No human relations programs were conducted to

insure that the bused children were properly integrated into the receiving schools and these Negro children are still taught in separate classrooms even though some of the white classes in the same building are small enough to amount to private tutoring.[53]

The West End Conference recommended that the Board of Education establish an independent commission to eliminate school segregation by redistricting, busing, use of open enrollment, and the equal distribution of "faculty and human relations programs" for parents, teachers, and children.[54]

The Board denied that any of its actions were intentionally discriminatory. Dan Schlafly, who served on the Board for twenty-eight years, reports that the Board hired a Washington University sociology professor who determined that fewer white children attended West End schools because the West End's white population was growing older, and many white residents in the area were childless or had grown children.[55]

To its credit, the Board participated in a series of question-and-answer sessions with citizens.[56] These meetings were packed, and the building where the Board met was typically crowded with citizens who could not get into the meeting room.[57] The Board defended its policies in part by citing a paragraph of the 1962 report of the U.S. Civil Rights Commission, which stated that the "administration deserves praise for the conscientious and intelligent progress it has accomplished with difficulty during the past eight years."[58] Citizen activists responded that the St. Louis schools had regressed to resegregation.[59]

In June 1963, another citizens' group, the Committee of Parents, organized by parents of "transportees" from the West End of St. Louis, urged a boycott of public school buses to protest intact busing and racial discrimination in the public schools.[60] Parents alleged that black and white children had separate lunch periods at "integrated" schools and drank from water fountains at designated times, that black children were required to wait for school buses outside of the schoolyard while white children played inside the yard, and that white children were taught by white teachers and black children by black teachers.[61] Others alleged that black children had to enter the school building through a separate door.[62] The proponents of the boycott asked the school administration to correct these conditions no later than September 1963.[63] On the last two days of the school year, a blockade was set up to prevent school buses from picking up black students from the West End.[64]

On June 21, 1963, the Citizens Advisory Committee, appointed by the St. Louis Board of Education, presented its recommendations to the Board. These included integration of professional staffs, open enrollment, new boundaries drawn for schools, the full integration of bused students into receiving schools, and the elimination of the so-called "German transfer," which had been used by white students to transfer out of Soldan (a predominantly black high school, which had no German-language instructor) to south side schools (predominantly white).[65] As a result of the report, the Board agreed to appoint four board members to serve with

Board President Schlafly to draft a new policy statement on integration.[66]

At the end of July, Superintendent Hickey submitted a series of his own recommendations to the Board, which the Board quickly approved.[67] Two of the most important of these recommendations asked for "Intensification of efforts on the part of all principals and teachers of schools receiving transportees to bring about fullest possible integration of pupils, parents, and teachers in all aspects of school life" and an expanded program of integrated classes for the study of basic skills, remedial reading, art and music, and physical education.[68]

Hickey's recommendations were far more conservative than the citizens' committees had hoped for. Hickey was not going to change any elementary school boundaries, but high school district lines would have to be altered because Vashon High was being moved to the old Hadley Technical High building.[69] Hickey agreed to assign a German-language instructor to Soldan High.[70] As for the intact busing policy, Hickey proposed "scheduling all pupils for the same lunch period and some classroom integration in several schools." He added, "I should point out, however, that the later return of the transported pupils to their home districts will mean that they will not have the protection of city-employed guards at major street crossings and that the children will be walking to their homes at the start of evening rush-hour traffic."[71] Hickey also recommended that open enrollment occur on a first-come, first-served basis after children had enrolled in their neighborhood schools.[72] No consideration of race or color was to be made, but students who chose the open-enrollment option would have to find their own transportation.[73]

On August 15, 1963, the Board tried to bar all demonstrations and bus boycotts proposed by St. Louis activists by seeking a court injunction.[74] A *St. Louis American* editorial read, "[I]t is quite apparent that the School Board is going into court not alone for a 'clarification' of the law as applied to its dilemma of daily shipping more than four thousand pupils to schools where they are jimcrowed, but that it is really playing for time—perhaps as much as two years before a final decision can be handed down."[75]

The general tone among the black community, as reflected in the newspapers, was that the Board was not doing everything within its power to protect the constitutional rights of St. Louis's black children. Later that month, Dr. William Kottmeyer stepped in as acting superintendent while Hickey recovered from a stroke. Kottmeyer was not well received by the black community, who believed that his policies would do little to mend the fractured public schools.[76]

In 1963, nearly nine years after *Brown I*, the NAACP reported that many school districts in southeastern Missouri had failed to desegregate.[77] U.S. District Court Judge James Meredith, responding to a complaint filed by parents and students against the Board of Education of Charleston, Missouri,[78] found that the Charleston schools continued to be operated in a racially discriminatory manner. He further held that a policy that permitted the Charleston Board of Education to "initially assign [students] by race and put the burden upon negro pupils to apply for a transfer to a particular school" was unconstitutional. He gave the school district thirty days to submit a plan for reorganizing the schools, including school bus transportation on a nonracial basis beginning in September 1963.[79]

Two years later, parent groups in St. Louis were still outraged. Although the Board ended intact busing in the fall of 1963, it failed to integrate black and white students in the south side public schools.[80] Instead, between 1962 and 1967, the Board had built nine new elementary schools in all-black neighborhoods.[81] In 1965, black children were being bused to predominantly black schools near the housing projects, hardly one of the goals of the desegregation program.[82] Still another parent activist group, the Citizens for Equality Education, presented a list of demands to the Board. This document gives a detailed "snapshot" of the state of St. Louis school desegregation at that time. It said:

1. We do not oppose busing as a sensible plan for utilizing the total school facilities of the community, but we do not find acceptable the fall plans for busing. . . . [P]resent an nounced plans include:
    A. Containment of the transportation of Negro children within the Negro community thereby extending de facto desegregation into administrative segregation;
    B. Transportation of children greater distances than necessary for available seats;
    C. Refusal to use all the schools for integrated busing that had been used for segregated busing two years ago;
    D. Refusal to admit that departure and return schedules can be adjusted to allow transported pupils full participation in the life of half-empty schools some distance away;
    E. Non-utilization of all the available school space in the St. Louis Public School System;
    F. Threatening to segregate bused pupils in receiving schools if further construction or rented facilities are not obtained within the Negro community.

2. We strongly oppose the current and future plans calling for the rental of marginal church facilities where the environment gives children the minimum of a seat and a teacher without the full use of necessary common facilities such as a library, gym, playground space, lunchroom, audio-visual facilities, etc.

3. We insist that the Board make public the amount of pos-

> sible classroom space available and establish a policy of
> utilizing such space. . . . [This should] precede any plans
> for new construction of schools, so that a full utilization of
> existing school facilities can save taxpayers the needless cost
> of new construction.[83]

The Board received praise for its handling of the St. Louis school segregation controversy in 1963–65, when a University of Chicago research study cited St. Louis as an example of "good government in action."[84] St. Louis was cited for having the most ambitious program of school integration among eight Northern cities, largely because of its busing program, ironically.[85] The Board was applauded for its reforms and response to "protests from Negro and liberal groups about the prevalence of 'de facto' segregation in the city's public schools."[86] After the Board had been criticized in 1963 by the West End Community Conference report, "the board moved to eliminate segregation in its busing system and took other steps that had the effect of undercutting civil rights militants," the study explained.[87] It continued: "St. Louis's integration of the busing program greatly increased the amount of integration. . . . In addition, St. Louis increased teacher integration, adopted open enrollment, and has a widely publicized and apparently successful compensatory education project."[88] Finally, St. Louis was praised for its record of "progressive race relations," Catholic leadership in integration, and its highly developed black business elite.[89]

It does appear that the St. Louis Board of Education managed to implement its cautious desegregation policies throughout the 1950s and 1960s without thoroughly alienating either the black or white communities. As researcher Amy Wells wrote, "It had built new schools for black children, made a token commitment to desegregation, and kept the southside schools' classrooms segregated."[90] Nonetheless, by the 1972–73 school year, very little actual integration had taken place in the elementary schools or the high schools.

On February 18, 1972, Concerned Parents, founded in the fall of 1971 by Minnie Liddell of St. Louis, filed their class-action lawsuit against the St. Louis School Board, its individual board members, the school superintendent, and district superintendents in the United States District Court for the Eastern District of Missouri.[91] The Concerned Parents group filed on behalf of Minnie's eldest son, Craton Liddell, then age twelve, and four other St. Louis public school students, asserting that the St. Louis public schools were administered in a manner that had the effect of denying equal educational opportunities to black citizens, in violation of the Constitution's Fourteenth Amendment. Mrs. Liddell recalled that Concerned Parents "selected five parents, and each parent used their oldest child, and so those five kids are on the suit; that's the way it came out."[92] Because Craton Liddell's name was first on the list, the case would thereafter be known as *Liddell v. Board of Education of St. Louis.* Mrs. Liddell remembers that when the lawsuit was publicized, "[M]y kids caught hell, my older kids. We filed this suit in '72. . . . There were black teachers who took offense and said that we were saying they couldn't teach."[93]

The case was assigned to Chief Judge James H. Meredith, the same judge who had decided the Charleston, Missouri, case. A graduate of the University of Missouri–Columbia School of Law, Judge Meredith had been in private practice until his appointment to the court by President John F. Kennedy in 1962, and he was made a chief judge in 1971. Judge Meredith would be the first of the four judges assigned to the *Liddell v. Board of Education* case.

The state has had to be dragged kicking and squealing into preparation of a voluntary school desegregation plan for the St. Louis area, and now that the U.S. Supreme Court has denied the state's request for a delay, there is no more room for procrastination.

–*St. Louis Post-Dispatch* editorial, April 20, 1981

{Chapter Six}

Progress and Opposition: 1973–1981

On May 25, 1973, the U.S. District Court denied, without prejudice, the plaintiffs' motion to proceed as a class action. On October 3, 1973, in response to a renewed motion, Judge Meredith granted the Concerned Parents' application to proceed as plaintiffs in their class-action lawsuit against the City Board. In December 1973, the Board's request to include the state of Missouri and the United States on the roster of defendants was denied. Judge Meredith gave no reason, but it is quite clear that he had decided to limit the case to the St. Louis School District only. The plaintiffs and defendants were ordered to build their cases by submitting facts, due on June 7, 1974.

Attorneys for the plaintiffs agreed to proceed without a fee, but the Concerned Parents group still had trouble raising the money for filing fees and other costs.[1] The Concerned Parents repeatedly missed deadlines, but Minnie Liddell remembered that Judge Meredith had been tolerant. "He could have kicked us out. We never met a filing date, we never met anything," she said. "We had no money, you know; we scrambled trying to find the money to file. And so he just was like, he just sat there and let it happen, and he didn't throw us out of court. So I have to thank him for that."[2]

On June 7, 1974, as promised, the parties filed a written stipulation of facts. Both the plaintiffs and defendants agreed on the following points:

- Prior to 1954, racial housing segregation prevailed in the city, and restrictions against blacks were enforced by the courts and agencies of the state of Missouri.[3]
- After 1954, racial discrimination in housing continued to exist. The city had failed to enforce its own building codes, insurance companies "redlined" certain neighborhoods, and

Students stepping off a bus to attend a new school on the first day of desegregation within St. Louis City. Photo courtesy the *St. Louis Post-Dispatch*.

    the Federal Housing Administration allowed discrimination in making home loans and in allowing newspapers to publish separate real-estate listings for whites and blacks.

- For many decades, the population of the city of St. Louis was predominantly white. From 1940 to 1970, however, the white population declined by approximately 500,000, while the black population increased by 150,000. At the same time, the population of St. Louis County increased by 677,000, and remained overwhelmingly white. Fewer than 5 percent of the county's residents were black.
- From 1940 through 1970, the proportion of black students enrolled in the city public schools was 50 percent greater than the proportion of black residents in the city, in part because more white pupils than black attended private and parochial schools.
- Prior to *Brown v. Board of Education* in 1954, Missouri public schools were segregated by state constitutional and

statutory law. But as of June 1974, segregation, although illegal, continued to exist in practice in the St. Louis public school system. Numbers showed that of the ten public high schools then in St. Louis, three had enrollments that were 100 percent black, and two were 90 percent black or more. Of the five remaining schools, three were 90 percent white or more. Only two schools had some racial balance: McKinley was 63 percent black and Central, 73 percent black. Of the city's elementary schools, forty-eight were 100 per-cent black, and fifteen were 100 percent white; forty-four were 90 percent or more black, and twenty-four were over 97 percent white. Twenty-one elementary schools were evenly divided between white and black students.

- An analysis of the data available for the years 1953 through 1973 revealed that once a school enrolled more than 50 percent black students, the ratio increased to 90 percent black students within three and a half years.

- The basic principle in assigning pupils to elementary schools since 1954 had been the "neighborhood school" concept, whereby children residing in a given neighborhood were the first to be placed in their neighborhood school. Transfers to other schools were permitted, if the parents assumed the responsibility of transportation.

- The problem of overcrowded schools affected far more black students than white students. Eighty-two percent of the students who were bused away from their neighborhood schools because of overcrowding were black.

- To its credit, the City Board had affirmatively sought out and hired black teachers, and had tried assigning new teachers to schools with pupils predominantly of a race other than that of the teacher. But teacher transfers to achieve "racial mixing" were not compulsory. Some principals did not want to work with personnel of another race, and objections by some teachers and certain factions of the community had limited the degree of racial mixing. Thus, in many instances, the faculty and administrators in elementary schools followed the racial patterns of the school's neighborhood.

- Of thirty-nine school buildings constructed by the City Board after 1954, thirty-five were attended predominantly by black students.

On December 24, 1975, without going to trial, the plaintiffs and defendants signed an agreement called a consent decree.[4] The consent decree was a compromise between the interests of the plaintiffs and the defendants. Under the decree, the school board was permitted to deny that it had knowingly operated a segregated school system, but it explicitly agreed to affirmative action that it believed would result in integrated schools. This included building new schools in areas where they were least likely to become segregated; realigning the school system to prevent racial isolation at city high schools, a move that would later result in the creation of "middle schools" for students in grades 6, 7, and 8; hiring more minority teachers; requiring the defendants to raise "the quality of education throughout the system, all within the context of reducing racial isolation in the schools and with the goal of desegregating the school system,"[5] and serious consideration of a concept called "magnet schools."

It was at Minnie Liddell's urging that magnet schools became part of the agreement. "I read about magnet programs and the magnet schools," she said. "And I had to read the articles; I didn't know what they were talking about. And when I read it, I talked to my attorney. I said oh, I said, 'I just read about a program that came out of Europe. I said, 'It is such a—it sounds so outstanding.' I said I would like for us to take a look at that and see, could we put this into our agreement for some things that we want. And Russell did some research and called some people he knew and that's how we got in on the magnet program. That came from me."[6] The merits and advantages of the magnet school concept were clear, and the St. Louis Board of Education began operating nine magnet schools in the city in the fall of 1976—seven elementary schools and two high schools. Specializing in fields such as business, science, and performing arts, they attracted both black and white students and soon developed long waiting lists.

The court ordered the plaintiffs to publish the December 1975 consent decree in the *St. Louis Daily Record,* so other interested parties could file any objections to it.[7] Objections were filed by the teachers' union and the St. Louis chapter of the NAACP. The union objected to the plan's intention to increase the percentage of minority teachers in the system to 10 percent in 1976–77, 20 percent in 1977–78, and 30 percent in 1978–79. This goal was mandatory and was to be achieved through voluntary teacher transfers, if possible, but otherwise teachers would be given mandatory assignments without regard to any contracts, tenure, or seniority agreements.[8]

The NAACP also filed a motion to intervene. While it agreed with the original goals of the *Liddell* lawsuit, it believed that the consent decree failed to comply with the constitutional mandate to create a unitary school system—a system in which every possible effort had been made to meet the goals of the class-action suit. They asserted that the original plaintiffs no longer represented the interests of all black parents and students. James DeClue, who then headed the St. Louis chapter of the NAACP later explained, "The original order said the St. Louis School Board was not guilty of illegal segregation of schools and they said nothing had been done wrong, which we knew was not correct, and that was the reason for the intervention."[9]

The NAACP came into the case on behalf of a mother named Earline Caldwell. Minnie Liddell said, "Caldwell was a woman with foster children . . . so the NAACP used her name and those foster children to enter in the case. And when at that time the NAACP came in, everybody came in. There was a group of parents called the South Side Parents for Neighborhood Schools; they came in. The White Citizens Committee, everybody—at one time [there were] so many parties to this case."[10]

The NAACP's petition for intervention represented a change of heart for that organization. Before Mrs. Liddell and the Concerned Parents commenced their lawsuit, they had spoken with the president of the local chapter of the NAACP, Joseph Clark, and asked the NAACP to assist them because theirs was a civil rights case. Mrs. Liddell recalled that Clark "looked at us like we was crazy. He said, 'Schools in St. Louis are not segregated. The NAACP took care of that in the '60s. We met with them and they changed their policy.' I [told Clark] they may have changed their policy, but that is all they changed."[11]

Although the local NAACP originally refused to help, Mrs. Liddell's lawyer, William Russell, was able to obtain ten thousand dollars from the NAACP National Legal Defense Fund to hire an expert witness, Dr. William B. Field, who visited St. Louis and computed demographic data that showed how segregated the St. Louis schools really were.[12]

The district court denied the NAACP's motion to intervene, holding that the NAACP's motion was filed too late. The NAACP promptly filed a notice of appeal.[13] On appeal, the United States Court of Appeals for the Eighth Circuit ruled that the NAACP's application had not been late.[14] The court did not decide whether the consent decree met the constitutional requirement of equal opportunity, because that was not the issue before the court. The Eighth Circuit did note, however, that unless the final plan submitted by the City Board provided for the desegregation of elementary schools, the plan would meet with serious constitutional objections. It then stated:

> In view of the difficult problems in working out a meaningful
> constitutional plan, we suggest to the district court that it invite
> the United States Department of Justice to intervene, and that
> the same invitation be extended to the Missouri State Board of
> Education. We recommend that the parties explore the creation of
> a bi-racial citizens advisory committee, which has worked so suc-
> cessfully in other areas of the country.[15]

Judge Donald Lay, writing for the Eighth Circuit, saw how difficult it would be to integrate the St. Louis schools solely by reassigning city students within the city school district. Judge Lay urged the parties to consider a voluntary interdistrict plan. In this plan, students from the city and the suburbs could choose to attend schools in either district. In effect, this plan would create a partnership between the city and the county school districts. If students were allowed to cross the borders each way, all the schools in the metropolitan area were more likely to be integrated.[16] This suggestion ultimately was embodied in the 1983 plan to comprehensively desegregate the public schools of St. Louis.

Finally, the Eighth Circuit directed that the district court promptly hear any objections to the City Board's January 1974 plan, a plan that was subsequently incorporated into the consent decree. The Eighth Circuit also directed that within a reasonable time, the parties should submit alternative plans, but "in no event should implementation of plans for a unitary school system be delayed beyond the commencement of the 1977–78 school term."[17]

The City Board, seeking to uphold the consent decree, disagreed with this ruling and promptly moved for a stay of mandate while it petitioned the United States Supreme Court. On January 28, 1977, the Eighth Circuit denied its motion. One month later the U.S. Supreme Court refused to take on the case.[18]

In July 1977, the roster of parties, both plaintiffs and defendants, was complete. The Concerned Parents for Neighborhood Schools (known as "the Adams plaintiffs"),[19] the United States,[20] and the city of St. Louis were authorized as plaintiffs, and the state of Missouri, the Commissioner of Education of the state of Missouri, and the Missouri Board of Education (State Board) were added as defendants. The case went before the court on November 17, 1977. The trial continued until May 26, 1978. The court gave the parties until August 1, 1978, to file more facts and legal briefs, and until September 15 to reply to them. The case was finally submitted to Judge Meredith on October 31. Oral arguments were held on February 2, 1979.

On April 12, 1979, Chief Judge Meredith handed down an exhaustive opinion.[21] He reviewed the history of education in the St. Louis public schools. He pointed out that housing in the city of St. Louis was clearly segregated, and that policies and actions of the federal government had been a major force in developing and maintaining housing discrimination.[22] He noted that since the Supreme Court's 1954 decision in *Brown v. Board of Education*, the St. Louis school system had changed from a majority white system to a majority black system, and a number of schools with formerly mixed student bodies had virtually all-black enrollments. He found that the primary reason for the current (1979) racial imbalance in the St. Louis public school system was adherence to a neighborhood school policy. The judge concluded that whatever resegregation had taken place since 1954 was not the fault of the city's Board of Education. Thus, he wrote, the plaintiffs had failed to prove there had been "any intentional segregation of students caused by the actions or inactions of the Board."[23]

Chief Judge Meredith rejected the NAACP's proposal to assign the district's children using a numerical percentage by race in each school, because in his view the end result would be more segregation. In reaching this conclusion, the judge relied on the testimony of an expert witness for the United States, Gary A. Orfield, who testified that a practical, stable plan of integration could not be achieved solely within the city of St. Louis, because city schools were 75 percent black and 25 percent white. Simply reassigning students to achieve that ratio in each school, Orfield said, would result in 100 percent black city schools within a short time. Adopting a recommendation previously made by Judge Lay of the Eighth Circuit, Orfield suggested that the City Board consider asking adjoining school districts in the county to find white students who would volunteer to be bused into the city for the purpose of achieving integration. The district court stated that it "had no objection to such an effort," but argued that "the only way it can be achieved is to offer such quality education within the City of St. Louis that cannot be duplicated in the County. This can be done by a continuation of the magnet school program which could attract white students from the County and from the private and parochial schools within the City, which will improve the balance between black and white students."[24]

Because Judge Meredith had found no constitutional violation, his decision imposed no remedy, stating that the criterion for the district's actions going forward "shall be quality education, which includes integration of the races, where practical and feasible."[25]

The United States, the Caldwell plaintiffs, the Liddell plaintiffs, and the Adams plaintiffs all promptly filed appeals. All of the judges of the federal Eighth Circuit Court heard the case and, on March 3, 1980, unanimously overruled the decision of the district court.[26]

The Eighth Circuit held that the City Board's "neighborhood school" policy failed to fulfill the defendants' duty to take whatever steps might be necessary to convert to a unitary system in which racial discrimination would be eliminated root and branch. The Eighth Circuit pointed out that when the neighborhood school plan was first implemented, the school attendance zones had been drawn to have the least possible impact on the students and on segregated personnel assignments. Moreover, the court stated that an intent to segregate could be inferred from the fact that school "attendance zones were drawn so as to correspond, with remarkable consistency, to the racially identifiable residential neighborhoods in the city."[27] Finding that "the continuation transfer option virtually guaranteed that the School Board plan would be an ineffective tool of desegregation,"[28] the court rejected the district court's finding that factors beyond the City Board's control were substantially responsible for the segregation in the St. Louis school system, and stated:

> The facts are that most schools in the heart of North
> St. Louis were black in 1954 and remain black today, and that
> most schools in South St. Louis were white in 1954 and remain
> white today. The Board of Education has simply never dealt with
> this overwhelming reality. If the Board had dealt with the problem
> in 1954–1956 and had implemented a plan for integrating the
> schools in North and South St. Louis, we would have a differ-
> ent case today. We would have to examine the question from an

entirely different point of view. But it did not; the schools remain segregated and we have no choice but to adopt a practical remedy to achieve an integrated school system. We have no alternative but to require a system-wide remedy for what is clearly a system-wide violation. [29]

The Eighth Circuit next considered the proposed alternatives. The City Board had proposed the creation of twelve junior high schools, with as many of them as possible enrolling an equal number of black and white students, and the rest being all-black junior high schools. The City Board also proposed building a new business and office magnet school, two specialty high schools, expanding enrollment at Metro High School, the successful alternative school opened in 1972; and turning O'Fallon Technical High School into a full-day comprehensive technical high school with "appropriate representation of both races." The Board proposed building an educational park to house a variety of magnet and specialty high schools, and seven new magnet elementary schools. Finally, the City Board proposed consolidating city schools with those in St. Louis County if something more was required, based on the City Board's view that county schools had been partially responsible for the segregation in the city schools.

The NAACP had proposed to integrate all the schools along the lines of the public school district's enrollment: 75 percent black and 25 percent white. Schools which came within 15 percent of the ideal percentage would be allowed to remain as they were. This, however, would allow a school 90 percent black and 10 percent white to qualify as integrated. This was the plan that Dr. Gary Orfield had concluded would soon result in an all-black school system.

The Liddell plaintiffs proposed to convert the public school system to a four-tiered system: Kindergarten through grade 3; grades 4–6, grades 7–9, and grades 10–12 ("the Colton plan"). The first tier (K–3) would continue as neighborhood schools. Second-tier students would be housed in the same building as the first tier, but would be assigned so as to achieve a 55 percent black, 45 percent white student population in as many units as possible, with the remaining units enrolling only black students. Students in grades 7 through 9 would be housed in existing school buildings adapted for use as junior high schools, with a racial mix of 60 percent black, 40 percent white, with one-third of the junior high schools enrolling only black students. Fourth-tier students would be housed in seven high schools. Five of them would be 60 percent black and 40 percent white. Two would be all-black high schools. Student assignments would be made so that no student attended both an all-black junior and senior high school, and every white student would be in an integrated school after the third grade.

The Department of Justice took the position that neither the Liddell group's plan nor the NAACP's plan would desegregate the system. It favored a plan developed in accordance with the views of its expert witness, Dr. Gary Orfield. Dr. Orfield submitted an 80-page report with his recommendations (called "the Orfield plan"). His plan would leave currently integrated schools alone and stabilize them for the foreseeable future. All-white schools and as many black schools as possible would be integrated with a 50/50 racial mix. Special programs in the neighborhood schools would keep students from being locked into a slow-moving curriculum. Free choice, intradistrict transfers, and interdistrict transfers would be permitted and encouraged. He believed that a voluntary city-county interdistrict remedy funded by the state would have the best chance of permanently integrating the schools in the St. Louis metropolitan area.[30]

Dr. Orfield predicted that two years from the date of his report there would not be "a suburban school district that did not wish it had a record of voluntary desegregation efforts" and "recommend[ed] that Judge Meredith order the state to develop and organize a voluntary pupil-swap procedure."[31]

After considering these plans, the Eighth Circuit rejected the intra-city plan proposed by the City Board, saying that it did little or nothing to integrate grades 1 through 6, would delay desegregation at the junior and senior high school level, and that its other proposals were but futuristic solutions to a current problem. In the court's view, the City Board's proposal offered too little too late.[32] The Eighth Circuit also found fault with the NAACP plan, stating it would desegregate the elementary and secondary schools only temporarily.

Having made these observations, the Eighth Circuit Court returned the matter to the district court. It instructed the City Board to develop a comprehensive integration plan within sixty days. The Eighth Circuit held that the district court should require the defendants to pay for the cost of integration and that the plan should be system-wide for integrating both the elementary and secondary schools under either the Colton approach (consolidating county and city schools) or the Orfield approach (voluntary interdistrict transfers). In support of the Orfield approach, the court noted:

> Anything that can be done to involve the suburban districts should be done. . . . St. Louis County suburban school districts, pursuant to state law prior to *Brown*, collaborated with the City of St. Louis to ensure that they had segregated schools. Included among the pre-*Brown* practices of these districts was the assignment and transportation of black students living in the suburbs to black schools in the City.[33]

The court directed that whatever plan was adopted, it should be in place and operating by the beginning of the 1980–81 school year. Under either the Colton or the Orfield approach, some all-black or virtually all-black schools in North St. Louis would remain. The City Board was responsible for ensuring that students in all schools received equal educational opportunities. Compensatory, remedial, and educational programs and integrated learning experiences would have to be established, particularly for students in all-black schools.

Significantly, the court also directed the City Board to create a comprehensive program for exchanging and transferring students between the city and the suburban school districts of St. Louis County. The City Board was directed to seek the cooperation of the county school districts, the State Board, and the United States in developing and implementing the plan, and to ask the state and federal governments for help with the costs.[34]

The court also asked for magnet and specialty schools to be maintained and additional ones to be established; that the Board permit students to transfer within the district, but not if the transfers would increase the segregated nature of either the sending or receiving school; that steps be taken to ensure that school personnel at every level were integrated; and that future school construction and abandonment of school buildings not be used to perpetuate or establish the segregated school system.

County school districts responded promptly and negatively to the Eighth Circuit's interdistrict exchange program. The *St. Louis Globe-Democrat* reported that county school superintendents would object to busing public school students between St. Louis and St. Louis County.[35] Attorneys for county schools said that only a landmark decision by the United States Supreme Court would get any of the twenty-four school districts in St. Louis County to participate in a court-ordered desegregation plan for the St. Louis school system. They hedged their bet by adding that a voluntary interdistrict plan might work if the county school districts cooperated.[36]

Many South Side white parents reacted immediately and predictably to the Eighth Circuit's order to integrate all predominantly white schools in South St. Louis. One parent leader told the *South Side Journal* that she had received between ten and twenty telephone calls in the days following the ruling, and "The parents are telling me there is no way they are going to tolerate any plan. . . . Not one parent I've talked to will put up with their child being bused. . . . From what I can tell, they don't think it's a racial issue as much as some court telling them what to do. They feel they're being robbed of a basic freedom to decide where their children will go to school."[37]

Some parents said that rather than follow the court order they would withdraw their children from the public schools. Between the 1971–72 and 1978–79 school years, the enrollment of white students in the city school system had fallen from thirty-five thousand to eighteen thousand. The attorney for the Adams plaintiffs predicted that the desegregation program would result in an immediate flight of yet more students from public schools, including a loss of 25 to 30 percent of the city's school population the first year.[38] The Catholic Archdiocese and the Lutheran schools office had already dealt with the swelling number of applicants to their parochial schools by refusing to admit public-school students who were trying to avoid desegregation.[39] George Henry, education director of the St. Louis Archdiocese, remembered that in 1978, Archbishop John May "called the pastors together in the city of St. Louis for a meeting, because obviously, from a pastoral viewpoint, here were some students who wanted to come to a Catholic school—and with that came dollars. . . . The Catholics that all of a sudden had had a conversion and wanted to go to Catholic schools. Our policy did not allow the school to accept Catholic or non-Catholic if they were enrolled in a public school. And that applied in the county, if they wanted to go there."[40]

On April 29, 1980, the City Board approved a desegregation plan. Under the plan, forty-four hundred white students and thirty-two hundred black students would be bused for integration, and an additional thirty-four hundred black students would be bused to alleviate overcrowding. Soldan High School, whose black enrollment had been 99 percent, would have a black enrollment of 39 percent in the fall of 1980. Roosevelt High School's black enrollment would change from 30 percent in the 1979–80 school year to 41 percent in the 1980–81 school year. Cleveland High School's white enrollment would change from 97 percent to 58 percent; and Southwest High School's black enrollment would change from 35 percent to 44 percent.[41] The remaining six city high schools would remain predominantly black. The plan also called for the creation of four new magnet schools, in addition to the eleven existing magnet schools, which enrolled thirty-eight hundred students.[42]

Many South Side parents reacted to the Board's plan exactly as they reacted to the Eighth Circuit's decision. One mother, whose daughter attended an all-white school in South St. Louis, said, "I think the people should have a right to vote on this. . . . The blacks don't want it, the whites don't want it. I wanted to get my daughter into a private (parochial) school. She was turned down. . . . I think we'll fight this thing completely until school starts next fall."[43]

A member of the white South Side group, Concerned Parents for Neighborhood Schools, offered an alternative: "Give the teachers more pay, forget about the busing."[44] As for the desegregation order issued by the Eighth Circuit, "We'll defy it," she said. She preferred to keep her "son at home rather than have him bused to another school."[45]

Promptly on remand, Judge Meredith appointed Dr. Gary Orfield as the district court's expert and held extensive hearings on the City Board's plan. In his May 21, 1980, decision, Judge Meredith found that both the city and the state of Missouri were responsible for the segregated St. Louis schools. He went a step further, however, finding that the state defendants were the primary constitutional violators. The court's order stated:

> [The state defendant's] efforts to pass the buck among themselves and to other state instrumentalities must be rejected.
>
> The state cannot escape responsibility for the racial discrimination disclosed in this case or the obligation to correct the effects of such discrimination by neatly compartmentalizing the authority and responsibilities of its various instrumentalities and then contending that no single instrumentality is wholly responsible for the unlawful segregation or has the power to correct the unlawful segregation.[46]

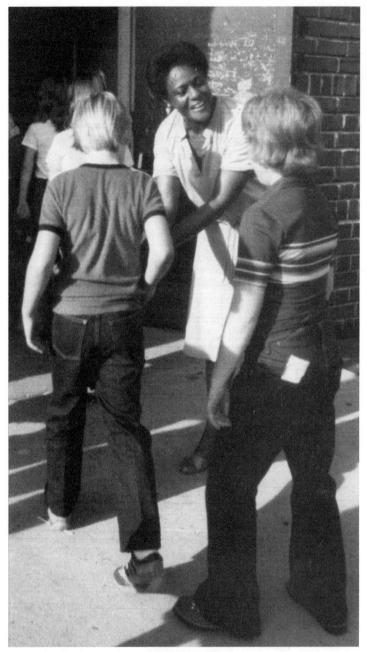

Principal Eula Flowers of Patrick Henry School greets students on the first day of school in 1980. Students were transported under school desegregation order. Photo courtesy the *St. Louis Post-Dispatch*.

The court's order approved a comprehensive desegregation plan to take effect that fall, at the start of the 1980–81 school year. The essential elements of the plan included:

- Reassigning students to achieve the greatest possible number of desegregated schools (defined as 30 to 50 percent black);
- Establishing magnet and alternative schools designed to attract students of all races from throughout the St. Louis area;
- Organizing a middle school system for grades 6, 7, and 8, to facilitate clustering, pairing and other integrative efforts;
- Instituting and expanding specialty and part-time integrated programs;
- Facilitating the student transfers that were allowable under the plan;
- Initiating cooperative interdistrict desegregation programs;
- Providing for integration of and special training for school personnel; and
- Developing a comprehensive community relations program.[47]

Under the plan, there would no longer be any all-white or predominantly white schools in the district, and it would be essential to transport both black and white students to accomplish this goal. Several all-black schools would remain.

Judge Meredith further ordered the integration of faculty, biennial reports to the court so it could assess the progress of desegregation, and the appointment of a monitoring committee. Any school construction had to first obtain the court's approval. Judge Meredith went beyond that, however, and, accepting the Eighth Circuit's earlier suggestion, directed the state, the United States, and the St. Louis Board of Education "to make every feasible effort to work out with the appropriate school districts in St. Louis County, and develop, for 1980–81 implementation, a voluntary, cooperative plan of pupil exchanges which will assist in alleviating the school segregation in the City of St. Louis." By November 1, the Board was "to develop and submit to the Court . . . a suggested plan of inter-district school desegregation necessary to eradicate the remaining vestiges of government-imposed school segregation in the City of St. Louis and St. Louis County."

Judge Meredith also called for the public schools to work with the Community Development Agency of St. Louis on a plan for insuring that federally assisted housing programs in the area would operate in a way that would facilitate school desegregation. He called for the merger and full desegregation of vocational educational programs in both the city and county.[48] And the defendants had to create and submit a plan "which expands programs and schools so that all the schools in the City of St. Louis may be eligible for Title I funding for the year 1980–81 under Title I of the U.S. Elementary and Secondary Education Act of 1965."[49]

Judge Meredith's May 21, 1980, order was clearly the most innovative and important order of the entire litigation. It laid the foundation for the successful, voluntary interdistrict transfer plan that was later adopted.

The state of Missouri promptly appealed the decision of the district court to the federal Eighth Circuit Court. The state argued that it had been required to pay too much toward the integration plan and that it should not have to help to develop either a voluntary or an involuntary interdistrict plan—unless and until the suburban districts had joined the lawsuit and had been found to have contributed to the segregation of the St. Louis City schools.

Two separate groups of plaintiffs also appealed. The Adams plaintiffs argued that the district court's decision was unfair to white students because previously all-white neighborhood schools would now be integrated. A black parents' group asserted on appeal that the plan did not go far enough, because some schools in North St. Louis would still be all black. All of the appellants said the court should have found that the United States had contributed to segregation in the St. Louis School District, and the United States should have been ordered to pay a substantial portion of the cost of integrating the system.

Although Judge Meredith knew that his decision would be appealed, he acted on his order immediately. He appointed an interracial citizens' advisory committee to promote community involvement in the proceedings and named as its chairman Edward T. Foote, dean of the Washington University Law School. Dr. Gary A. Orfield, the court-appointed expert, was asked to continue providing expert assistance in preparing a desegregation plan. The committee established an office, hired staff, retained a consultant, approved a budget, and arranged finances for its first year of operation. It retained Price Waterhouse, Inc., to monitor the City Board's Information Retrieval System and to objectively assess the City Board's management. A contribution from the Danforth Foundation helped to finance its activities.

The committee focused on making sure that all transferring students arrived at their schools safely. Toward this end they secured the cooperation of the police department, persuaded the City Board to hire one monitor to ride each bus each day, and approved the City Board's plan to transport 14,500 students within the city. It arranged with the League of Women Voters for volunteers to assist during peak travel periods and persuaded an interfaith coalition of 124 clergymen, of many religions, to ride the school buses on opening day and serve on welcoming committees at schools.[50] The coalition also met with parents and students to urge peaceful and constructive responses to desegregation. The Desegregation Monitoring Committee worked with the Coalition for Peaceful Implementation, created by St. Louis's Civic Progress organization and the Regional Commerce and Growth Association to demonstrate business and labor support for peaceful integration.

During the summer of 1980, Dr. Edward Foote, chairman of the desegregation monitoring committee, met informally with the state commissioner of education and his staff, lawyers for the county school districts, St. Louis school officials, and people with experience with voluntary interdistrict transfer programs in other cities. Commissioner of Elementary and Secondary Education Arthur Mallory assigned Dr. Susan Uchitelle of his staff to work on a voluntary metropolitan plan. When school opened in the fall, no county district had formally agreed to accept any city children, but most had adopted a policy of refusing to accept any transfer that would increase segregation. Only one county district had accepted a black child, and the city had accepted fifteen white children from the county into its magnet schools.

At the end of October 1980, Dr. Foote reported to the court that discussions among those directly concerned with the voluntary interdistrict plan had moved past the shrill response that dominated the headlines and beyond the question, "Are you for busing or against it?"[51] Foote reported that representatives of several county districts seemed genuinely interested in exploring a voluntary interdistrict plan, but they were hesitant because paragraph 12(c) of the court's order suggested that participation in the plan should be mandatory. He said that the county representatives were understandably unsure about whether to concentrate on cooperation or on preparing for years of litigation.

Foote also noted that Commissioner Mallory had proposed financial incentives for cooperating districts. Foote's report frankly stated:

> It would be premature and misleading to report that there is a groundswell of enthusiasm in the County for interdistrict cooperation. . . . Increasingly, however, the realistic alternatives are crystallizing in the minds of those following not only developments in this case, but also the unfolding case law elsewhere. . . .
>
> Increasingly, those in the County . . . see the alternatives . . . like this:
> 1. Do nothing, probably get sued and either win or lose. . . .
> 2. Seriously explore a voluntary, cooperative plan that is educationally and legally sound, and carries with it some protection against further desegregation litigation.
>
> All seem to concede that a county district cannot be forced into a remedy unless it is found guilty of a violation. . . . [T]he present parties presumably are assessing the strengths of their own potential next steps. . . .[52]

In response to the question, "Can a voluntary plan protect participating districts against further litigation?" Foote received and circulated an opinion from a St. Louis law firm that this was indeed possible, and that substantial protection would be provided by incorporating a resolution to this question in a court-approved settlement of the class action.[53]

Foote's October 1980 report to Judge Meredith presented a framework for an interdistrict transfer plan that: (1) would be completely voluntary, (2) would offer new and attractive educational alternatives to all students, (3) gave participating school districts substantial protection against desegregation litigation, (4) preserved the autonomy and independence of any participating district, (5) get county districts whose students were predominantly white to agree to a substantial, but a minority, percentage of black students, (6) offer free transfer across district lines for students moving from a district in which they were in the majority race to one in which they were in the minority, (7) would include transportation, (8) reimburse participating districts at least for their additional out-of-pocket costs and perhaps more, (9) would receive active state support ranging from expertise to funding, and (10) would set up an administrative structure able to supervise a metro-wide plan and provide for continuing review and improvement, and coordinate long-range educational planning.[54] The settlement agreement reached between the parties and approved by the district court followed this framework very closely.

While Dr. Foote looked into voluntary interdistrict transfer programs, the City Board put into place its intradistrict program on the first day of school in September 1980. Fifteen magnet schools opened with a total enrollment of 4,241 students, 1,907 of whom were black. Fifty-seven black students and 62 white students were on the waiting list for admission to magnet schools. Enrichment programs were developed for nonintegrated schools.

Absenteeism appeared to be the only expression of opposition. There were no organized boycotts, no protest demonstrations, and no public displays of hostility.[55] Attendance the first day was 46,524, but it increased to 52,754 the second day.[56] By the end of the third week, 62,059 students were enrolled in the public school system, only 3 percent below official projections.[57] White students enrolled in fewer than expected numbers at many of the 24 integrated schools.[58] All 3,940 qualified teachers in the system were assigned by the opening of the school year. However, 35 schools were short a total of 81 teachers and related staff.[59] By November, this number had been reduced to 49.[60]

The first year of court-ordered desegregation was largely peaceful, but not without some initial confusion. Juanita Doggett, a principal, remembered, "In 1980, when the district reorganized and set up middle schools, I was called to open up King Middle School as principal with all bused-in children. I think I had twenty-six buses of sixth, seventh, and eighth grade students, all black students. . . . The[ir] school was closed downtown. In three days I got furniture [and] left-over staff, and teachers who did not have positions were sent into my building to conduct this program. Teachers were all unhappy because no one wanted to be in a middle school—very few opted to go to middle schools. It was a real challenge." The school's capacity was 240 students; 600 students came.[61]

In the second week of school, there were reports of sexual harassment of white girls by black boys at Cleveland, a south city high school. Cleveland's 97 percent white student population had dropped to 58 percent in the 1980–81 school year. The day following the reports, 404 white students and 129 black students stayed

City school students gather near buses on the first day of transporting students for integration. Photo courtesy the *St. Louis Post-Dispatch*.

out of school. The Department of Justice organized student response teams, the police department assigned thirty-seven additional officers to the area for a few days, and sixteen additional staff members were sent to the school to help work through the problems of security and communications. Georgia Nicolaison, a former science teacher who eventually became Cleveland's principal, began working there in September 1980. She called those first few weeks at Cleveland "awful." "I can remember it because I was a new administrator and it was very tense," she said. "I had come from Soldan, which was all-black, where you could concentrate on education. You know, we were all so worried about—well, two black kids, 'Is it a black issue or a white issue?' rather than 'Is this an educational issue?' It was a lot of wasted effort."[62]

On September 19, 1980, the Desegregation Monitoring and Advisory Committee reported to the court:

> In summary, some incidents of unpleasantness occurred but were exaggerated in the climate of tension and anxiety generated, at least in part, by desegregation. Many students missed a day or so of school, but most returned by early this week. Communications among all concerned, especially students, parents and school officials, have increased, for the better. Some deeper problems of antagonism remain, but for now, what could have been a significant blot on implementation has been handled reasonably and appears under control.[63]

The principal of Cleveland stated that the brief boycott by white students was "a way of protesting over no special incident. It released frustrations of parents who have demonstrated [against desegregation] over the years."[64] Unfortunately, the opposition to a traditional, integrated public high school in what was then a nearly all-white section of the city persisted for many years. Eventually the City Board looked for an alternative use for Cleveland High, and in 1994, the school became the Cleveland Naval Junior ROTC Academy.[65] The Academy continued to enroll both white and black students.[66]

As the school year began, groups of city parents organized against the desegregation plan. The South County Association of Neighborhood Schools met on September 6, 1980, to start a chapter of the National Association of Neighborhood Schools (NANS), a group that opposed busing as a method of desegregating schools.[67] Their goal was to protest the busing already taking place and to head off any move to involve the county suburban schools in any program that would bus city students to county schools, or vice versa. A group of North Side parents organized under the banner of "Save Our North Side Schools" and also opposed the court-ordered plan.[68] The third anti-busing group was known as the United Parents of North and South St. Louis. This biracial group of twenty to thirty parents was reported to have planned a protest for the opening day of school, but no one besides the founder and her husband showed up.[69]

In the fall of 1980, what had been obvious to Dr. Orfield and other leaders—that an interdistrict transfer program was necessary—became clear to all who were seriously interested in offering an integrated education to students attending the St. Louis schools. With a ratio of 75 percent black to 25 percent white, it simply was not possible to integrate the St. Louis school system without the voluntary or involuntary busing of students between the city and the county as a part of a court-ordered plan. Opponents of integration also realized that an interdistrict transfer program was essential to meaningful integration. They seized on opposition to busing as the most effective way to slow the integration of the all-white, South Side schools and to resist the interdistrict plan.

On December 19, 1980, Judge Meredith issued an order reviewing the plan submitted by the state of Missouri for the voluntary interchange of students between the city and county school districts.[70] The judge acknowledged the state had encountered problems in trying to obtain the voluntary cooperation of the county school districts. He then declared that the plan submitted was insufficient for the court to determine whether it was feasible. Judge Meredith stated, "In one last effort to promote a voluntary plan, this Court will order the state of Missouri . . . to submit another voluntary and cooperative plan on or before February 2, 1981."[71] He directed that this plan should set forth:

1. The number of students that each district in the County can accommodate. . . .
2. Specific details for each district on the number of teachers, available space, and the desirability of its location. . . .
3. The present racial mixture of each school district in St. Louis County.
4. A plan providing for the interchange of students between the districts of the County in order to achieve more integration, and between the County and the City.
5. Specific recommendations for locations of magnet schools and the manner in which they may be implemented both on a part-time and a full-time basis for students within the County and from the City.
6. Specific financial estimates of costs and the means whereby the plan may be financed. The burden of financing will be borne primarily by the state of Missouri. . . .[72]

The state of Missouri appealed Judge Meredith's orders to the Eighth Circuit, which affirmed Judge Meredith's ruling on February 13, 1981.[73] The court stated:

Although the plan reflects the fact that it is not possible to fully integrate every school in the St. Louis system, the district court faithfully followed the directions of this Court by provid-

ing a variety of integrative experiences and enhanced educational
opportunities for students remaining in the [predominantly] black
schools.[74]

In response to the state of Missouri's claim that the district court had no authority to order it to contribute to any interdistrict plans unless and until the suburban districts were joined as parties to the lawsuit, the Eighth Circuit Court held that
the voluntary exchanges contemplated by paragraph 12(a) of the district court's May
21, 1980, order must be viewed as a valid part of the attempt to fashion a workable
remedy within the city. The court stated:

> to the extent that segregation was imposed by County school
> districts which are not parties to the lawsuit and which have not
> been designated as constitutional violators, [the segregation]
> cannot be considered to be "government imposed." But to the
> extent that any such segregation was imposed by the state or other
> defendants, and to the extent [they] have the power to remedy the
> violation, it is proper for the district court to order them to take
> steps to do so.[75]

The Eighth Circuit recognized that the City Board and the Caldwell plaintiffs
had petitioned the district court to add as defendants the suburban school districts
in the three-county area surrounding the city of St. Louis. The court expressed no
opinion on the merits of those motions but emphasized that the current parties
were to comply with the terms of the district court order, including the interdistrict
provisions. The court rejected the state's contention that it should have no part in
paying for the costs of integration, because the court had found the state to be the
primary constitutional wrongdoer. The court also found that the district court had
not acted wrongly in refusing to grant the NAACP's motion to amend its complaint
to seek relief against the United States. The court stated, "In its order approving the
plan, the district court expressly recognized that a substantial portion of the funding
for integration would come from the United States government. . . . Moreover, the
evidence in the record gives us no reason to believe that similar funding will not be
available to continue implementation of the plan for the foreseeable future."[76]

The court's opinion that federal funding for integration would continue proved
to be inaccurate. The United States, through the Justice Department, participated
actively as a litigant in desegregation cases and provided funds for school desegregation only through 1982. In that year, under a newly elected administration, it
declined to state the theory under which it intended to proceed; that is, it pleaded
that it took no position in the case, and therefore was not liable if the ruling went
against it.[77] The court responded:

IT IS HEREBY ORDERED that on or before January 10,

1983, the United States shall disclose with particularity, either in its own pleading or by adopting another party's pleading, its position regarding the 12(c) liability phase of this case, or the United States shall not be allowed to present evidence or cross-examine witnesses at the 12(c) liability hearing herein.[78]

The United States responded:

It is the position of the Department of Justice that the interests of the United States are best served at this time through our efforts, in cooperation with the Special Master [attorney Bruce LaPierre, appointed in 1982], to obtain a voluntary settlement of the 12(c) proceedings in this case. That effort would not be promoted by our taking an adversarial position on the claims or defenses raised with respect to the 12(c) proceedings.[79]

In other words, the United States would not continue as a defendant in the case.

On February 16, 1981, children wearing T-shirts that said "Stop Forced Busing" presented to a congressional delegation petitions with sixty thousand signatures of area residents who favored a constitutional amendment against court-ordered busing.[80] The petitions had been circulated by St. Louis affiliates of the National Association for Neighborhood Schools.[81] Three Missouri congressmen accepted the petitions: Richard A. Gephardt (D-3rd Dist.), Wendell Bailey (R-8th Dist.), and Bill Emerson (R-10th Dist.). The *South Side Journal* reported that Congressman Gephardt "called busing to achieve racial balances, a 'futile pursuit,' and said that as a remedy, it 'simply does not make good sense.' . . . While enacting a constitutional amendment to stop federally court-ordered busing would be an arduous process, Gephardt said he thought it was a 'do-able process.'"[82]

Congressman Bailey said that a "majority of Congress would like to see court-ordered busing as a 'remedy' discontinued."[83] John Heffern, representing Senator John C. Danforth, reported that "the senator was 'absolutely and unequivocally' opposed to court-ordered busing and was interested in 'constitutional remedies' to that end."[84]

On February 18, 1981, Barbara Mueller, chairman of the South County Association for Neighborhood Schools, said that she had expected the Eighth Circuit's decision to favor voluntary interdistrict school desegregation. She said, "The courts are going to do what they want to do. It's not like we're holding our breath waiting for it. . . . I really believe it's almost a vindictive order. They are leaving no room for discussion. There's not a single voluntary aspect to it. They have a gun to your head. They've already found we're guilty. Now they're trying to find the loophole to hang us on."[85]

Besides affirming the substance of the district court's decision, the Eighth Circuit refused to issue a stay to delay development of city/suburban integration plans until the orders could be reviewed by the U.S. Supreme Court. Missouri Attorney General John Ashcroft said, "If the stay is refused, we're prepared to go before the Supreme Court within two weeks."[86] However, his petition to the Supreme Court for a stay was denied.[87] This was the third time the Supreme Court had turned back attempts to halt desegregation in the St. Louis schools. After the denial, Ashcroft said he would continue the fight and take the matter to the Supreme Court for a decision on the merits. He added, "Although I have not seen the court's decision, it appears the Supreme Court has ignored the law it announced in some of its previous decisions. Specifically, I am referring to . . . decisions which do not permit a lower court to order an interdistrict remedy without finding an interdistrict violation."[88] An editorial in the *St. Louis Post-Dispatch* stated:

> The state of Missouri has had to be dragged kicking and squealing into preparation of a voluntary school desegregation plan for the St. Louis area, and now that the U.S. Supreme Court has denied the state's request for a delay, there is no more room for procrastination.

The editorial also noted that school districts were not being compelled by the courts to participate in the interdistrict plan; participation would remain voluntary. It pointedly added, "In view of its historical role in practicing segregation, the state might be expected to welcome a voluntary way out of the results."[89]

On December 22, 1980, after nine years of presiding over the case, Judge Meredith resigned from the case for health reasons. Judge Meredith continued to believe that his original order, based on the consent decree signed by the City Board and the Liddell plaintiffs, was the best way of desegregating the city schools. Nevertheless, he had followed the decisions of the Eighth Circuit in letter and in spirit.

When Judge Meredith resigned, the responsibility for desegregating the St. Louis schools fell into the hands of Judge William H. Hungate. Judge Meredith, along with Judge Donald Lay of the Eighth Circuit Court of Appeals, must be recognized as architects of a comprehensive plan to desegregate the schools in a major metropolitan area.

'Follow That Bus!'

Every politician objected to the St. Louis School Desegregation Plan. Illustration courtesy Dan Engelhardt.

This [plan] is not perfect, but the sun has its spots, a diamond has its flaws, gold will not rust, and the good will shine through.

–Judge William L. Hungate[1]

{ C h a p t e r   S e v e n }

Reaching a Settlement: 1981–1984

Judge William L. Hungate did not volunteer to take on *Liddell v. St. Louis Board of Education*, nor was he selected by lottery. He was appointed by Chief Judge H. Kenneth Wangelin, who perhaps saw that Judge Hungate's forthright manner suited him for the job of breaking up the logjam that had developed in the school desegregation case.

Believing that "the goal of all lawsuits is to bring them to an end,"[2] Judge Hungate acted swiftly and decisively, prodding twenty-three reluctant suburban school districts into agreeing on a finely negotiated interdistrict desegregation plan. He weathered the outcries that greeted his orders, the state's attempts to minimize its fiscal responsibility, and the politics that reduced the issue of equal educational opportunity to a matter of "busing." By 1983, Judge Hungate had helped put into place what became the nation's most extensive effort to integrate the schools of a major metropolitan area.

Born on December 14, 1922, in Benton, Illinois, Hungate graduated from the University of Missouri in 1943 and entered the U.S. Army as a private that same year. He graduated from Harvard Law School in 1948 and practiced law in Troy, Missouri, for twenty years. From 1964 to 1977, he represented Missouri in Congress. Nominated by President Jimmy Carter on May 17, 1979, for a new seat on the United States District Court for the Eastern District of Missouri, he had been on the federal bench for scarcely a year, from October 1979 to December 1980, when Judge Wangelin assigned him to preside over the *Liddell* litigation on December 22.

Almost immediately the NAACP asked Judge Hungate to give up the case, asserting that while in Congress Hungate "consistently cast votes in opposition to public school desegregation."[3] In one speech before Congress Hungate declared, "I am proud to state that schools in my congressional district were at once promptly

Judge William Hungate had the courage and integrity to issue the correct but controversial court order during the fight of the school case. Photo courtesy the *St. Louis Post-Dispatch*.

integrated and are so operated today."[4] The NAACP did not go so far as to file a motion to disqualify the judge. On February 18, 1981, Judge Hungate entered an order stating that because no party to the case had filed a formal complaint of personal bias or prejudice against him he would proceed with the *Liddell* case.

Judge Hungate expected all parties to comply with the district court's orders and to respect the court's deadlines. On March 4, 1981, he rebuked state of Missouri officials for not having filed a voluntary city/suburban school desegregation plan within the sixty-day time limit set by Judge Meredith. Judge Hungate gave the City Board and the Justice Department thirty days to file an interim plan or plans or risk an order of contempt. To ensure that at least one voluntary plan was produced on time, he ordered Tad Foote, the chairman of the court-appointed Desegregation Monitoring Committee, to file a separate plan by March 27 and ordered Dr. Gary Orfield, the court-appointed expert, to review and comment on Foote's proposal by April 6.[5] Judge Hungate's order then cut to the heart of the matter:

> The . . . public record reveals extraordinary machinations by the state defendants in resisting Judge Meredith's orders. In these circumstances, the Court can draw only one conclusion. The state

has, as a matter of deliberate policy, decided to defy the authority of the Court.

Let there be no misunderstanding. This is not a simple case of a private litigant failing to take proper measures to comply with the Court's orders. This case is quite different. The public interest is involved to a much greater extent when a party's actions serve to undercut the implementation of the Court's desegregation orders.

The constitutional dimensions, so important and so far-reaching in dealing with the rights of children and their parents and guardians in school desegregation cases, demand full respect of the federal court system.

To grant the State defendants a stay would permit the State to escape triumphantly from the consequences of its defiance of Judge Meredith's orders. . . . If this Court's orders are complied with, there will be no need for contempt proceedings. If they are not executed, the Court will order the State defendants, the City Board of Education and the United States to show cause why they should not be found in contempt.[6]

Finally, Judge Hungate stated that any facts or assertions brought up while the state, city, and county developed a voluntary city/county school desegregation plan could not be used as evidence against any party to the case.[7] This freed the county school districts from the fear that their participation might reveal whether they had contributed to segregation in the city schools.

After the March 4, 1981, order, all parties submitted their plans on schedule. Tad Foote said that he had worked closely with all interested parties, and two fundamental principles governed his plan. First, the plan allowed choice, and second, it was designed to be fair to all.[8]

Foote's plan was voluntary. No students would be forced to attend a school outside their neighborhood. Students, parents, and school districts would be given incentives to participate. If enough school districts in the metropolitan area agreed to participate, Foote said, the plan would lead to an educationally sound, relatively quick conclusion to the case.

Foote's plan called for:

- "Permissive transfers" giving students who were in the racial majority at their school the right to transfer to another school where they would be a racial minority.
- Allowing transfers only if the host district had space available.
- The host district would not have to pay any more to educate the transfer students than it spent on its own students.
- Each participating district with fewer than eight thousand

students had to open up at least fifty spaces for transfer students, and each participating district with an enrollment of more than eight thousand had to open one hundred spaces. After those were filled, each participating district would accept as many black, permissive, interdistrict transfer students as it took to bring to 15 percent of the total population of black students in that district, with an upper limit of 25 percent black students. This ratio reflected the racial composition of students in the city of St. Louis plus the three adjoining metropolitan counties: St. Louis County, St. Charles County, and Jefferson County. Bruce LaPierre, who helped design the plan, pointed out that in this cautious first step, "It was all an outflow [of black students from the city to the county], no inflow."[9]

- Transfers were to be made on a first-come, first-served basis, with priority given to: (a) black students living in the city of St. Louis, (b) any student attending a school that was 90 percent or more of the student's race, and (c) all other qualified applicants.
- Transfer students could attend the school they preferred.
- Interdistrict transfer students were to be held to the same academic and disciplinary standards as students of the host district. They would have the same eligibility for all host-school programs, and transfer students would not be re-segregated for non-educational reasons.
- Magnet schools and programs would continue to expand and achieve racial balance in their enrollments.
- Participating districts would be encouraged to set up educational or other programs that would bring together students of different races for constructive and enjoyable experiences.
- Transportation would be provided to all students. (Foote did not say who would provide the transportation and pay for it.)
- The plan would allow for voluntary teacher and staff involvement, with provisions being made for professional development and interdistrict teacher assignments.
- A Participating School Districts Coordinating Council, made up of one representative from each participating district, would coordinate and oversee the plan and make recommendations. The council would have the power to hire staff, establish an office, and take any necessary administrative steps.

- The United States and the state of Missouri would share the cost of the plan, with the state contributing toward the cost of transportation according to its existing formula.
- Fiscal incentives would be established for both the home and host districts.
- The court would have to approve the plan, which would be in effect for six years[10] and remain voluntary during that time.

Dr. Gary Orfield commented that neither the sending nor receiving schools would willingly put any additional funds into such a program, and a successful plan would need funds from the state or federal governments or both. He also suggested that the monitoring plans were insufficient because all the districts opposed having any coordinating authority with any real power. And under the Foote plan, receiving schools did not have to integrate their faculty or provide human relations training for their staffs. The plan did not ensure that students would know about their right to choose. Finally, he found the number of guaranteed spaces for the first year to be too few.[11]

The state of Missouri informed the court that it was preparing a petition for a writ of certiorari to the U.S. Supreme Court, requesting that it reverse the court order requiring the state to submit an interdistrict desegregation plan.[12] Nonetheless, the state indicated that it would still try to come up with a viable, voluntary plan that could be implemented by September 1981. The state had already drawn up a plan, submitted in 1980, but it was not as extensive as that agreed to by the United States and the City Board. According to the state, the City Board was more than willing to spend the state's money freely, even as the state faced a budget deficit of $250 million. To save the community from protracted, costly, and emotional litigation that could only harm the children of the metropolitan area, the state asked the district court to approve Foote's plan, with the following changes:

1. The state would be primarily, but not entirely, responsible for the transportation costs involved in the plan. Limits were set by the existing state formula for transportation. The state estimated that the first-year costs for transportation under its formula would be approximately $320 per pupil. (The actual cost turned out to be more than $1,000 per pupil, because the students came from a large geographical area and were transferred to several county districts.)
2. The state would provide the following fiscal incentives to participating districts: For each student who transferred out, each home district would receive half of the state aid allocated by the established school foundation formula.

The other half of the state aid would "follow the student" and be paid to the student's host district. The state of Missouri would pay to the host district the difference between half of the state aid and $1,250. State aid would be determined annually based on appropriations from the Missouri General Assembly.[13]

3. Finally, the state plan anticipated that federal funds would help finance transportation, fiscal incentives, magnet schools or programs, and administrative coordination. The state also took the position that the magnet programs should be financed in part by the United States, the City Board, and the county districts.

The United States and the City Board's plan was patterned after Tad Foote's plan, and incorporated Dr. Orfield's comments on that plan. The principal elements of the U.S./City Board's plan were:

1. No time limit on the duration of the desegregation plan, in contrast to Foote's proposed limit of six years.
2. Making the state fully responsible for funding transportation costs, even if those costs exceeded those that would be paid under existing state transportation policies.
3. A recruitment and counseling center would be established in a central location in St. Louis County with a full-time staff of six.
4. For each student who transferred, the host district would receive regular state aid for the student plus an amount equal to the per-pupil state aid of the sending district. Under this formula, no limit was set on the amount of aid a host district could receive.
5. Additionally, each student who transferred would receive from the state a half-year of tuition-free education at any Missouri state university for each year completed in a host district.

The plan also set forth in some detail the magnet school programs and educational programs it would implement.[14]

Judge Hungate held an evidentiary hearing on all the plans and, on July 2, 1981, approved a voluntary plan very similar to the City Board–United States plan. Suburban districts participating in the plan would not be held liable for actions that might have contributed to school segregation. Their voluntary acceptance of the plan counted as a formal commitment toward furthering desegregation.[15]

The plan had three broad segments: permissive interdistrict transfers, specialized magnet schools and magnet programs, and educational programs designed to increase and promote constructive experiences for students of different races. The educational component extended the existing part-time educational programs in the St. Louis schools to the participating suburban districts, and increased the number of programs. Students would be admitted to new part-time specialty programs in art, music, public safety, transportation, and mass media on a first-come, first-served basis, with consideration given to racial balance.

The plan also called for staff exchanges between the city and suburban districts, for parental involvement centers and recruitment and counseling centers throughout the city and county, and for a coordinating committee with representatives of the city and county schools. The Missouri Department of Elementary and Secondary Education was given responsibility for student transportation.

Importantly, the state would pay all costs and expenses of the plan for the first year. The State Department of Education would have to distribute a detailed explanation of the plan to all school districts in the metropolitan area. The court declined to adopt the part of the plan that gave voluntary interdistrict transfer students one year of free college education in a Missouri institution for every two years of transfer but stated that it might consider approving something similar in the future.

Districts were given until August 6, 1981, to decide whether to participate in the court-approved plan in the school year 1981–82. Judge Hungate's decision stated that he would "countenance no further delay in elimination of the vestiges of racial segregation in the St. Louis public school system," and that if too many districts rejected the voluntary plan the court would consider imposing a compulsory plan.[16]

The state, predictably, appealed Judge Hungate's decision. The Eighth Circuit Court of Appeals affirmed that the state had to share in the cost of desegregation.[17]

Unfortunately, by the end of July 1981, only five school districts had conditionally agreed to participate in Judge Hungate's plan for the upcoming school year: Kirkwood, Clayton, Pattonville, Ritenour, and University City. Eighteen school districts rejected the opportunity.

In response, on August 24, 1981, Judge Hungate entered two orders. The first recognized that only five school districts had agreed to participate in the voluntary plan. The second order stated that because the voluntary plan had been overwhelmingly rejected, the court would begin legal proceedings leading to a mandatory interdistrict desegregation plan.

The court named as defendants the St. Louis County school districts of Affton, Bayless, Brentwood, Ferguson, Florissant, Hancock Place, Hazelwood, Jennings, Ladue, Lindbergh, Maplewood–Richmond Heights, Mehlville, Normandy, Parkway,– Riverview Gardens, Rockwood, Valley Park, Webster Groves, and Wellston. The lawsuit would probe into the question of whether these districts had violated the law by contributing to segregation in St. Louis City schools. Also named as defendants were several state officers, including the St. Louis County executive, the governor, attorney general, state treasurer, commissioner of administration, and the

Missouri Board of Education and its members. The court also ordered the state and the City Board[18] to develop and submit to the court another plan for interdistrict school desegregation for the city of St. Louis and St. Louis County. The court set a hearing date for March 1, 1982, to address both alleged constitutional violations and proposed remedies.[19]

The Caldwell plaintiffs and the City Board moved to add Clayton, Kirkwood, Pattonville, Ritenour, and University City to the list of defendants, but the motion was stayed because those five districts had volunteered to participate in the plan. Those districts were delighted with Judge Hungate's order.[20] The eighteen other school districts were shocked and outraged. In effect, Hungate's order gave them two choices: participate as volunteers in the court's city-county desegregation plan or be forced to do so after a legal battle they would almost certainly lose. The Missouri Commissioner of Education, Arthur Mallory, said, "I can't believe he did that. . . . Nobody has been found guilty of anything. Nobody had a day in court."[21] St. Louis County Executive James McNary, named as a defendant by the court, announced, "We're going to put every ounce of our energy into reversing the course of this federal court. . . . We may even look for different approaches to bring this Judge to his senses."[22] McNary said the culprit was the Eighth Circuit, which in March 1980 had ordered the district court to begin desegregating the city schools. "[W]e'll take it to the U.S. Supreme Court," he declared. "It's the only chance. No lawyer knows how to deal with a completely improper and unlawful order."[23]

Not everyone shared McNary's views. In an editorial, the *St. Louis Post-Dispatch* stated that McNary "will be doing the entire community a grave and potentially dangerous disservice" if he campaigned "to poison the minds of the people against the district court's attempt to eradicate racial segregation in the schools."[24]

The new U.S. attorney general, William Bradford Reynolds, appointed by President Reagan, sided with the opponents of Judge Hungate's order. On September 3, 1981, the U.S. Department of Justice asked Judge Hungate to strike the part of his August 24 order "requiring preparation of a 'suggested plan of interdistrict school desegregation' by Feb. 1."[25] Missouri Governor Christopher S. Bond and Missouri Attorney General John D. Ashcroft, who had lobbied the Justice Department to reduce its involvement in the case, praised the Justice Department's action. Ashcroft said the Justice Department's motion "goes straight to the heart of the fact that the judge is seeking to develop a mandatory remedy before proof that there is a malady to be corrected."[26]

On September 10, 1981, twelve county school districts, stepping up their opposition to the plan, asked Judge Hungate to disqualify himself from the case on the grounds that he "'has prejudged and predetermined' the facts in the dispute and that Hungate 'is not a neutral and detached judge of the facts.'"[27] To support this motion, they cited a statement Judge Hungate reportedly made on May 20, 1981: "We all have bosses and the Eighth Circuit is mine. I have to do what they say and if enough people do not participate with the voluntary plan, I will have to enter a mandatory plan."[28]

**'Our Work Would Be A Little Easier If We Didn't
Have To Listen To The Tantrums'**

Politicians fought vigorously against the St. Louis school desegregation plans. Illustration
courtesy Dan Engelhardt.

In an affidavit filed with their motion, the county districts also cited statements made by Judge Hungate during the proceedings:

> If I may, in an aside, talk about the different sections [of the court's order regarding the development of an interdistrict plan:] we have–12(a)'s, 12(b)'s, 12(c)'s; we have voluntary or mandatory.
>
> In World War II . . . you could volunteer. Some of us had that opportunity. You could volunteer to go to the Air Force.
>
> If you volunteered, they would put you there. You could volunteer for the National Guard. You could volunteer for the Navy.
>
> Some of us didn't do that. Later we were drafted, and we were placed in the infantry. You'd be surprised at what interest the sergeant would have in what you then would like to volunteer for.
>
> Now the reception was not too good at that time. I hope that's helpful.[29]

Judge Hungate denied the motion to recuse himself, stating that on January 23, 1981, in a conference with all the counsel of record for the parties to the case, he had invited affidavits of bias or prejudice if any counsel or their clients believed he should be disqualified. He reminded them that no party had filed such a motion.

Despite the heated opposition to Judge Hungate's order, the Eighth Circuit Court found no basis for Judge Hungate to remove himself from the case. It said that at most his statements "indicate a view on his part that if a successful voluntary plan could not be put together, he would be required to enter a mandatory plan at some date in the future," and "the orders and statements do not indicate any personal prejudice on his part but, instead, are simply an expression of what he considered his duty to be."[30]

The Eighth Circuit did note, however, that the chief judge could opt to assign the interdistrict phase of the case to another judge.[31]

In the same opinion, the Eighth Circuit reiterated the state's liability for desegregating the St. Louis schools.[32] The Eighth Circuit also found that desegregation was progressing. Previously all-white schools in South St. Louis had been integrated. Thirty thousand black students still in all-black schools had been provided with some integrated educational programs and opportunities, and efforts were being made to improve the quality of education in those schools. A number of integrated magnet schools had opened, and there had been a modest beginning toward voluntary interdistrict desegregation. It concluded that the district court could and should determine what actions the state or City Board had to take.

After the Eighth Circuit's February 25 decision and remand, Judge Hungate's actions were critically important. He chose actions that forced the parties to balance the merits of a voluntary settlement against the costs of lengthy litigation.

Asked about his thoughts on the case, Judge Hungate expressed frustration with having inherited a case that had already been in the court system for seven

'... And People Think We Missouri Mules Are Stubborn!'

Illustration courtesy Dan Engelhardt.

years.[33] Further, he remembered meetings regarding desegregation that took place in the 1950s and was surprised and unhappy to discover the high degree of segregation that remained in the St. Louis school system twenty-five years later. His own experiences influenced his view of the case. In the military, he "learned that it's not very nice to be treated a certain way just because of your rank."[34] At Harvard Law School, because of alphabetical seating, he sat next to a black student who became one of his good friends. This friend talked with him about "he and his wife driving to California from Ohio and taking their children and they would have to buy lots of fruit because they couldn't eat in those restaurants. We're talking 1946, 1948, and that wasn't right. I could feel those things."[35]

As it stood, in the winter of 1982, only five districts had joined the voluntary plan. Judge Hungate was looking for some movement toward a settlement, because he wanted to resolve the case before "the kids had gone to school and got out already."[36] He did not want a trial because "that would have been a mess, it would have gone on forever, and the appeals would have gone on forever."[37]

So Judge Hungate pushed the remaining parties to settle by establishing a trial date of February 14, 1983. He also set deadlines so the parties would not "just keep discovering [evidence] forever," a risk when so many parties were involved in such a complicated case.[38] As 1982 wore on, one by one, more districts joined the voluntary plan until the number rose to ten. But more than half the districts still were not on board.

What Judge Hungate did next certainly drew the attention of the remaining non-participating districts. On August 6, 1982, the district court issued another interim order telling the districts what they could expect if they were found to have contributed to the segregation of the St. Louis schools.[39] The order warned that they could expect "abolition of the presently existing school districts and their consolidation into one unified metropolitan-wide school district," a uniform tax rate throughout this consolidated district, and mandatory student reassignments by race.[40] As Judge Hungate put it later, "I wasn't saying they [the districts] had liability, but, if they had liability, this was what was going to happen."[41]

The suburbs responded immediately and with passion. White suburban parents were alarmed that their school districts might be abolished. In a *St. Louis Post-Dispatch* article titled "Hungate Accused of Using Threats on School Merger," representatives from some of the districts expressed anger. One said that Judge Hungate had already found the districts liable without the benefit of a trial and that Judge Hungate announced the remedy at that particular time "because school's about to open. It's a definite threat aimed at getting more districts to volunteer before school does open."[42] Attorney General John Ashcroft agreed that the order was a pressure tactic "to force districts" to settle; he said, "There's little doubt that this is meant to threaten a set of conditions that could happen if they don't [settle]."[43] State Representative Jean Matthews said she was "very, very angry" about the plan and that "Judge Hungate's plan to create one massive school district and dissolve local school boards and boundaries is a classic example of the continuing erosion of the constitutional rights of the people."[44]

Judge Hungate recalled that he received several death threats after the order: "One time someone came to me, I was on the bench, and [was told that the] FBI got a report that 'there's a contract on you, and we don't think the guy's drinking,' and so they sent . . . the marshals . . . for about a week, and they had somebody opening my mail for about that length of time." He was also called "Attila the Hungate," and worse. As he remembered it, he could not even eat at a local Steak 'N' Shake because a "woman in a fur wrap" would call him "a lousy son-of-a-bitch."[45]

Judge Hungate did not let the pressure distract him from preparing for trial. As he put it, "What they would have loved best is if I would get real mad and say anything. That would get me out of the case and that's what they wanted."[46] On October 25, 1982, he appointed D. Bruce LaPierre, professor at the Washington University Law School, as a special master to assist the parties in negotiating a settlement agreement. LaPierre had previously worked with Tad Foote, dean of the law school, on the initial interdistrict voluntary plan, which had involved only five suburban school districts.

Five months of negotiations led by Bruce LaPierre finally produced a settlement.[47] LaPierre said that he practiced "shuttle diplomacy"; that is, he talked with groups individually and then relayed suggestions to opposing groups. He credited Larry Marshall of the Missouri Attorney General's office; John Gianoulakis,[48] who was an attorney for two of the school districts; and Judge David Tatel, an attorney for the St. Louis School Board at that time, for being particularly helpful. LaPierre noted that the Justice Department, which by now was only an amicus in the case, did nothing but create difficulties. "I went to Washington early on, probably in November of '82, to talk to William Bradford Reynolds, who was Reagan's ironic choice for the Civil Rights Department, civil rights guy, and I took his testimony where he gave me the Republican version of how schools should be desegregated. And I said, 'Here's what I'm proposing to do. Everything's voluntary . . . and I would very much like to have the Department of Justice sign on because it helps my odds getting the school fairness hearing with Judge Hungate.' . . . Reynolds heard me out politely, and thereafter the Department of Justice did nothing but create difficulties. They spoke to people behind my back, they inflamed passions at all possible times."[49]

Gianoulakis remembered that the attorneys involved debated everything, even spending four hours on defining the word "student." He said, "On the one hand we had people who believed in busing to achieve racial balance, and on the other hand, we had people who [thought] that the concept [was] particularly abhorrent. Still we reached an agreement."[50]

Negotiations were intricate, lengthy, and political. Lawyers representing all school districts met for hours and days. The superintendents had to work with their boards of education and meet with their communities to convince them that this plan was far superior to a lengthy legal battle in which the districts had very slim chances of coming out unscathed. Even the most recalcitrant districts began to realize that they might not be able to escape consolidation of their districts and loss of local autonomy and control. Bruce LaPierre recalled, "I think Bill [Hungate] was perceived, particularly by the county lawyers, as a wild man, unpredictable. What the devil was he going to do? . . . Bill Hungate had made it clear, at least to the county lawyers, that if there was a finding of liability, and he sure was interested in making a finding of liability, that he loved the idea of the massive interdistrict—actually one metropolitan school district . . . in which we'd have—horror of all horrors—we'd have a unified tax base. Everybody would pay the same tax rate, and every school in the district would, with some variations, essentially have the same mix of African American students and white students."[51]

In negotiations, LaPierre found that the abiding concern of the county school districts was that "'we can take almost anything as long as there are no mandatory transfers of white students into the [city] school system.' That was their bottom line, and what I'd promised them from the outset, that they'd never pay a penny. . . . They needed reassurance on the no-white-transfer-in [policy], which, of course, meant that the burdens of desegregation were going to be borne by . . . those who had been victimized by segregation."[52]

However, it became evident that black parents and students did not consider the policy a burden but rather an opportunity to attend a high-quality integrated school at no cost, because as many as thirteen thousand black students annually took that opportunity when it opened up.[53]

Throughout the negotiations, dozens of lawyers represented the desires of twenty-four school districts—twenty-three from St. Louis County, and then St. Louis. About twenty outstanding issues made reaching a consensus seem almost impossible. Finally, with the trial date fast approaching, the suburban school districts chose an attorney to meet one-on-one with the St. Louis attorney to try to come to some agreement in order to avoid a trial. Their attorney was Henry Menghini, a trial lawyer who represented several school districts. One district had purchased a policy to pursue legal action should it be sued. Menghini had first become involved in the case when he had been asked to defend this district. Menghini had worked closely with Ken Brostron, who represented the St. Louis City School District, and throughout the negotiations they had worked to get as much consensus as they could. Now an impasse was imminent. In an interview, Menghini remembered that "there were several lawyers who had become out of control with their demands, and nothing was getting accomplished."[54]

Menghini talked with all the attorneys. Some would consider nothing less than that their districts be reimbursed by the state for 100 percent of their per-pupil costs. Others were less insistent on this issue but went along. The attorneys also demanded that transfers be purely voluntary and that the state pay the full transportation costs. The state had talked with the districts at the beginning of the negotiation process and urged them not to settle, claiming it would be ten times more expensive if they settled with a voluntary resolution. Yet the districts wanted to settle and get their full per-pupil costs.

As the arguments became increasingly intense, Menghini continued to serve as an intermediary. He and Brostron would "receive daily telephone calls from [the state's] attorney up to the very end urging that we not settle. . . . The State of Missouri was always opposed because of the cost. They fought every claim including paying for legal fees."[55] Summarizing his experience, he said, "This was the most interesting thing I have ever worked on. It touched more lives than anyone can imagine. While I could not ever do it again because of the time and energy it took, I never would have given up this opportunity."[56]

Like the state, some county school districts strongly opposed a settlement. The lawyer for the Hazelwood School District, Robert P. Baine, Jr., faced a dilemma.[57] His district did not want to participate, and he personally believed that Judge Hungate's court really did not have the constitutional authority to give the orders that it did. His position was that in 1954 when *Brown v. Board of Education* was decided, the Hazelwood School District barely existed and did nothing to include or exclude black children. He felt Hazelwood had a "*de minimus* impact" on school segregation. He knew, however, that the district court was not likely to accept his views. So he would have to work hard to convince his district to accept a voluntary interdistrict transfer program.

When he had first started to represent the school district in 1978, it had a 7 percent minority population. By 1981, it was 17 percent minority because many African American families had moved out of the city of St. Louis to North County communities such as Hazelwood, which shared a boundary with St. Louis. "Any black person with a sense of justice wanted a good place to educate their kids," Baine said.[58] The Hazelwood district finally agreed to the settlement, largely because it limited African American student enrollments to 25 percent, and Hazelwood's counsel was able to further negotiate reimbursement and local autonomy provisions.

Earl Hobbs, former superintendent of the Clayton School District, remembered that his district accepted the program early on.[59] Clayton school board members voted overwhelmingly (with one dissent) to participate. But Dr. Hobbs thought that the "saber rattling of City Board and their legal threats at trying to strong-arm the county schools districts was a disadvantage to getting a settlement."[60] He thought the court would search legal records to find proof that each district had practiced or supported segregation. To convince other county superintendents that settlement was their only real option, he advised them that a long legal battle would drain their resources and divert attention from their mission.

Dr. Hobbs saw the interdistrict program as an opportunity "to do something meaningful for kids, which is the school district's business, rather than have a ten-year legal battle and community uproar."[61] His board members saw it as "the right thing to do" and voiced the opinion that the problems of the city of St. Louis were also theirs.[62] Hobbs saw that Clayton's students, 95 percent of whom were white, would be part of a heterogeneous culture in the future. Hobbs also believed that "a generation of black students would benefit tremendously in developing self-confidence, setting academic goals, and being in an environment where high expectations were the norm."[63] He remembered, "There were some frightened teachers, but also some self-confident teachers. One teacher had taught in the city for many years and convinced the faculty that African American children are just like any other children. She helped many teachers make the transition to meeting needs of the students who were transferring."[64]

Jay Moody, the superintendent from the Ritenour School District, one of the original five county participants in the 1981 voluntary transfer plan, represented a district whose school board members did not favor any cooperative efforts with St. Louis. They were certain, he said, that "voluntary" meant "involuntary" and that "they would have no say about what would happen with their students."[65] Superintendent Moody, however, said he was always "confident that it would work. I never once had a second thought about it. I never felt we were doing anything but the right thing."[66] Slowly his board began to understand his perspective.

"Once we began to participate," Moody said, "I made certain that we never commingled the funds, so that we would never depend upon this desegregation money to run the district. In fact, I used the funds we received for computers, and was one of the first school districts to have computers throughout our schools. When our district became supportive, I felt good about it because I never had any misgivings even when my colleagues felt I had betrayed them and broke ranks. Initially I was considered a traitor."[67]

Finally, after months of tense negotiations, the parties agreed in the spring of 1983 on the three elements of the plan: first, the voluntary transfer of fifteen thousand African American city students to suburban school districts; second, the establishment of additional racially balanced magnet schools with a total enrollment of up to fourteen thousand students; and third, for those schools in the city that would remain all-black, remedial and compensatory programs to improve the facilities and the quality of education. On February 22, 1983, the plaintiffs of all St. Louis County school districts, except Riverview Gardens, signed an agreement in principle. By April 4, all of the county school districts except University City had unconditionally accepted the settlement plan. The agreement was reached with all St. Louis County's school districts by June 1, 1983, and finalized over the next several months. Although the state of Missouri and the U.S. Justice Department refused to sign the agreement, their refusal was not enough to invalidate it.

The 1983 settlement agreement—signed by the Caldwell and Liddell plaintiffs, the St. Louis City School District, and the suburban school districts—was the nation's most extensive effort to integrate the schools of a major metropolitan area.

The settlement agreement made it clear that by signing the agreement the suburban school districts in St. Louis County were resolving the pending claims against them. No mandatory, court-ordered, interdistrict busing of students would occur, and the districts would remain independent. These provisions removed the possibility that Judge Hungate might consolidate the city and county schools.

State Attorney General John Ashcroft vehemently opposed the plan, stating that it was "an outrageous expenditure of public funds, unwarranted in magnitude, which threatens our ability to mobilize financial resources across the state for educational purposes."[68] Notwithstanding his objections and the state's refusal to sign the settlement agreement, the state was to share in the costs of the intradistrict aspects of the plan and was required to pay 100 percent of the interdistrict transfer costs.

The settlement agreement established both "plan ratios" and "plan goals" for minority enrollment in the suburban school districts for the next five years. Suburban districts with low minority enrollment agreed to increase their percentages of black students to at least 15 percent beyond their current minority ratio up to a 25 percent maximum. The plan was capped so that minority students, resident and nonresident combined, would not make up more than 25 percent of student enrollment. Unlike the earlier desegregation proposals, under this agreement a suburban district could not use "lack of space" as a reason for denying an African American student a transfer if that district was below the 25 percent cap or "goal." The settlement agreement also allowed African American students residing in a suburban district with a minority enrollment higher than 25 percent to transfer to another suburban school. (That decision was overruled by the Eighth Circuit Court of Appeals, which did not allow county-to-county transfers to be part of the agreement since no liability had been found in the county districts.)

The settlement agreement also set forth some ground rules for city students transferring to suburban schools. The transferring students were to be held to the same standards as any other student. For example, a transfer student could not have a record of serious disruptive behavior. Transportation would be provided for students who participated in after-school extracurricular activities. City parents would receive information so that they could make informed choices about their children's schooling.

The Voluntary Interdistrict Coordinating Council (VICC) was established to coordinate and administer student transfers and voluntary teacher exchanges. Each school district selected one representative to the VICC. Also, one person would be selected by the NAACP and the Liddell plaintiff group and one person employed by the State Department of Elementary and Secondary Education. The VICC had the power to select an executive director and a director of student recruitment and counseling and was empowered to enter into written contracts. The state of Missouri would finance the VICC subject to approval by the district court. The VICC would also counsel city students participating in the program as well as collect research data.

Under the plan, both the host and home schools stood to benefit financially if a student transferred into a suburban school. If a St. Louis City–based African American student would have been assigned to an all-black city school and made the decision to transfer to a suburban school, then the city school would have one less pupil. But the city school would continue to receive half the state aid and the full local monies for the student who was no longer there. Thus, transfers to suburban schools would dramatically increase the money available for the pupils remaining in city schools. The suburban district would be reimbursed for the transfer pupil by

A "tea party" demonstration against Judge Hungate, October 3, 1983. The Party Alliance group held the demonstration at Kiener Plaza. The guest of honor was a no-show. Photo courtesy the *St. Louis Post-Dispatch.*

receiving the average cost of educating a student in that district. Because of economies of scale, a suburban district could make a profit on hosting transfer students, and use the extra funds to benefit all students, transfer and resident alike.

The settlement agreement set a goal of fifteen thousand students from the city and sixteen hundred from the county to be enrolled in city and county magnet schools.[69] Twenty-four city magnet schools, including those previously opened, were to be operating in the city in September 1983 with an enrollment of 8,734. The settlement asked for five additional magnet schools to be established by September 1984. The state was required to pay one-half of the cost of operating the magnet schools that existed on the date the settlement agreement was signed and to pay the full cost of any magnet schools established after the settlement agreement date. The settlement agreement created a Magnet Review Committee to evaluate magnet programs and to approve future magnet schools. The magnet schools were to be racially balanced at 50 percent black and 50 percent white with a variance of 10 percent.

The drafters of the settlement agreement realized that a number of the city's schools would remain all black, even after the transfer and magnet school programs were in place. The settlement agreement acknowledged that many of the city schools were older buildings that had fallen into disrepair. It called for "buildings and grounds which are safe, clean, attractive, . . . healthful, efficient and functional."[70] The plan required that positions in maintenance and groundskeeping that had been cut for lack of funds be reinstated, and that buildings with problems be renovated and modernized.[71] To facilitate learning and classroom management, the settlement agreement contained a provision to reduce city class size to the pupil-to-teacher ratio of 20 to 1.[72]

The settlement agreement provided the city schools with more nurses, counselors, and social workers, as well as funds so that principals could institute "school of emphasis" programs. These funds were designed to allow each city school to have its own academic specialty, like a smaller version of a magnet school. Remedial programs, Saturday classes, summer school, and motivational and role-model programs were also listed in the settlement agreement.

The settlement agreement established an affirmative-action plan for faculty and administrative hiring in suburban schools, setting a goal of recruiting a workforce with 15.8 percent black teachers and 13.4 percent black administrators.[73] Lists of qualified black applicants were to be kept on hand and used to fill openings as they became available.[74]

Finally, and most importantly, no time limits were placed on the duration of the plan.

In May 1983, Judge Hungate held a hearing to determine whether the settlement agreement the parties had signed was fair and to determine how the programs listed in the agreement would be funded.[75] On July 5, 1983, Judge Hungate issued an opinion that approved the settlement agreement as "fair, reasonable, and adequate and constitutionally sufficient."[76] The court placed the burden of the costs on those parties responsible for maintaining school segregation—the state of Missouri and the Board of Education of the city of St. Louis.[77] As Judge Hungate stated:

> For twenty-nine years [from 1954 to 1983], black school children of St. Louis have been urging the fulfillment of the promise of constitutional equality. For twenty-nine years, Missouri has created new programs and expanded old ones with funds that should have gone to students whose constitutional rights have been violated. The constitutional responsibility must now be faced.[78]

The court ordered the state specifically to pay the full costs of voluntary interdistrict transfers and part of the costs for the magnet schools and remedial and compensatory programs.[79] The district court enjoined, or halted, a planned property-tax rollback in St. Louis to make money available for the rest of the plan. Yet the court did not make any findings about what the total budget would be, although it noted that estimates ranged widely.[80]

Again seeking to have Judge Hungate's ruling overturned, the state appealed the district court's ruling to the Eighth Circuit Court of Appeals. The state asserted that it could not be forced to pay for the desegregation plan because it was not liable.[81] According to the state, it had met its constitutional obligations when the state laws that mandated segregation were repealed in the 1950s. State Auditor James Antonio attended a "Tea Party" rally opposing Judge Hungate's order, in which the organizers compared Hungate's treatment of the property tax rollback in St. Louis to the "taxation without representation" that the colonial patriots had suffered under British rule.[82]

Meanwhile, as the 1983–84 school year began, increased numbers of African American city students began participating in the voluntary transfer plan. Local religious leaders urged, for the sake of the children involved, that the detractors of the plan relent and support the plan for its first year.[83] One black student who decided to participate in the plan in the fall of 1983, fourteen-year-old Kimberly Perkins, described the morning bus ride from her home in North St. Louis as the "longest hour" she had ever spent: "I was scared. I didn't know what to expect. I didn't know how the people would be, and I was afraid I would get lost."[84] The school she transferred to had an orientation program that made the transition easier.

While the school year was starting, the state was appealing Judge Hungate's ruling to the Eighth Circuit. On February 8, 1984, the Eighth Circuit, sitting *en banc*, issued an opinion that approved the settlement agreement with minor modifications. In essence, it rejected the state's appeal. In addition to other smaller adjustments, the Eighth Circuit's decision also excluded suburb-to-suburb transfers and plans to establish suburban magnet schools. Although the changes slightly reduced the amount the state would have to pay, the changes did not "alter the central character of the plan,"[85] which was to desegregate the St. Louis City schools and integrate the suburban schools. The modifications aligned the settlement with constitutional law and Supreme Court precedent and filled in some of the more important details that had been left open by the original agreement and the district court's opinion.

One of the changes made by the court involved funding and budgeting. The Eighth Circuit ordered a Budget Review Committee to develop a long-range financial strategy and help resolve any budget disputes.[86] As far as the sources of funding, the Eighth Circuit upheld the district court's power to enjoin the property tax rollback in St. Louis. However, the Eighth Circuit held that for the school year beginning in 1984, a similar injunction could be entered only if the district court found that no other funding alternatives were available.

The Eighth Circuit approved most of the voluntary interdistrict transfer component, as its previous holdings had alluded it would. However, it limited the number of students participating to fifteen thousand.[87] It also stressed that because the purpose of the transfers was to desegregate the city schools, which was where constitutional violations had been found, any new state-funded magnet schools would have to be built within the city's boundaries.

Although federal courts do not have the authority to order increased general funding for disadvantaged schools, the Eighth Circuit determined that it did have the authority to order remedial programs designed to remedy the effects of past discrimination.[88] Noting that a number of the city schools had long been all-black and were to remain all-black, the Eighth Circuit found that the agreement's proposed 20-to-1 teacher/student ratio, enrichment programs, additional staff, and the "school of emphasis" program were remedial in nature and "may be included as a means of ensuring equal educational opportunity" in all-black schools.[89] The court further reasoned that improving the city schools increased their appeal to all parents, thereby promoting integration.

Although the state would pay slightly less for the plan, the Eighth Circuit ruling ensured that "no party found to have violated the Constitution will be permitted to escape its obligation to provide equal educational opportunity to the black children of St. Louis."[90]

Attorney General John Ashcroft appealed the Eighth Circuit decision to the U.S. Supreme Court. At the time, Ashcroft was campaigning to become Missouri's governor and opposition to the desegregation plan was part of his political strategy. He stated during the campaign that the plan was too expensive and would harm the suburban districts' budgets.[91] However, the Supreme Court refused to hear the appeal. After the Supreme Court allowed the Eighth Circuit decision to stand,[92] Ashcroft said that the Eighth Circuit's decision usurped legislative authority, and he vowed to "continue to fight to keep the costs of the busing plan at a minimum."[93]

By 1984, the state's appeals were exhausted. At long last, after twelve years, Minnie Liddell's lawsuit to change the St. Louis public schools had succeeded. Although not without controversy, the settlement agreement had established the framework for desegregation in St. Louis. How the settlement agreement would operate in practice over the next sixteen years forms the next part of the story.

I was surrounded by kids who had goals and aspired to go on to college. It was a cultural enlightenment. I got to know Jewish and Asian people and learn about their lifestyles. The counselors made me feel proud of my accomplishments and encouraged me to pursue my dream of becoming a doctor.

–Jameson Dickson, "Fulfilling the Dream," VICC pamphlet, fall 1994

{Chapter Eight}

City and County Students Go to School Together

The plan to desegregate the St. Louis public schools was by far the largest and most comprehensive plan in the nation to desegregate an inner-city public school district. It was twice as large as the Milwaukee program; twenty times the size of the Hartford program; and five times the size of the Boston program. It was also the only plan that required the state to pay the full cost of transporting students who chose to transfer to neighboring public school districts and to pay the receiving county schools a sum equal to the full cost of educating the transferring students.[1]

The decision to participate in the voluntary interdistrict transfer program was left to individual African American families in St. Louis. According to the 1983 settlement agreement, a family's school-age children could either stay in the "neighborhood school" that was closest—whether it was an integrated school or an all-black school—or attend an integrated city magnet school, or participate in the transfer program and be transported from the city to the suburbs.

The making of the actual decision to transfer to the county schools differed from family to family. Some parents said that their children had brought up the idea; the children wanted to go to the schools where their friends were. But most children in the transfer program, when asked why they participated, said, "Mama made me."

Given the three choices that African American city students had, why did a quarter of the families pick the transfer plan? Interviews confirmed that many parents believed that county schools were safer and offered better educational opportunities. As one parent said:

> I felt like it was a better opportunity for them to go into this program than going to the [St. Louis] public schools. Because I felt like the public schools would not take as much time, and I

just felt like . . . this school would have been better for them. . . . I
felt like they would be under control, they would be able to watch
them and they would be able to help them and they had more
advancement, you know, as far as clubs, as far as computers and as
far as everything.[2]

Parents often mentioned county physical facilities as a reason for opting into
the interdistrict transfer program. Many described city schools as ill-maintained and
complained that the peeling paint and lack of air-conditioning detracted from learning. Some saw the city schools as unsafe, undisciplined places. As one parent stated,
"You might be able to deal with prejudice, but you can't deal with knives or a gun or
this kind of thing."[3]

The number of students participating in the interdistrict program increased
each year, one indication that African American families saw the program as a success. By the end of the 1983–84 school year, the first year that the court-approved
plan was in effect, approximately 2,886 St. Louis City students had transferred to
county schools.[4] Many more had requested a transfer—4,489 applications were on
file—but the Eighth Circuit Court, sitting *en banc*, had issued on September 13,
1983, a temporary stay on additional transfers pending legal appeals.[5] On February
8, 1984, the Eighth Circuit lifted the stay.[6] The transfer program steadily grew, rising to more than 14,500 students in the 1998–99 school year, when the final settlement agreement ended the court's supervision and limited the number of students
who could take advantage of the interdistrict program.[7]

At the county's public schools, African American city students found high
expectations for all students. They could take a variety of electives and college
preparatory courses. The physical facilities did not detract from learning. Yet at the
same time, the transfer students also had to deal with the lasting effects of racism
and segregation, the differences in the discipline meted out by school administrators, and feelings of isolation and "difference" from their white peers.[8] Suburban
students, both white and black, also had significant adjustments to make.

The Voluntary Interdistrict Coordinating Council, also known as the VICC,
gathered in the summer of 1983 to begin developing guidelines, policies, and procedures that would give substance to the interdistrict desegregation plan.[9] The first
meeting took place on July 20, 1983, at offices in a Ladue school building. Caution
and courtesy prevailed at that initial meeting. At this meeting, Dr. Susan Uchitelle
was appointed as permanent director of the VICC.[10]

The VICC met regularly throughout the summer, in an atmosphere of uncer-
tainty, because the transfer program was being initiated under court order, and some
parties to the *Liddell* litigation, including the state of Missouri and the South Side
Parents group, remained opposed to the program. St. Louis County suburban school
districts and the St. Louis School District disagreed on several points about how the
settlement agreement should be implemented, and the VICC staff had to negotiate
with the districts in order to build consensus.

By the beginning of the 1984–85 school year, the VICC had four subcommittees. Dr. Dolores Longley chaired the Policies and Procedures Subcommittee, Jerry Elliott, Jr., chaired the Staff Development Subcommittee, Doug Cormack chaired the Staff Exchange/Transfer Subcommittee, and Tom Krebs chaired the Transportation Subcommittee. Also, the settlement agreement provided for the establishment of the Magnet Review Committee, which was chaired by Dr. Max Wolfrum.[11]

Inside the VICC organization, politics played a major role. The St. Louis School District and suburban school districts vied for equitable staff distribution. The settlement agreement had allowed for two VICC directors, one to be the overall director of the VICC and the other to direct the recruitment and counseling center. Both would report to the VICC governing body. Thus, the VICC operated with two staff flow charts. This structure opened up questions as to who was in control of the organization, and it caused tensions that abated when the director of recruitment and counseling (a city employee) left the position and her position remained vacant.

While the formal organization of the VICC and its policies and procedures were crystallizing, its staff was placing the first wave of transfer students into the suburban schools. During this period, the VICC approved the procedures and the criteria for accepting transfer-student applicants. Notwithstanding the plain language of the settlement agreement, some districts wanted to choose among the applicants and accept only those with good academic records. The VICC refused to allow this.

Many other unforeseen issues arose and were dealt with. For example, the VICC staff had to obtain library cards for interdistrict transfer students so that they could use the public libraries in their school districts. The VICC and the State High School Activities Association worked together to guarantee that transfer students would be allowed to participate in inter-school athletic programs without the usual waiting period required for students who were new to a district. During its early stages, the VICC was frequently in court, because the state of Missouri continued to object to the funding requirements of the desegregation program, particularly its responsibility to pay for the interdistrict aspect of the settlement agreement.[12]

After the first year of the program, the VICC identified several weaknesses. Staff exchanges did not meet expectations, so the VICC took measures to encourage teacher applications. Notwithstanding the efforts, by the end of the second year, only fifty-five transfer applications had been received and only seven transfers had taken place. Six teachers from the St. Louis public schools went to the county school districts, and one teacher from the county transferred to the St. Louis public schools.[13] In fact, the staff exchange program never realized its potential. In 1998, the VICC reported to the court, "There were no staff exchanges or transfers this past year. Until school districts see this as a priority it will not happen. There is nothing more the VICC staff or the Staff Exchange Subcommittee can do to facilitate this program at this time."[14]

Another problem was the transportation system. The state tried to fulfill transportation needs without adequate staff and equipment. Buses were often late or failed to arrive. Transportation was seldom available for students participating in extracurricular activities before or after school, and students had to walk long distances in the dark to return home from bus stops. Parents and school districts worried about their safety.[15] It took four years for a reasonably efficient transportation system to be put into place.

The VICC published reports highlighting the numbers of students transferring, school district activities, withdrawals, promotions, graduation rates, attendance, and general activities for the year.[16] The reports emphasized special programs and detailed school district efforts to accommodate the needs of all students. Simultaneously, the VICC staff developed curriculum for school district use and trained teachers and counselors. They also worked in the school districts with students, parents, and staff on critical issues in the lives of the transfer students. These issues ran the gamut from achievement to racism to acceptance in an alien environment to understanding the culture of the schools and adapting to new rules and guidelines.

VICC counseling-staff programs included Improving Race Relations, Girls Within Reach, and Freedom Rising, which highlighted famous African Americans from the region and their contributions to America's heritage. Materials for these programs, including a videotape and full curriculum for the Freedom Rising program, were developed by VICC and disseminated to all participating school districts. Advocacy for fair treatment of transfer students and their parents was also a major responsibility of VICC.

Not only did the interdistrict transfer program provide the opportunity for black city students to benefit from an integrated education, it provided county students with the same opportunity. In 1983, six of the participating school districts had minority ratios of less than 5 percent.[17] Four more had less than 9 percent.[18] By June 30, 1999, minority enrollment at county suburban schools had dramatically increased. Nine districts had minority enrollments of more than 21 percent, and no participating school district had a minority enrollment of less than 13 percent.[19]

From the fall of 1983 through the spring of 1999, over fifty-two thousand students transferred from city to county schools or from county to city schools. According to Tom Jones, director of Desegregation Services of the Missouri Department of Elementary and Secondary Education, as of 1995, the cost of the interdistrict transfer program was $75.5 million per year, including transportation costs, bringing the gross cost per pupil to $7,257. Because this sum included one-half of the state aid of approximately $1,250 per student,[20] the net cost for the interdistrict transfer program was $6,000 per student. Of that sum, $1,300 represented transportation costs. The cost for the educational component was thus $4,700 per student per year, a sum less than that spent to educate the students remaining in the St. Louis School District.[21] Spread across the state, the interdistrict program added only thirty to forty dollars to the per pupil statewide average cost of educating students.[22]

By 1998, more than six thousand of the city transfer students had graduated from high school, with a significant percentage attending a broad array of post-secondary institutions.[23] Moreover, more than eighty-six thousand city and county students benefited from an integrated education.²⁴ Many times this number benefited from such an education over the sixteen-year period the interdistrict program was in effect.

Given the large number of African American students participating in the program, no one experience can tell the whole story. However, interviews with graduates of the transfer program indicate that many African American transfer students found that they were academically challenged for the first time in the county suburban schools they attended. For some, school became an escape from a violent neighborhood. Others made plans to attend college and achieve their career goals.

Not that transfer program participation was always easy. Students and former students reported long bus rides to and from school, being treated as "outsiders" in the majority white schools, and having to deal with the reality that racism existed in those schools, whether it was because of differential treatment by disciplinary figures or more subtle remarks by white students. Transfer students also had to contend with peer pressure from their city friends and neighbors, who questioned whether they were losing their black identity by going to school in the suburbs. Most of the students, however, were able to cope with these adversities. They learned that dealing with different types of people, attitudes, and even racism could assist them in managing these issues throughout their lives.²⁵ Although no experiences were identical, the following interviews of participants in the program are representative of transfer student experiences.

Charlie Bean, an African American city resident who later became a counselor in the St. Louis schools, relates his experiences in the Lindbergh School District:

> Why did I decide? I was at Sumner High School . . . and it wasn't challenging for me. I needed something that was going to really work with me. . . . I needed someone to really tell me, Charlie, this is how life is really. You need to get out and at least start thinking before you do anything. You know, it's not about money. You have got to have that knowledge upstairs before you EVEN think about getting the money.
>
> I was treated like family [at Lindbergh]. . . . I was in the drama club so we did a lot of performances. And one performance we did was *Fame*. . . . During that week . . . it was hard for them to give us transportation at the end of the performance, so we had to pair up with one kid. . . . Some of them said you come stay with me. . . . So I went and stayed with one family and that family . . . treated me like, Charlie . . . welcome to the house. . . . This is your home, home away from home. I will never forget that. . . . I think it was the love. . . . They didn't look at me being a city student. . . . [I]t wasn't just the teachers, the counselors, the administrators, but a lot of the city and county parents, especially the county parents, they really got out there and said, well, we're

going to work with you. . . . And I think that was the thing that really made me really focus more on this is what I want to do. I want to be a counselor.

We had a lot of racial things that happened. . . .

Lindbergh was a struggle, it was a real big struggle. But you have to [know] . . . how to fight . . . without using the fists and one thing I did, I . . . was using what I had upstairs.

I don't think I would be a counselor if I had stayed in the city. . . . Lindbergh held on to me. . . .[26]

Karen Swain, also an African American student from the city, commented on why she chose to stay in the transfer program.

I didn't mind the hour bus trip. . . . I felt extremely comfortable at Webster Groves High School. I just felt like I could relax in the environment. You know, I felt like it was okay to be smart. . . . You could go off campus to lunch. . . . [T]hey have more of the little extras. . . . I thought it was neat that we had air conditioning. It was kind of like you're proud of your school.[27]

Ms. Swain stated that she experienced good relationships with the people in the county school she attended.

I [had] good relationships with everybody and I think that had a lot to do with the type of person I am. . . . I really can't think of any negative relationships with the students. . . . [I]t was my senior year and I was filling out a scholarship, and the secretaries were encouraging me to fill out this scholarship. I said, I'm not eligible because it said you had to be a resident. They said, you are not a resident? And I said, no. Now, I'm about to graduate. And they said, I didn't know you were a city girl. [28]

The interdistrict transfer program took Derrick Brooks from the north side of St. Louis to suburban Kirkwood, and later to the chemical engineering program at Washington University. Like many other transfer students, Brooks's enrollment in the transfer program began with a decision made by his mother:

[M]y mom made that decision. . . . [I]n kindergarten I went to Dunbar Elementary School in the city. . . . [W]e were in walking distance. And there I finished all my work pretty, pretty fast; and I was always asking for more work to do because I was sitting there twiddling my thumbs. . . . So the teacher there gave me upper level work to do in order to keep me busy. . . . [T]oward

A county parent in a school district resistant to the transfer program kept transfer students at her home after an athletic contest. Photo courtesy the *St. Louis Post-Dispatch*.

conference time . . . my teacher suggested to my mom that she remove me and my brothers from that school district and put us into a county school, because she didn't want my learning to be hampered or impaired because they didn't have . . . whatever it took for me to excel academically. . . . And she wanted to make sure I got the most out of my education. So that began the pursuit . . . my mom was searching out a county school for me to develop academically, me and the rest of my brothers.[29]

Although his mother seemed to be motivated by a desire to assure an enriched classroom experience, Brooks saw the interdistrict transfer program as more than just an opportunity to escape struggling city schools, even if his peers in the city viewed him as "trying to be, quote, unquote, white and trying to fit in with another class of folks."[30] He focused on the transfer program's ability to expand the world views of urban African Americans like himself:

To me the driving force and key to this whole deseg program was to give students the opportunity of experiencing life the way life really is up front and personal at an early age. There's no way in the world that you would be in an environment to where you only would have to deal with people of your same race, which would have been the case if I were to go to a city school. Everybody I saw would have been black.

Going to a voluntary desegregation school that has a melting pot of different cultures and backgrounds and socioeconomic classes . . . gives you an idea of how to adapt and how to see . . . people's differences and not exploit them, but to recognize that we are different people. And these differences are what make us unique and not to fight against it, but to go ahead and accept these differences and move on. And I think that you are better adapted in society whenever you . . . go into the workplace if you were to go to a deseg school because all of this stuff is in your face. You already feel comfortable with communicating with people of the opposite race. You don't feel the apprehension, . . . which is what I initially felt when I switched from the city school to a county school. . . . [Y]ou gradually become accustomed to being comfortable with people that are not like you, which is essential if you do well in society today.[31]

I formed very significant [relationships with white students]. I guess a good example is . . . where a friend of mine, Marty, just ended up being really, really good friends throughout high school. [H]e showed me a different side of life, things that they do to have fun. I showed him a different side of my life, what we do to have fun. . . . But that bond shows me that it doesn't necessarily matter what a person looks like on the outside, it's what that person is on the inside, how that person puts himself or herself out there as far as success. People latch onto people that want to be successful in life; and if you show them, if you're sincere about what you have to do and do everything that you can in an honest way, not being selfish but also be willing to give back to those other individuals and help out other causes for people that are not as fortunate as one, and people see that and they add to it.[32]

Brooks was convinced the transfer program was influential for the white suburban students as well:

I think it was definitely a give-and-receive type of thing. I gave of my energy and my time and my dedication, and they did the same to me, and I think we all shaped each other to become the positive individuals that we are today.[33]

Brooks observed that life as a transfer student involved a demanding schedule, especially for those who, like himself, were also involved in extracurricular activities:

> On an average day, I woke up at 5:00 o'clock in the morning
> . . . got quickly prepared and walked to the bus stop down the
> street. . . . I had to be at the bus stop at 6:18 in the morning be-
> cause I was one of the first stops. So I usually slept on the bus; or
> if I didn't finish my homework for some reason, I'd do homework
> on the bus.
> We'd get to school around about 7:30, . . . 7:50, class starts.
> We . . . got out at 2:50. . . . [B]asketball practice started right
> around 3:15 [and ended] . . . at about 5:30. The activity bus . . .
> left our school at 5:45, . . . then I wouldn't make it home until
> about 6:45. We'd have something to eat then. . . . I would do my
> homework [and] I would be up 'til 12 o'clock or whatever doing
> everything I had to do and then getting to bed, getting five and a
> half hours of sleep at best a night.[34]

He attributed his success, and that of other high-achieving transfer students, to
a drive and determination that enabled them to take advantage of the increased opportunities available in suburban schools, despite the hardships entailed by the daily
commute:

> I think what connected us, at least the ones that did well in
> the deseg program, was the determination. We had to be up at
> five o'clock in the morning . . . just to get ready, prepare to get on
> the bus at six o'clock in the morning to make a drive for about an
> hour just to get a basic education. . . . This . . . effort . . . showed a
> certain level of dedication that we were serious about our academ-
> ics, and we . . . wanted the most out of life especially in regards
> to our education. That and also enduring another long ride home
> from school. And then if you were to be involved in any type of
> sports, school activities, this delays the amount of . . . free time
> that we have because so much time is being dedicated to getting
> to and from a school. . . . So the dedication among these people
> is the tie that brings, I think, all of us together, especially the ones
> that wanted to do well and did well in the deseg program.[35]

Brooks, however, conveyed no regrets at having spent a considerable part of his
high school days riding the bus:

> I was just sowing seeds for my life later on. . . . I'd rather put
> the time in now for me to enjoy a better quality of life later on.
> That's like my driving force. I want to enjoy life after my educa-
> tional experiences at a better degree than my parents were able to
> do so, and so that constant push that started getting me set in my

ways along middle school and high school continue to progress in
my college years, and I think it's what's gotten me to the point . . .
where I'm at today.[36]

Brooks noted that placing white students and black students in the same school
did not always create an integrated environment:

> A prime example of [students separating themselves by race]
> was in the lunchroom. You walk across the lunchroom and you
> can see very, very few tables are integrated. . . . Does that mean
> everybody's racist? No. You sit with people that you feel comfort-
> able with. [I]n the classrooms you're so discouraged because all the
> classes I was in there was maybe two, three very, very rare cases
> where there were blacks in the class. Everybody else was white. So
> when you have that chance or opportunity to get with some of
> your other friends that you don't see during the course of the day.
> . . . [L]unchtime . . . you want to get together. . . . I think that is
> more so a driving force than trying to resegregate on purpose. . . .[37]

Brooks indicated that transfer students initially had to overcome some obstacles
presented by some suburban teachers:

> [W]hen you come from a city school, which is . . . basically
> not in the most promising of neighborhoods, then they feel that
> these students are here basically spinning their wheels, they really
> don't want to learn, and they will try to distract from everyone's
> education if they had the opportunity. But my . . . initial impres-
> sion that I give everybody is not that. So then their behavior
> towards me . . . would change automatically.[38]

Perhaps as a result of his experience with a largely white suburban faculty, Brooks
spoke of the importance of the integration of the faculty as well as the students:

> If I only went to a school [where] every single instructor was
> white, what does that tell me about my capabilities? Does that
> say that blacks are not well-educated enough to where they can
> actually be giving the lecture instead of just being the recipients
> of what comes out of the white person's mouth? Subconsciously, I
> think you become formulated into that. Well, how come I can't be
> here? How come there's not people that look like me . . . deliver-
> ing this much information to us for us to soak up?

Brooks attributed his substantial academic success to his parents' determination to see their son succeed, and to his own ambitions, which increased with the heightened expectations generated by his participation in the transfer program:

> I think first and foremost my success . . . is directly associated with parents' . . . drive for me to do well. . . . The second takes place in me, my personal drive, my personal benefits, my personal goals and me not settling for mediocrity. That coupled . . . with the environment of the education is what really just sends it over.
>
> I don't think that I would have been afforded the same opportunities . . . if I went to Beaumont [a city school]. . . . Washington University is my first choice. I went in for early admissions. And when you check Washington University's record, I don't think anybody from Beaumont ever went here.
>
> The minimum criteria that has to be achieved to graduate from Beaumont doesn't even come close to what you need to do in order to even submit applications to the schools. So that automatically changes what my choice is for college, which ultimately changes my whole lifestyle, the things that I do. . . . [A]t Kirkwood [a county school], everybody was expected to go to college. . . . [In] the city schools, if you go to a college, you've done something amazing. . . . So that whole atmosphere subconsciously is like, well, . . . just graduating is good enough, so I don't necessarily have to go to college. I can just get a good job. . . . [W]hen you go . . . to a county school, you're expected to go to college. . . . [The] push is for you to go to graduate school, but college is expected. . . . So me going to college is like, well, I just did the next thing that I'm supposed to do. Now, the only biggie is which college to choose and how well I'm going to do on which college that I choose.
>
> The counselors were right there willing to help, and they help you with step-by-step plans to get where you want to be as far as your educational standing.[39]

Brooks speculated that even if he had not participated in the transfer program, he would likely have gone on to college anyway, but his experience as a transfer student caused him to set his goals higher than he would have otherwise:

> If I didn't go to a county school, I'd graduate from Beaumont; and the way that my mom is, I would have still gone on to college because that was her push and this degree is very much my degree and my mom's. . . . I wouldn't have gone to Washington University. . . . I don't think my major would have been chemical engineering. . . . I don't even think I would have reached chemistry level

until my senior year according to the curriculum that's going on in the city school.[40]

Asked about the future of the transfer program, Brooks hoped that students would continue to have the option to attend school in the county:

> [Y]ou shouldn't make everybody go to a city school. Transfer either way from city to county or county to the city, but that option should always remain there and whatever they can do, because you cannot begin to put a dollar sign, to put an amount on, the value that you gain from an interracial learning experience. I wouldn't have changed it for the world. You just can't beat it, especially if you're planning on a career instead of just going to a job, punching a clock, coming in and out. . . .
>
> And I don't think I would have been as comfortable around people. So many of my friends too or associates here at Wash U . . . are not black. . . . You see no color barriers. . . . I just don't believe that that level of comfortableness would be the same if I didn't go to a high school or middle school or grade school that wasn't racially integrated.[41]

Another early participant, Anthony Brown, was mentored by a band director at Mehlville High School who used to drive him home after late practice. "Mr. Dennison talked a lot about music and colleges during those rides home. He talked and I listened. I learned a lot. He's still my mentor." Anthony, a gifted clarinet player, believes Dennison "put the bug" into his ear about a college that had a good school of music. Anthony received a full tuition scholarship, qualified for the dean's list, and played in a college's top band. Being part of an environment where studies were emphasized was motivating for him. "That helped to push me along. It was contagious being around achievers who wanted to excel in both high school and college." And when finished with his training, Tony chose to return not only to St. Louis but to Mehlville High School as the band director, fulfilling a career goal he had set for himself.[42]

Transfer student Brian Griffin went to Ladue schools, where during high school he was on the football team and also the Honor Roll. He believes his Ladue education helped him get into Notre Dame on scholarship. His exposure "to so many cultures gave a realistic picture of life. I learned to communicate and be comfortable with all people." He also participated in the Principal's Leadership Cabinet; INROADS, which is a career development organization for minority youth, and the National Honor Society. This background gave him the ability to get the degree he wanted, which is "a ticket I need for a good job and a promising future."[43]

As the numbers of African Americans grew in the schools, teachers became more successful working with African American students. There were fewer discipline problems and more attention was paid to a multicultural curriculum and student academic growth. All of those dimensions made the program increasingly successful as the years progressed, as measured by teacher effort to reach minority students academically, students feeling as if they were an integral part of the school system rather than strangers to the system, and students' increasing participation in school-related activities. Additionally and equally important, more transfer students were winning awards and scholarships for their academic achievements, their participation in school functions, and their athletic participation.[44]

As the interdistrict program continued to attract students from the city, more and more students not only excelled at their transfer schools, but they also parlayed their transfer experience into future dreams. Among those who excelled was Teas Sexton Steele, who was one of ten students nationwide to receive Washington University's prestigious John B. Ervin Scholarship. Ms. Steele credits her St. Louis County alma mater: "The research and study skills I learned at Clayton are definitely helpful to me now."[45] Her upper-level courses, which included honors and advanced placement classes, gave her the background in math and science she needed to proceed toward her goal of becoming a neurosurgeon. The reputation of her high school aided in her admission to Johns Hopkins University and the six-year medical program at the University of Missouri at Kansas City. She stated that an important benefit of attending Clayton High School was that "it allows you to dream. We interact with Clayton kids, see their lifestyles, and know they are headed for success. We say to ourselves, I'm on the same track as they are, so I have a chance at making it too." In addition, she felt that the atmosphere allowed her "to make connections with influential people."[46]

Tiffany Rainsville, a 1998 graduate of Pattonville High School, went on to Columbia University in New York City. She returned to Pattonville after her first semester at Columbia to express her appreciation to her chemistry teacher, who had helped prepare her for her academic success. "Attending Pattonville schools was very beneficial to my life. The thought of going to college at Columbia University was at first intimidating. Once there, I realized my high school teachers—especially chemistry and calculus—had prepared me well. The helpful faculty and staff at Pattonville gave me the confidence to believe in myself. Columbia University is my new home, but Pattonville will always have a special place in my heart."[47]

One early participant, Gabrielle Lambert, says that her school experience in Clayton "definitely well prepared me." She attended Georgetown University on a Westlake scholarship, with the goal of becoming a pediatrician specializing in trauma. Ms. Lambert found that cultural diversity was something she appreciated because she learned from her past exposure how to be comfortable in a college setting where only about 10 percent of the students were minorities. "I learned a lot from the exposure I had. It's beneficial to break away from the nice, safe environment you might be used to."[48]

Not all students were successful. Many returned to the city schools because they could not adjust to life in suburban school environments. Others felt unwanted or simply preferred their neighborhood school. Some were suspended and required to leave the program. A focus group study conducted in 1993 demonstrated that initially many children felt that there were not enough transfer students.[49] Many of the students interviewed said that it was hard being in a situation with more white students than black and that the environment was very new to them. Many spoke about racially discriminatory incidents in their classrooms and during extracurricular activities. For example, one student remarked:

> The white kids make it harder for us because we have to work in groups and act all silly and stuff and they're not serious about it and the whole group gets graded for it and the teacher looks at the black kids and tries to blame it on us when we were really the ones who were working.[50]

Over the years many receiving schools made a concerted effort to meet the needs of transfer students, resulting in an increased retention rate. The focus group study concluded that in most situations the effect of the transfer program was positive. The parents were pleased with the education their children were receiving in the county schools, and the students were thankful for the integrated experience and for the future career opportunities available to them. These findings are consistent with the anecdotal evidence and confirm the value of the interdistrict program to African American students.

Views of White Suburban Students

The white suburban students who were interviewed in the early 1990s as part of the focus group study had a wide variety of views about the transfer program and the African American students who participated in it. For the most part, the white students interviewed did not demonstrate the apprehension or hostility that many white suburban students exhibited when the program started. Most of the white students interviewed felt positive about the program, because it gave them a chance to interact with students from diverse backgrounds and learn about different cultures. However, they also reported that racial problems still existed and transfer students (because of their long bus rides) often did not participate in school activities as fully as their suburban peers.

One white student said that without the transfer program "we would have hardly any black people in our school and I think it's good that we have [the transfer program], because if we didn't, then we probably would never be around anybody different."[51] Other students discussed how meeting black students in school would prepare them to interact with people of different races and nationalities in the workplace. Some students said that the transfer program helped them discard stereotypes that they had held about African Americans. For example, one student said he met a number of transfer students through playing football who were "really nice guys. A lot of them, you know. Then there's some who are just troublemakers. But that's the same thing, people from the county, too, I mean. It's just you get a cross-section of everybody."[52]

Some of the students interviewed acknowledged that they had many opportunities in their schools that were not available to students in the city. When asked this question, one student compared his school to those in the city and said:

> I was just thinking about . . . a school . . . it's a dominantly
> African American school closer to the inner-city. And I look at
> them and sit there and think, these are people who don't have
> control because whereas we're in the county, we have little more,
> we've got choices, we're getting good classes. . . . There's . . . a
> lot less money, and people there aren't getting the chance. They
> can't, they're applying themselves but they're going to get nowhere
> because there's nowhere to go. They're not having control, they got
> no way out almost.[53]

Some white suburban students came to recognize that they had advantages they thought everyone had before they met people from the inner city. For example, one white student said that from talking with an acquaintance he met through the transfer program, he realized that many of the students "go through a lot of stuff each day where they live. . . . [T]here's gunshots. . . . [W]indows are broken. . . . [T]here's gang fights. . . ."[54]

The white students acknowledged that racial problems still existed in their schools but felt that matters were improving. One student remarked that "racism . . . it's probably like one of the biggest problems. I mean, actually the most dangerous one, where people actually get hurt over it, things get blown out of proportion."[55] Other students confirmed that blacks and whites were treated differently in terms of discipline:

> If you're in our school basically you're not like white . . .
> preppy looking . . . just normal looking, I mean, I don't know how
> you define normal. You know, sort of normal looking, then, you
> know, you're not really going to get bothered. But if you look dif-
> ferent, and if you're black, . . . if you have your head shaved, or if
> you've got on weird clothes, then they [school security] are going
> to tend to follow you more and make sure that you're not causing
> trouble.[56]

One white student in the group commented on the cost of the program and also asked why the suburbs should shoulder the burden of dealing with the social problems associated with the inner city. Responding to the earlier comments about violence and other bad situations in the city, one student asked, "If things are so horrible there, why are they bringing it to us?" Yet another student observed that everyone needed to address the social issues of violence and poverty, because "if you're not exposed to it now, . . . it's going to be a worse culture shock if you're exposed to it later when real life is around you."[57]

African American County Residents Offer Their Perspectives

The African American students living in the county for whom suburban schools were their "neighborhood schools" offered yet another perspective on a voluntary transfer experience. A 1993 VICC focus group study interviewed black students whose families lived in the suburbs. To a large extent, all the students expressed some anxiety about feeling caught between two different worlds. Living in the predominantly white suburbs, they felt they did not fully belong with either white suburban students or the African American transfer students from the city. The consensus was that African American city students viewed them and their families as "sellouts" for leaving the city and that at the same time suburban white students and teachers did not fully accept them because of their skin color. One student put it this way: "Your peers are telling you that you're not black enough, and the teachers are just telling you, 'Well, we don't think of you as being black.'"[58] Another student expressed a similar feeling: "It's almost like we're stuck in the middle, . . . [y]ou know, like the city students think we act white . . . [a]nd the county students think we want to be white."[59]

Many of the county African American students spoke about the assumptions and stereotypes that they had to confront at school from whites and from the black city students. Two students mentioned that white cafeteria workers would assume that they received a free lunch because of their skin color. At the same time, many city students would assume that the families of resident black students must be exceedingly wealthy. One resident county black student observed, "The black city students, they automatically think [you're] like a sellout once [you're] staying out in the county," and noted that city students had a nickname for the rest of the black students, "County Rodney."[60] Another student reported being treated more favorably by a white teacher after the teacher found out that his family lived in the county.[61]

Despite difficulties fitting in with the transfer students, the African American county residents, for the most part, had positive comments about the voluntary transfer program. The black students' presence helped them feel as if they were not such a small minority in the school. Although the resident students still felt isolated at times and mentioned being "singled out" to talk to the class during Black History Month, they agreed that the presence of the African American city students eased this burden somewhat. One student remarked, "You get everything in that school when you have a desegregation program. If they take it out, I mean, it's like something will be missing. . . . And the white people in our school can tell you, they learn something from the black kids who come from the city too."[62]

Administrators and Principals See Both Positives and Negatives

Many administrators and principals in the St. Louis school system believed the voluntary interdistrict transfer program adversely affected the city schools. Vera Atkinson, principal of Cote Brilliante Elementary School, agreed that although the transferring students did not differ in ability from those who remained in the city they were nonetheless the "best and the brightest."

> [W]hen the desegregation case first came about, my biggest complaint about it was that the St. Louis city schools were going to lose the best and brightest of the children, and it happened. . . .
>
> Note I say the best and brightest because they may not have been IQ-wise . . . the highest scoring, but they were children who knew how to act in the classroom. They were children whose parents were interested in what they were doing.[63]
>
> [A] lot of times a parent who takes an interest in his child's education will say, okay, the deseg program says we have the opportunity to send these children to the county, so the county must be better. We have sent a subliminal message . . . out that said, the city schools are not good enough so transfer to the county. . . . And that, I feel, is one of the biggest things that happened to the city schools in the desegregation program.[64]

Ms. Atkinson was also concerned that children with a discipline history were not permitted to transfer.

Terre Johnson, principal of Webster Middle School in St. Louis, agreed with Ms. Atkinson that the city schools lost many of their motivated students.

> I feel that [the magnet schools and the transfer program are] a brain drain and a family drain, because the children who are geared from the home to think "education," the parents will go the extra mile to make sure their children are prepared, those are the parents who take the time to be put in the lottery to get their children in these schools. I see nothing wrong with it. I did the same thing. But the problem for me is, once the children in this area are in the magnet schools, then I have the children who I would normally have anyway, but I have a larger population of the children who are just not grounded in education in the family or just not dedicated to education as the other children who are in the magnet [or interdistrict] program.[65]

Steve Warmack, principal of Roosevelt High School, said, "At the secondary level, we're not only talking about losing a level of kids who are academically capable, but in many instances, it was the school leaders . . . and the athletes."[66] Mr. Warmack added that 90 percent of the outstanding athletes in the county schools were transfer students from the city.[67] This was due, in part, to recruitment.

Joyce Roberts, principal of LaClede Elementary School, observed that her school lost about 30 percent of its third- and fourth-graders to the magnet schools and the county schools.

> The high-achieving students are the ones that go in the county. And the county has instituted a screening process, in my mind. They send an application out to the counties, and then we receive a document back indicating, we want you to mark these spaces on the children. And if [there] are any discipline problems, they don't go. If they're a discipline problem in the county, they kick them out and they send them back to us, the neighborhood schools.[68]

Ms. Roberts believed that the African American students attending the county schools were doing no better than those in the city schools.

Sandra Wilson, principal of Ashland Elementary School, did not agree with the teachers who referred to the transfer program as a brain drain.

> I cannot look at it as brain drain, okay? Because what you're saying is that the children who are left in the ordinary schools are not capable, and which one among us can really say that? I have a problem with—and my staff knows this—if you were to take my background and use all those wonderful statistics that they want to say: "Single parent"—my mother was divorced—but then she was a single parent. I was a girl and growing up, by 15 I should have been pregnant, on welfare at 16, and with ten children at 20.
>
> But I didn't, so if there's one Sandra Jean . . . Wilson out here, . . . there's got to be a whole lot more, and we're going to teach them that way. We're going to treat them that way, because somebody cared. Somebody cared enough about me; I didn't just shine because I was a brilliant student. I was not *cum laude* over my graduating class, no. So I was not the brilliant student, but somebody encouraged me along the way. Not just one somebody, a whole bunch of somebodies. . . .
>
> About the brain drain, I think that's a very poor way to look at the number of children who are left, I really do. And I have to look at our parents.[69]

Emma Cannon, principal of Banneker Elementary School, said that children did not get a better education in the county, but they did benefit from an integrated education. She said, "I resented them saying the children would get a better education in the county. For exposure it is good. One problem with segregated school[s] is lack of exposure. Their whole world consists of a few blocks."[70] She also complained that children could be returned to their neighborhood school after funds had been allocated to the county schools to educate the students:

> [T]he child could be returned to the neighborhood school for failure to achieve academically. Children were returned in November and March. Money was earmarked in September and students would be returned in March. The city schools end up having the student but did not get the money. The students were returned to the city schools in March right before testing.[71]

Other complaints about the program included the disparity in the marketing efforts for different schools. Jimmy Irons, principal of Farragut Elementary School, said:

> [T]he way the magnet schools and the county schools were marketed, they had posters on buses that said, if you want a good education, send your child to. . . . If you want a choice education, you either went to a magnet school or you went to one of the St. Louis County schools. There was no kind of public information, positive public information about the all-black schools, I mean, none whatsoever. When we raised the question concerning that, we were told, you have to publicize your own schools yourself. You can send articles to the newspapers, but my concern at that time and the concern of some of the other principals is that the federal government and part of the deseg program had put out three or four hundred thousand dollars a year for someone to promote the nonintegrated schools as well—just as they promoted the others, but that was never done, is all I can say.[72]

Mr. Irons also complained about funding disparities, saying that city and county teachers received different bonuses for transferring.[73]

Webster Middle School Principal Terre Johnson also believed that the county schools benefitted far more than the city schools. "They built new plants, they had all kinds of things. And that's one of the reasons I feel that the county schools really didn't jump to get out of the deseg plan because of the amount of money they" received from the state.[74]

LuVerne Cameron, associate director of the Desegregation Monitoring Committee, viewed more positively the overall impact of the interdistrict program. According to Ms. Cameron, there was no significant objection to the interdistrict program. It allowed choice and exposure to a world with different people and different resource allocations. Nonetheless, she believed that there were mistakes in the implementation of the program:

> I think the tragedy of the interdistrict program is that implementation occurred before you readied the environment to receive those children. Many a day I cried because parents would call, stories unbelievable, things that happened to their children. The most infamous and fairly well known was the suspension from the bus but not from school, and yet if you reside in a city project area, you don't have a car. How in the world are you going to get the kids to school? [There was] no mechanism in place to deal with that kind of thing. Children who were "A" students in the city find themselves in special-ed classes in the county. Now, was that because these children had needs, special-ed needs? How much of it was the perception of the individuals they were dealing with? Some parents were strong enough, had the interest of their kids well enough in mind and in heart, they challenged it and won out. But the majority did not. They trusted the school to do what was best.[75]

Studies of the Transfer Program

The reflections of individual students and educators are supported by a study undertaken after the desegregation program had been in effect for a year.[76] The study found general consensus among "St. Louis educators and community leaders that the voluntary interdistrict transfer program is working well for participating students. Significant educational advantages are being gained by black city students transferring to suburban districts and white suburban students enrolled in city magnet schools."[77]

The study recommended: (1) no screening of students should take place, because the program was designed to desegregate public schools, so all children should be eligible; (2) human relations workshops were much needed by all staff working in multicultural settings; (3) orientation for transfer students was critical in every school district where students were transferring; (4) transportation should be reviewed periodically and modified when circumstances warranted it; and (5) adjustment of transfer students to their school environment should be an ongoing activity and comprehensive for both the students and their parents.

In 1988, after the voluntary transfer program had been in effect for five years, the *St. Louis Post-Dispatch* commissioned a series of polls by an independent research organization to gauge community reaction to the program.[78] Because no polls had been taken before the program started, it was difficult to determine if attitudes had shifted. Nevertheless, these polls provided a "snapshot" of the attitudes of suburban teachers, suburban students and parents, and city students and parents toward the program as it existed in 1988.

Although African American and white students experienced the same interactions in the suburban schools, the polls showed that the perceptions of the program were vastly different depending on the race of the student. The answers to a series of questions that asked respondents to quantify the amount of social mixing between African American and white students provide an example. Seventy-six percent of African American transfer students agreed that there was "a lot" of social mixing between black and white students. Only 46 percent of white suburban students agreed with this proposition.[79] Likewise, 82 percent of African American high school transfer students responded affirmatively that blacks and whites worked together in the classroom, whereas only 38 percent of whites replied affirmatively to this question.[80] The suburban teachers, when asked to comment on the levels of interaction between students of different races, replied with the following answers: 6 percent agreed that there was a "great deal" of interaction; 37 percent said that there was a "moderate" level of interaction; 33 percent said that there was "little" interaction; and 7 percent said that there was "no" interaction.[81] Despite the differences in perception between black and white students of how often those interactions occurred, interaction took place.

The polls also revealed gaps between African American and white students and parents when these groups were asked whether they thought the program was a good idea. Only a slim majority of white suburban parents who replied said that they supported the program, indicating continuing resistance to integrated schools in the suburbs. The polls also revealed more resistance to the plan among white parents than among white students. Seventy-one percent of white students either agreed or partially agreed with the statement that it is "a good idea to try to mix black city kids with white county kids," whereas only 54 percent of white parents felt this way.[82] The polls revealed overwhelming support for the program among African American students and parents.

According to the polls, suburban teachers, on average, thought that the transfer students were at least one year behind grade level when they entered the suburban schools.[83] The teachers' opinion supports the anecdotes related by the transfer students interviewed for the focus groups. Nearly all the students said that they had some difficulty adjusting to the pace of work in their new schools, and that they had to work harder to maintain the grades they had previously achieved in the city.

At the same time, however, suburban teachers expressed optimism that the longer the city students stayed in the suburban schools, the better their situation would be. Twenty percent of suburban teachers said that transfer students had made a "great deal" of progress after two or three years, and 64 percent said that they had made some progress.[84]

From 1983 through 1999, when an agreement to end court supervision of the desegregation program was reached, the interdistrict transfer program was the most visible and controversial aspect of the entire desegregation program. If one believes that parents and students should have some choice as to where the students will attend elementary and secondary school, the voluntary interdistrict transfer program was clearly a success. The program not only enrolled as many as thirteen thousand students a year, but it also gave students and parents, irrespective of their race or economic status, a real choice as to where they would attend school, empowering many families with the belief that they could improve their children's educational opportunities. State transportation was provided for all students, and the receiving districts were paid the full cost of educating the students they received from other districts, benefits not present in most school choice programs. Thus, the receiving schools were willing to accept a significant number of transfer students and provide them with a high-quality education. Further, a student's economic status did not affect his/her exercise of choice, because families were not required to pay transportation costs.

It is important to note that the city schools did not lose money by virtue of the fact that thousands of students chose to transfer to county schools. In fact, the St. Louis School District received substantial additional resources to provide a competitive education to the students who remained, and as a result, they had more dollars to educate fewer students. The city schools were able to increase their adjusted expenditures per pupil from $3,682 in the 1983–84 school year to $8,071 in the 1997–98 school year. Unfortunately, the city schools were affected by a loss of students to the county and magnet schools. Dr. Gary Orfield, a professor of Education and Social Policy at Harvard University, agreed with the views expressed by St. Louis educators that removing motivated students from the city schools erased some positive peer-pressure influences on the students who remained.[85]

Dr. Orfield, however, also believes that the benefits participants in the transfer program received outweigh the effect the program had on the city schools. The graduation rate of city transfer students was on average two to three times as high as the graduation rates in the city schools, particularly in those schools where the graduation rates of all students is high.[86] More significant, however, is the anecdotal evidence from African American city students confirming the advantages that individual students gained from participating in an integrated school where the norm was to graduate and attend college.

Given this success, it appears obvious that the transfer program should have continued at 1999 levels. This was not to be, however, as the 1999 settlement agreement programmed an enrollment decline of about 25 percent for the interdistrict transfer program. The state of Missouri was behind the efforts to limit future participation in the interdistrict program. The state opposed the program because it was required to bear the full cost—$4,700 per pupil, per year—and because an integrated education was a goal of the program, a goal not shared by many Missouri voters and officeholders. The state apparently viewed choice in education as a valuable option to enhance student achievement, but it did not want to fund this option. If it did not, poor black students could not choose to attend a county school unless their transportation was paid for. And primarily white county school districts would not accept large numbers of black city students unless they were reimbursed for the full cost of educating these students.

[T]he district court . . . has done everything within rea-
son to make sure that the plan to desegregate the St. Louis
schools is carried out. This has not been an easy task,
particularly because the state generally likes to do less and
pay less and the School District wants to do more and
have the state pay more.

–Liddell v. Board of Education[1]

{Chapter Nine}

Enhanced Opportunities for City Students

Between 1954 and 1980, the St. Louis public school system changed from a predominantly white district to an overwhelmingly black district, making it impossible to desegregate the city schools by simply busing students from one part of the city to another. The interdistrict city-county program and magnet schools were two ways the federal court found to provide integrated educational opportunities for more than half of the city students.

St. Louis pioneered the concept of specialty schools by establishing Metro High School in 1972 as an alternative, integrated high school. Betty Wheeler, principal of the school from its inception until her retirement in 1999, described it as 50 percent black and 50 percent white.[2] "The students were the ones who selected the colors for the school, and their colors were black and white because they said we are completely integrated," Ms. Wheeler remembered.[3] She continued:

> [W]e called it a school without walls. . . . [T]he city was our classroom. The students went out in the streets, and they would interview people and find out about their background. . . .
>
> From the beginning we had a community service component . . . where the students would have to give sixty hours each year . . . [to] a nonprofit agency. . . . [A]nd we asked that the students be evaluated on attendance, getting along with others, having initiatives, and things like that. . . .
>
> [W]e took all of the kids to camp one week. This was so that they would get to know each other.[4]

The student body was comprised of 60 percent gifted and 40 percent non-gifted students, because Wheeler believed children who were gifted learned as much

153

Children sharing secrets at a school that was completely white before the transfer program began. Photo courtesy the *St. Louis Post-Dispatch*.

from those who were not gifted as the non-gifted students learned from them.[5] Metro initially enrolled 112 students and had grown to 240 students by 1999. Five percent of the students were from the county and the remainder were from the city. During the years she was principal, the attendance rate was 98 percent, by far the best in the city. Metro had a 100 percent graduation rate, and nearly all Metro graduates went on to higher education.[6] Housed in a new building, Metro became recognized as one of the state's best high schools. In 2001, black Metro High students had test scores in communication arts and math twice as high as the state average for black students. White students' scores were 50 percent higher than the state average for white students. The Missouri Assessment Program (MAP) test scores for both black and white students were higher than the scores of any high school—in the city or in the suburbs.[7] There was no significant difference in test scores between the black and white students; a minimal "achievement gap."

Wheeler offered a few lessons to be learned from the successes at Metro: schools need to be smaller; there must be a strong curriculum; students should be involved in decision-making and should have a chance to evaluate the teachers; and everyone—administrators, parents, teachers, and students—should be held accountable.[8] She emphasized that the principal had to lead the school.[9] Students needed to know that somebody knew them and cared about them, and parents had to be involved.

After the tenth week of school, parents of Metro students were required to come to the school to receive periodic grade reports.[10]

Hoping to draw on the success of Metro, on December 24, 1975, Judge James H. Meredith ordered the City Board to report to the court on or before May 1, 1976, as to whether having elementary and secondary magnet schools would reduce segregation.[11] After the report concluded that they would, the City Board began operating magnet schools in the fall of 1976: seven elementary schools and two high schools. Ideally, each school would enroll 50 percent white and 50 percent black students. Most of the elementary magnet schools were located in South St. Louis.[12]

Of the seven elementary magnets opened in 1976, two were academies of basic instruction. The other schools offered action learning and career education, computer-managed learning, individually guided education, investigative learning, and a visual and performing arts center. These schools enrolled a total of 3,851 students; 68 percent were black. Only one magnet school, the Academy of Basic Instruction at Loring, was an all-black school.[13]

The magnet schools attracted many white students who previously attended private or parochial schools, but white enrollment still fell short of the Board's expectations.[14] However, to maintain racial balance, significant numbers of black students were denied admission to the magnet schools during 1976. On August 10, 1977, the City Board adopted a new policy, concurred by the U.S. Office of Education, that magnet schools must be between 50 and 70 percent black.[15] Applicants from non-public schools remained eligible for admission.

By the 1978–79 school year, three secondary magnet schools were operational. Each had a focus: math and science, visual and performing arts, and business. Together they enrolled 1,011 pupils, of whom 65 percent were black.

Chief Judge Donald Lay, writing for the Eighth Circuit Court in *Adams v. United States*, noted with approval the value of magnet schools as an element of desegregating an urban school district, qualifying his opinion by quoting the expert testimony of Dr. Gary Orfield:

> A Magnet School plan in itself has never been successful in desegregating a big city. It almost always produces no significant white transfers into predominantly black or Latino schools. . . . [It] will not produce substantial desegregation without a compulsory plan backing it.
> [I]t is valuable in desegregation because it builds in educational choice for parents, and . . . you ought to take advantage of it in any good desegregation plan. . . .[16]

Chief Judge Lay ordered that additional magnet schools be created to meet constitutional standards and expand the opportunities for an integrated education.[17] Judge Lay's decision required the City Board to seek the help of the state and federal governments in financing the magnet schools,[18] which made possible the comprehensive magnet school program that was eventually put in place.

On remand, the district court required the City Board to submit a constitutional plan to desegregate the city schools. It further required the state of Missouri to fund one-half of the cost of the magnet schools,[19] a sum significantly larger than city schools would otherwise receive under the basic state aid formula. The Board promptly submitted a plan in the spring of 1980 that continued the existing magnet schools and added six new magnets.[20] Under the Board's plan, the magnet schools were expected to enroll 5,125 students, 70 percent of them black.[21] By the 1982–83 school year, both the enrollment figures and the number of magnets had grown beyond the Board's proposal: the district had 21 magnet schools enrolling 6,488 students, 45.9 percent of whom were white.[22]

The settlement agreement approved by the district court on July 5, 1983, enshrined the magnet schools as an essential element of the plan to integrate the city schools. The agreement, as finally approved by the Eighth Circuit on February 8, 1984,[23] set a goal of fourteen thousand students in the city magnet schools, to be racially balanced with a variance of 10 percent. In approving the magnet schools, the Eighth Circuit Court had emphasized the importance of taking care to ensure that the magnet schools contributed to the overall integration strategy.[24] New magnet schools needed the approval of the Magnet Review Committee and the district court, and they had to demonstrate a "reasonable probability" of attracting white suburban students.[25]

The City Board and the state split the costs for the existing magnet schools in the city. The state, however, paid all the costs for any new interdistrict magnet schools.[26] Glenn Campbell, who was then the executive director of the Desegregation Planning and Monitoring Office, remembered that during the first three or four years "[a] number of magnet schools had been approved. We were trying to develop those magnet schools and outline them and define them and describe them and get budgets for them, and indicate the spaces used. All that had to go to a magnet review committee, and the state had a representative on that committee, and they never were in favor of any of the proposals."[27]

Nonetheless, by the opening of the 1983–84 school year, 7,000 students were enrolled in the city magnet schools, 3,300 of whom were white students. But of those white students, only 407 were from the suburbs. Attracting white county students to city magnet schools proved very difficult. No in-depth studies were made to determine why. It is likely that many parents lacked confidence in the quality of the schools. Some opposed the long bus ride the students would have to take each day, and others who had moved to the suburbs to avoid integrated city schools were not about to send their children back.[28]

The City Board adopted a program to expand the magnet schools by another three thousand students for the 1984–85 school year with admission on a first-come, first-served basis. March 19, 1984, was the deadline for parents to enroll their children in the expanded magnet schools, and competition for the additional spaces was intense.

The City Board and the state immediately began wrangling over the true nature of the new magnet schools. The state asserted that the City Board was trying to convert existing magnets into interdistrict magnets so that the state would have to pay their full cost.[29] The City Board replied that the state was simply attempting to avoid its responsibility to fund new interdistrict magnets. The state also complained that the City Board was establishing new magnets without careful study.

The district court referred the disputes to Warren Brown, an expert on school finance, who had been named by the district court as chairman of the Budget Review Committee.[30] Brown sided with the state and reduced the City Board's request for state money from $40.9 million to $11.5 million.[31] In an order issued in July 1984, the district court adopted Brown's recommendations and approved only part of the City Board's proposed magnet program. It approved two new magnet schools, rejected two others, and withheld ruling on a fifth. The court also held that two other magnet programs—the visual and performing arts high school and the Naval Junior ROTC program at Cleveland High School—could be expanded, but costs were to be evenly divided between the City Board and the state.[32] The City Board, seeking 100 percent state funding for the expanded magnets, promptly appealed to the Eighth Circuit Court.

On February 1, 1985, Judge William Hungate, who had done so much to further the progress of the *Liddell* case, resigned after presiding over the case for four years. Chief Judge Nangle assigned Judge Stephen N. Limbaugh to the St. Louis school desegregation case. Judge Limbaugh had been appointed to the United States District Court for the Eastern District of Missouri in 1983 by President Ronald Reagan. Prior to his appointment, he had served in the U.S. Navy, had been the prosecuting attorney for Cape Girardeau County from 1953 to 1957, and had served as the city attorney for Cape Girardeau from 1964 to 1968.

Shortly after Judge Limbaugh's appointment, the Eighth Circuit issued its opinion on the City Board's appeal.[33] The Eighth Circuit did not rule on each of the individual disputes over the planning, funding, and operation of the magnet schools. The court found that the physical condition of magnet schools existing during or prior to the 1982–83 school year had to be improved and that the City Board and the state must share the costs of the improvements.[34]

Believing that expanding the magnet program was of prime importance, the Eighth Circuit clarified the principles for magnet schools approved in its 1984 *en banc* opinion. It held that intracity magnet schools should enroll approximately eight thousand students, with adjustments to be made by the City Board depending on the students' needs. It limited enrollments in interdistrict magnet schools to six thousand students but reiterated that "the state is obligated to pay the full operating and capital costs of these magnet schools."[35]

One year later, in 1986, despite the Eighth Circuit's ruling, necessary capital improvements for the magnet schools still had not been made.[36] Interdistrict magnet schools had failed to meet enrollment and racial percentage expectations. The 7 interdistrict magnets enrolled only 2,016 students, 1,039 black and 977 white. Fewer than 6 percent of the white students were from St. Louis County.[37] The failure to fully implement the capital improvement program for the magnet schools deprived many additional students of the opportunity to attend them.

The dispute in the 1986 appeal was whether facilities for five new interdistrict magnet schools should be constructed at a cost of $20.2 million; whether the Humboldt visual and performing arts program and the Roosevelt foreign-language program should be continued at a cost of $2 million; and whether $4.8 million in architectural services for Humboldt should be approved. The Eighth Circuit noted that the City Board, the state, and the suburban school districts were obliged to work together in planning and operating interdistrict magnets, stating, "Until now, the state has mainly reacted to the City Board's proposals, usually negatively, and the suburban school districts have been largely indifferent to the planning and operating process."[38] The goal was to have at least two thousand more students enrolled in the interdistrict magnets by the opening of the 1987–88 school year and a total of six thousand students in these magnets by the 1988–89 school year. The court stated, "Unless these goals are met, the burden of integrating the St. Louis schools will have been primarily borne by the black students of St. Louis. This cannot be tolerated."[39]

The Voluntary Interdistrict Coordinating Council (VICC) was directed to play the leading role in recruiting county students, with the state providing the resources to the VICC. The Eighth Circuit made it clear that to provide an effective learning environment the intradistrict magnet schools must have a student/teacher ratio of no more than 20-to-1.[40]

In March 1987, Judge Limbaugh responded to the Eighth Circuit's September 5, 1986, order by revamping the entire magnet program. Stating that the "'helter-skelter' magnet school system had virtually shut out white students in the city and disrupted education," he rejected six proposals for new interdistrict magnet schools, saying that they had been insufficiently analyzed by the court-appointed Magnet Review Committee.[41] Judge Limbaugh criticized the City Board and the state for quarreling over finances, noting that they "do not meet to discuss, but rather meet to do battle."[42] He also saw that the magnet schools were becoming favorite replacements for city schools because they relieved the city of fiscal responsibility for the students' education. He added that "white city students were 'virtually being forced out of a city public education' because they are low on the priority list for admission to magnet schools."[43]

On May 14, 1987, Judge Limbaugh relieved the existing Magnet Review Committee of its responsibilities and appointed a panel of three nationally known educators to develop a long-range plan for the magnet schools in St. Louis. Appointed to the panel were Charles V. Willie, professor of Education and Urban Studies at the Harvard Graduate School of Education; Eugene Reville, superintendent of Schools in Buffalo, New York; and John A. Murphy, superintendent of Prince George's County Public Schools in Maryland.[44]

On July 7, 1987, the Eighth Circuit Court indicated satisfaction with the district court's newly constituted magnet panel.[45] The Eighth Circuit emphasized, however, that the plan to be adopted by the district court must increase enrollment in the intradistrict magnets from sixty-five hundred to eight thousand students and in the interdistrict magnets from two thousand to six thousand.[46] In a change of position, the Eighth Circuit accepted the district court's holding that the state was required to pay one-half of the intradistrict magnet specialty costs rather than one-half of the general curriculum costs. It reiterated, however, that the state was responsible for the total operating and capital costs of the interdistrict magnet schools. Regarding the "low priority" allegedly given to white students applying to magnets, the Eighth Circuit pointed out that when more facilities were made available, the magnets would accommodate an additional 750 white city students in intradistrict magnets and an additional 1,800 white city students in interdistrict magnets.[47]

The panel appointed by Judge Limbaugh submitted its report on September 1, 1987. The panel's report called for (1) changing racial goals in magnet programs to 60 percent black and 40 percent white rather than an equal enrollment split with a 10 percent leeway; (2) linking magnet schools with cultural institutions, businesses, and universities; (3) establishing the same financing formula for both types of schools; (4) changing the city's only vocational school, O'Fallon, into a math, science, and high technology magnet high school; and (5) establishing several additional magnet schools at the elementary, middle, and high school levels. Simplified enrollment procedures would ensure that students enrolled in a particular specialty would have an opportunity to attend a higher-level magnet school with the same specialty.[48]

The *South County Journal*, a St. Louis County publication, commented on the plan:

> The magnet program has been without direction for more than a decade. Its troubles can be blamed on the courts, which have allowed two magnet systems to develop: one serving the city and the other also including St. Louis County students. . . .
>
> Students have been subjected to an inexcusable lack of continuity in their education. There are elementary and middle magnet schools for which there is no corresponding high school; there are high schools without a related middle school. . . .
>
> Several feeble attempts to straighten out the mess—by the Magnet Review Committee, as well as state and city school officials—have been aborted by U.S. District Court Judge Stephen N. Limbaugh.
>
> Limbaugh took the right step in asking outside experts to revamp the magnet system. The outsiders are objective; they can make controversial suggestions without being accused of taking sides.
>
> The panel members saw right away that separate magnet programs are foolish. They made a sensible suggestion to consolidate

schools, allowing a "stream" of education. . . .

Magnet schools, and the students attending them, have been lost in the land of confusion long enough.[49]

The district court received the panel's report on September 14. From then on, efforts were made to resolve differences between the parties with respect to the plan. The court also held hearings on the plan and enlisted the aid of financial advisors Warren M. Brown and Jay Moody.

After an obviously careful and thoughtful analysis, on August 4, 1988, the district court filed a comprehensive plan to achieve student desegregation and a financially prudent approach to school improvement.[50] Specifically, the district court's plan allocated a higher percentage of magnet seats for black students (55 percent black, 45 percent white, with an allowable variance of plus or minus 5 percent). As for county students, at least 1,640 white county students must be enrolled in the magnet schools, with at least 12 percent white county students in each school.[51] It adopted major magnet "themes" so that any student who completed a final grade in a magnet of a specific theme was guaranteed a seat at the magnet school with a similar theme at the next educational level. It linked magnet schools directly with respected local institutions, including the Science Museum, the St. Louis Zoo, and the Missouri Botanical Gardens. A lottery system would replace the first-come, first-served system for placement of students.[52]

Perhaps most importantly, the plan changed the funding responsibilities. The new plan removed the distinction between intradistrict and interdistrict magnet schools. The state was to pay 71.5 percent of all capital costs for all magnet schools, and the City Board was to pay the rest. The court also approved a capital budget of $51.5 million, with the state to pay 71.5 percent and the City Board to pay the remainder.[53] The City Board and the state would each pay 50 percent of the schools' operating expenses.[54]

Importantly, Judge Limbaugh stated that the revised desegregation plan would be considered to be fully implemented when the following measures of success were met:

1. . . . enrollment of approximately 14,000 students.
2. Determination that each magnet school has the necessary resources for effective program implementation (including completion of appropriate building renovations and provision of necessary resources).
3. Determination that each magnet school is providing a high-quality educational program consistent with its theme.
4. Stable racial balance in each magnet school.
5. A total enrollment (in all magnets) of at least 1,640 white county students.[55]

Stating that 12 percent white participation in the magnet program was a reasonable goal, the court said that if fewer than 1,640 white county students were enrolled in magnets, the "state may petition the Court for a change in the unified funding formula or seek termination of any magnet that fails to seek a significant percentage of suburban white students."[56]

By the fall of 1989, enrollment in the magnet schools had increased to ninety-five hundred. The first lottery was held in March 1990 for admission the following September.[57]

On March 2, 1990, Judge Limbaugh considered staffing for the magnet schools, a concern raised by the state. The district court made it clear that a magnet school was not automatically entitled to staffing beyond minimum AAA–accreditation rating requirements.[58] Beginning with the 1990–91 school year, AAA staffing levels would serve as the standard level for magnets, even though this order contradicted earlier decisions requiring magnets to maintain class sizes at twenty students or fewer.[59]

In April 1990, Judge Limbaugh, not satisfied with the progress in the magnet program, entered an order stating that the City Board was defying court orders to expand magnet programs.[60] He demanded that school officials tell him why they should not be relieved of their duties. He called six school officials to his chambers to give a "'plausible, intelligent answer' to one question: How will the school district meet its court-ordered goal of enrolling more pupils in magnet programs?"[61] The City Board, at a hearing held on April 27, 1990, explained that the system had been delayed by construction problems, renovation problems, difficulty in buying new sites, and changes in some schools that affected other schools. The City Board projected that the goal of fourteen thousand students would be met by the 1992–93 school year. It suggested that Judge Limbaugh meet with city officials and board representatives to discuss the new Gateway Elementary and Middle Schools,[62] that he meet with the representatives of the St. Louis Science Center concerning the court-ordered science magnet school, and that he rule on motions of the City Board to approve plans for three other magnet schools.[63] Judge Limbaugh or his designees held the suggested meetings, but they did not result in the early opening of any of the schools in question. In March 1991, the *St. Louis Post-Dispatch* reported the shortage of spaces in the magnet schools resulted in the admission of only half of the black and white city students who applied, and two-thirds of the county students who applied.[64]

Despite the district court's prior effort to settle the funding issues, controversy continued. On August 30, 1991, Judge Limbaugh ruled that the state need only pay certain magnet school costs.[65] Any item to be funded, stated the judge, "must withstand close scrutiny as to its absolute need in order to carry out a specific magnet program."[66]

The City Board appealed this decision, and the Eighth Circuit agreed that the district court had adopted too stringent a test for state funding assistance.[67] The Eighth Circuit noted that magnet schools were thoroughly integrated and enrolled ninety-two hundred students, but that was short of the goal of fourteen thousand students. The court called for cooperation between the school district and the state of Missouri so the goal could be met as soon as possible.[68]

On September 4, 1991, the case was transferred from Judge Limbaugh to Judge George F. Gunn, Jr. As he left the case, Judge Limbaugh published his reflections on the progress that had been made, and the challenges that remained:

> The case is 19 ½ years old. . . .
> The issue of fault was tried and retried by Judge Meredith, with the Court of Appeals ultimately holding that both the Board of Education for the city of St. Louis and the state of Missouri were wrongdoers. In the simplest of terms, the Appellate Court ordered the Board and the state to atone for their policy of segregating black students in the school system, and directed the Board to integrate the schools and the State to help pay for the cost of doing so. . . .

Judge Limbaugh wrote about the deplorable state of many school facilities, adding that the Board had set aside no funds for renovation, so that "the original 150 schools over a period of 30 years lapsed into a severe state of deterioration." He cited Central High School as a model of what a magnet school could be. "Much remains to be done," he continued, adding:

> In any event at some point the Court must withdraw. Constitutional decisions have been made and are now being implemented. Unfortunately, the trial courts and the appellate courts, under the guise of constitutional redress, have been making educational decisions, as well. We are and always have been ill-equipped to do so. It is time to return the business of education to the professional educators. . . .
> As originally suggested, this is not an order binding on the parties, or my successor. What is said herein are only reflections and should be treated in that vein.[69]

Judge Gunn had been appointed to the United States District Court for the Eastern District of Missouri by President Ronald Reagan on April 17, 1985.[70] Judge Gunn had just taken over the case when he was faced with ongoing disputes about the as yet unbuilt Gateway Elementary and Middle School magnets. Judge Gunn ordered that construction of these schools start no later than August 15, 1993, that the schools be fully operational by the beginning of the 1995–96 school year, and that costs be limited to $14.6 million (excluding design and administrative fees, furniture, and equipment).[71]

Construction of the Gateway Elementary and Middle Schools did not begin until February 1994, four years behind the original schedule and a year later than the date set by Judge Gunn.[72] Even then, the state and the City Board were still arguing about the site costs and who should pay what. This dispute reached the Eighth Circuit Court in the spring of 1994. On March 29, 1994, the Eighth Circuit expressed its frustration that after ten years of court orders and plans, the parties had yet to fully implement the magnet school program:

> Ten years ago this court in an *en banc* opinion established an enrollment goal of 14,000 students for the magnet schools in the St. Louis School District. We subsequently stated that this goal was to be achieved no later than the 1989–90 school year. When this goal had not been met in 1990, we admonished the parties to accomplish it at the earliest possible time. We reiterated the need to reach the goal of 14,000 students as recently as 1993. Yet here we are in 1994 and there are still fewer than 11,000 students enrolled in the magnet school program. During the past ten years, the magnet school issue has been before this court on at least six occasions, and in the two most recent opinions we repeated the fourteen thousand–student goal.[73]

Sympathizing with the district court's efforts and regretting the delay in improved educational opportunities, the court went on to state that it would tolerate no further delays in reaching the fourteen thousand–student goal.[74]

After the Eighth Circuit's decision, construction of the magnet schools continued, and by the fall of 1996, the magnet school plan as developed by Judge Limbaugh was virtually completed.

Then, the future of the plan to desegregate the St. Louis public schools, including magnet schools, was called into question. In 1996, Missouri Attorney General Jay Nixon advanced a plan to end court supervision of the St. Louis schools. Nixon's proposal would have cost the magnet schools approximately $30 million per year and delivered a mortal blow to the program. The Eighth Circuit Court rejected the Nixon plan.[75]

In 2000, the City Board operated 5 magnet high schools enrolling 4,453 students: Gateway, Metro, Soldan, Central, and Cleveland. Seven magnet middle schools enrolled 3,227 students, and 14 early-childhood centers and magnet elementary schools enrolled 4,557 students. The total enrollment in the full-time magnet schools in 2000 was 13,275 students,[76] 725 fewer than the goal established by the Eighth Circuit in 1982.

There have always been more applicants for admission into the magnets than the schools have been able to accept. This is particularly true for black applicants and their parents, who view the magnet schools as providing a better educational opportunity than either the traditional integrated or non-integrated schools. Recruiting white students, especially those from the county, was still a problem.

Magnet schools attracted some white students from private and parochial schools in the city but not in the desired numbers. In 2000, approximately 65 percent of the students enrolled in full-time magnet schools were black, 32 percent were white, and the balance were other minorities.[77]

Results from recent state-conducted achievement tests indicate that students in two of the five magnet high schools (Gateway and Metro) scored at or above state-wide averages in all subjects tested. In fact, Metro had the highest scores of any high school in the state. Black students in six magnet middle schools (Gateway, Busch, Bunche, Carr Lane, Compton Drew, and McKinley) scored at or above statewide averages in all subjects tested. Black students in seven of the thirteen elementary schools (Gateway, Dewey, Kennard, Lyon, Mallinckrodt, Mullanphy, and Waring) scored at or above statewide test averages in all subjects tested. Students in the magnet schools did significantly better on the MAP tests than students attending non-magnet schools. Even though magnet school students generally did better than students in the non-magnet schools, the achievement gap between black students and white students remains in the magnet schools.[78]

Some arguments why magnet school students do better than those in the other public schools in St. Louis include:

1. The students tend to come from families that are "wealthier" and more educated than families in non-magnet city schools;
2. More resources are allocated to the magnet schools; and
3. Attendance rates are higher and dropout and mobility rates are lower.

Minnie Liddell had championed the magnet school concept during the negotiations for the December 1975 consent decree. Her own children who were still of school age attended and graduated from St. Louis City magnet schools. "Once we got the magnet schools going, it was—for the first time—it was something that the parents really appreciated. It changed the face of education in St. Louis," Liddell later said. "But it didn't do anything for those forty-some-thousand kids who were not involved in the magnet program."[79]

Only a small number of city schools were magnets. For the students who remained in the city's non-integrated or all-black schools, the City Board was to offer remedial and compensatory programs.

Upgrading the non-magnet, non-integrated city schools was of prime importance in the 1983 settlement agreement.[80] In a controversial order, Judge Hungate had ordered the City Board to certify the amount it needed to meet its one-half share of the cost of the settlement agreement, as well as the tax rate necessary to fund the costs. The City Board was further ordered to submit to the voters by February 1, 1984, a proposed bond issue sufficient to meet the most pressing capital improvements of the city schools. If the bond issue failed to obtain the required two-thirds majority, the court would consider an appropriate order to obtain the funds through other means.[81]

The state immediately asked the Eighth Circuit for a stay, pending appeal, and the city of St. Louis filed a petition for a writ of prohibition, arguing that the district court did not have the authority to control school tax rates.[82] The Eighth Circuit deferred action until it considered the other appeals that had been filed.[83]

After an *en banc* hearing was held in November 1983, the Eighth Circuit approved the funding of capital and other improvements to the city schools. To remedy the effects of discrimination, the court ordered higher standards and improvements for the non-integrated or all-black schools than for the integrated schools, and improvements including reduced class size, restored art, music, physical education and extracurricular programs, more staff including nurses and counselors, and better curriculum.[84] It then noted that any of the programs already in place could be continued, and the rest begun at the start at the 1984–85 school year. Perhaps the most radical change, the reduction in class size in all-black schools from thirty-five pupils per teacher down to twenty, "should be made over a period of four years beginning in 1984–85. . . ."[85]

To reach this goal, many more teachers would have to be hired. The schools could not bear the additional expense without an infusion of new tax money. As Judge Limbaugh had noted when he resigned from the case, St. Louis voters had defeated thirteen proposed school bond issues in the previous twenty-four years. The last two bond issues had been approved by a simple majority but lacked the two-thirds approval required by law. The Eighth Circuit, in its turn, observed that the state did not question the need to improve the facilities or its obligation to help pay for them. The state argued, however, that if the city bond issue failed, the whole plan would have to be shelved for lack of funding, "because it is unfair to expect the state to pay the full costs of the improvements."[86] The state also argued that federal courts were "without authority to enter an order requiring a tax levy to fund the City Board's share of the improvements."[87] The Eighth Circuit rejected the state's argument with respect to funding and gave detailed instructions as to how capital improvements to the city schools would be funded.[88]

In only a matter of months the district court was again called upon to resolve disputes about funding. It entered a series of orders, which were immediately appealed to the Eighth Circuit by the City Board and the plaintiffs, and cross-appealed by the state of Missouri.[89] The state questioned whether it could be required to pay for programs in nonintegrated schools that were not necessary for the schools to retain their AAA certification status. The Eighth Circuit responded that the state had to pay one-half of the cost of all programs that were in effect in nonintegrated schools on February 8, 1984, and one-half of the cost of preschool centers, all-day kindergarten, parental involvement, desegregation, and long-range planning.[90] Again the question of financing the bond issues came up, and the Eighth Circuit resolved the dispute by directing the City Board to prepare a building program not to exceed $40 million, "with emphasis on the all-black schools and the magnet schools.

... We recognize the need for long-term planning, and that should proceed, but the needs of the all-black schools appear to be so obvious that they should be met at the earliest possible time."[91] Regarding Judge Limbaugh's decision about funding needed to reduce the pupil/teacher ratio, the Eighth Circuit ordered the state of Missouri to pay half of the cost. Teachers employed in the new court-ordered remedial and compensatory programs were not to be included in determining pupil/teacher ratios.[92]

In the spring of 1987, the City Board told the district court that it had neither the space nor the money to reduce the pupil/teacher ratio to 20 to 1 by the beginning of the 1987–88 school year.[93] The district court denied the Board relief from this requirement, stating that it would not interfere with the Eighth Circuit Court's directives.

The case came before the Eighth Circuit again on July 7, 1987, on appeal by both the City Board and the state. The Eighth Circuit promptly entered an interim order, noting that as of the date of appeal the student/teacher ratio remained at 25 to 1, and directing that immediate steps be taken to establish the 20-to-1 pupil/teacher ratio. On September 17, 1987, the Eighth Circuit ordered that the 20-to-1 ratio be reached by the beginning of the 1988–89 school year.[94] Capital improvements were needed to reach that pupil/teacher ratio by the following fall. The Eighth Circuit's order was in accord with the $144.7 million district-wide capital program, which had been ordered a few days earlier by Judge Limbaugh.[95]

After reviewing the earlier Eighth Circuit orders requiring a $40 million bond issue to meet the most pressing needs of the all-black schools, Judge Limbaugh concluded that "the mechanics and the cost for preparing a building program for $40,000,000.00 to meet urgent capital needs of the district with emphasis on all-black schools . . . would require not much less effort than if the planning was directed to the entire school system."[96]

Accordingly, the district court undertook its own study of the capital needs of the entire St. Louis school system. Judge Limbaugh personally visited at least forty-three schools. He examined the physical facilities, observed classroom teachers and students, and talked with principals, teachers, students, and maintenance staff. The judge also directed the court's financial advisor, Warren Brown, to inspect all of the schools, analyze the architectural reports, project future enrollments, and consider budgetary requirements for capital improvements.[97]

After this review, Judge Limbaugh developed a comprehensive plan. He recommended that 104 city schools be rehabilitated, 21 schools be eliminated, and 19 additional facilities be retained and used for purposes other than instruction. Judge Limbaugh estimated the cost of rehabilitation at $144.7 million[98] and directed that the state pay one-half, or $57.4 million, over a three-year period.[99] He gave the City Board nine years to pay its share of the improvements in eight installments of $7 million and a ninth installment of $1.4 million.[100]

In June 1988, the City Board submitted two property tax proposals to the voters. Proposition 1 would prevent for one year a rollback mandated by the statewide sales tax for education. Property taxes would have remained at the current level.

Proposition 2 would increase the school tax rate to $3.75, the highest rate permissible under existing law with a simple majority vote.[101] Proposition 1 received 58 percent of the votes and Proposition 2 received 53.8 percent. In wards dominated by black residents, both propositions were approved by 85 percent of the voters. In wards dominated by white residents, both propositions failed by a large majority.[102] The proceeds from these propositions, together with other City Board funds, were sufficient to meet the City Board's obligation without a bond issue.

Although the matter of the City Board's funding responsibilities was thus resolved without further court order, class size remained a problem. The City Board did not take the steps necessary to reach the 20-to-1 pupil/teacher ratio in the all-black schools by the beginning of the 1988–89 school year. The pupil/teacher ratio remained at 24 to 1.[103] As a result, on August 26, 1988, the district court found the City Board to be in contempt of both the district court and the Eighth Circuit Court. Judge Limbaugh stated:

> The court will not hesitate in replacing key administrative personnel with persons more receptive to court supervision. The court could appoint an administrator of desegregation with broad authority to implement specified remedial orders. . . . Finally, the court could place the school district in receivership and name a receiver to carry out this court's desegregation orders. . . .[104]

The threat of sanctions caused the City Board to meet class-size requirements on time and to otherwise comply with court orders regarding school desegregation. No further cases came before either the district court or the Eighth Circuit with respect to class size in the all-black schools in the ten years from 1988–89 to 1999, when the school desegregation case was finally settled. Under the 1999 settlement agreement, however, class size was permitted to rise to 24 to 1 in the elementary schools and 27 to 1 in the high schools.[105]

The state and the City Board ultimately complied with the court-ordered remedial and compensatory programs for city schoolchildren. Compliance, however, did not come easily. The City Board and the state disagreed constantly about how to implement various programs, especially the reduction in class size, probably because this was the most expensive element of the programs.

Minnie Liddell was exhausted by the seemingly endless case. She remembered, "Every time I tried to quit this case, I just couldn't. I was tired of it and everything else. I got to the point where I think we'll never resolve anything, and then every time you change judges, you know, something different would happen."[106] The docket of the district court reveals that during the sixteen years of court-ordered desegregation the judges who presided over the case devoted substantial time to it. Since the Eighth Circuit's *en banc* decision on March 5, 1984, there had been 675 docket entries during the time Judge Hungate supervised the case; 3,545 docket entries during the time Judge Limbaugh supervised the case; and 2,838 docket entries from the time Judge Gunn was appointed to oversee the case until May 28, 1998, when the docket entries began to be made electronically.

When the district court and the Eighth Circuit had approved the 1983 settlement agreement, it was impossible to integrate all of the schools. It was believed, however, that if strong remedial and compensatory programs were adopted in the large number of all-black city schools, student achievement could be improved.[107] However, the results fell short of expectations. Possibly, first, this is because the court did not require, and the parties themselves did not adopt, accountability standards. It was not until after the final settlement agreement was reached in 1999 that the state mandated consequences for those schools whose students did not meet expected state standards, as measured by the MAP test.

Second, there was confusion and misunderstanding at all levels in the schools. According to LuVerne Cameron, associate director of the Desegregation Monitoring Committee, "One requirement, for instance, was that there be team teaching [and] that the regular classroom teacher accompany each class to an enrichment lab. The teachers were not provided with any training, for instance, on how to team teach. More often than not, while the enrichment lab teacher conducted the class, the regular classroom teacher sat in the corner grading papers. . . ."[108] Some school personnel did not realize that summer classes and all-day kindergarten were required by the settlement agreement and court orders.[109]

The faculty and staff also did not realize that the city schools had twice as much money to spend as they had before the desegregation plan went into effect.[110] Moreover, even though money was allocated, the schools did not always get the money. According to LuVerne Cameron, sometimes the funding would not appear until mid-year.[111] Because the teachers and principals did not understand the essential elements of the desegregation plan, the people in the community did not understand it.[112]

Cameron said that in her opinion the school district really viewed desegregation not as an operating principle but as a "burden imposed on the school district by the court."[113] She explained:

> I always said, you know, if the court were to back out of the case right now and all these funds were to be eliminated, business would go on as usual, because it has never been seen that we should come in and undergird and permeate the way the district operates and the way these programs are to function. It was always viewed as an add-on . . . that burden imposed on the district by the court. Never mind that the remedy was fashioned by the district, a specific response was fashioned by the district. . . . We were always seen as the entity that was causing the burden to be put on them. [114]

When the school district did buy into the program, many administrators did not. Numerous principals and teachers couldn't distinguish between what was the desegregation program and what was not.[115] In many instances, the programs were not implemented, and in other instances, implementation was unnecessarily delayed. This was particularly true in reducing class size in the all-black schools.[116] Glenn Campbell said, "[I] wasn't out supervising every day, you know, but I did see evidence that some [teachers] were teaching just as if they had forty kids. You know, 'Go to page ten and do those problems,' or something of that sort. There's no advantage in having a smaller class if you're not spending more time with individual students."[117]

Some schools, of course, did better, including LaClede, Stowe, Hempstead, and Arlington.[118] Staff at these schools underwent specific training early in the desegregation case, and the training changed the way the staff viewed themselves and their relationship with their schools, and led to higher expectations for students.[119]

The school system also continued to be plagued by many administrators', principals', and teachers' low expectations for student achievement. Too many accepted the view that poverty, a high percentage of single-parent homes, dilapidated school buildings, and a long history of neglect of the inner-city schools made it extremely hard, if not impossible, for them to improve student achievement. Fortunately, a number of educators in the St. Louis school system believed that every child could learn and excel and must be expected to do so. While recognizing the difficulties, they have proven that the goal could be met.[120]

I think black kids can and do achieve at the same high levels that white kids do, if you equip them with the same kind of background and experience, if you make sure they've got the basic skills they need to be successful, if you vary the time it takes for anybody to learn, whatever race you might be, and if you have high expectations for all kids.

–Chris L. Wright, Ph.D.[1]

{Chapter Ten}

The Educators Speak

Did the *Liddell* litigation improve the quality of education for students in the St. Louis metropolitan area? Does the state-mandated standardized test fairly reflect student achievement? If it does, why do students of color generally score lower on the test than white students? To answer these and related questions, the authors interviewed several St. Louis educators during 1999, 2000, and 2001. We heard how they dealt with the difficulties of providing a good education. The educators reflected on the effect of the standardized tests, recognized the effect of frequent changes of residence and drug abuse among students and their families, and acknowledged that a long history of racism kept students from reaching their full potential.

We initially note that Missouri has had a long history with the accountability movement. Since 1963, the state has utilized a variety of measures designed to assess and improve the quality of education provided to Missouri's children. Initially, the accountability legislation stressed the importance of investing in schools' programs and facilities. The schools were rated based on class size, the availability of school counselors, the offering of art and physical education classes, as well as the adequacy of library and media facilities. The St. Louis public schools' ranking fell because of deficiencies in these categories, but the system regained its top ranking again as a result of the 1983 settlement agreement, which required a significant new investment in magnet schools and remedial compensatory programs in the all-black schools.

Like Missouri's first accountability legislation, the 1983 settlement agreement focused on improving a school's programs rather than improving its test scores. Even though Missouri children had been taking standard tests since at least 1979, the emphasis on standardized testing as a tool to track a school's performance did not begin until the early 1990s. Several different tests have been administered over the years, with varying success—the Basic Essential Skills Test (BEST),[2] the Missouri Mastery and Achievement Test (MMAT),[3] the California Achievement Test (CAT),[4]

Court-appointed Citizens Committee say "We Shall Overcome" after submitting their desegregation plan to the federal district court. Photo courtesy the *St. Louis Post-Dispatch.*

and currently the Missouri Assessment Program (MAP). Not until 1999, however, were serious consequences imposed on schools whose students did not meet state proficiency standards.

Student achievement is influenced by many factors. The principals generally agreed, however, that socioeconomic conditions in a student's home affect student achievement the most. Dr. Chris Wright, superintendent of Riverview Gardens School District, said flatly that the gap between black and white students' test scores was not "a function of race. I think it's a function of poverty and culture."[5]

Vera Atkinson, principal of the all-black Cote Brilliante Elementary School, agreed that poverty sustained the black/white achievement gap. She said, "[A] child coming to me from an educationally deprived home, a child coming to me from a home where he's lucky if he can get to bed with something in his stomach, that child can achieve . . . but he's going to take longer because he comes to us farther behind."[6]

Emma Cannon, a teacher and administrator for twenty-eight years before she became the principal of Banneker, an all-black elementary school, said that in her experience "poverty does make a difference, because there is not a focus on education."[7] Dr. Cleveland Hammonds, interviewed while he was superintendent of St. Louis Schools, said, "If [a student] comes from a poor environment . . . then your home isn't as rich as far as language is concerned. There aren't people who are stimulating your vocabulary, and so you come to school with a deficit."[8]

Dr. Hammonds estimated that 50 to 60 percent of the students in the district came from single-parent families.[9] Dr. Wright said that most children in her district went home to empty houses because their single parent, most often their mother, was working. There was no funding to provide a free after-school program.[10] Vera Atkinson said that urban children saw "drug dealings going on around them day in and day out," and therefore, a "level playing field . . . does not exist."[11] Dorothy Ludgood, principal of Vashon High School, said poverty forced students to focus on other issues besides school. "Our kids bring in a lot of baggage with them," she said. "They are dealing with a lot of personal needs that interfere with the learning process."[12]

Another reason the principals cited lower achievement in urban schools is that "the mobility rate is as high as 90 percent . . . [which] means that 90 percent of the kids came in sometime during that school year," according to Chris Wright.[13] Only 80 percent of the students attending Vashon High School began and ended the school year there,[14] a statistic the principal, Dorothy Ludgood, was unable to do anything about because district policy said that only high school seniors could opt to stay with the school if their families moved.[15] She explained, "The kids are so transient in terms of their social needs. They might be with grandmother this week, who lives in our district so they come into our school. They might be over with their real father, who lives in somebody else's area. . . . Then they move back here."[16]

Principal Cannon said the neighborhood served by her elementary school had a sizeable transient population, but, she said, "[S]ome families like this school, and they've had some kids here, and they want them to go here. Even if they move, they try to sneak them back in if they can."[17]

On the other hand, black city students who transferred to suburban schools could remain in the same school. Barbara Kohn, former principal of Captain School in Clayton, a suburban school district participating in the transfer program, said, "We had pretty many kids who moved in and out, residential kids, but the kids from the city tended to stay no matter where they lived; they would stick with us."[18]

Although most principals did not discuss racism at length, Carmel Hall, principal at Cardinal Ritter High, a Catholic school, said that racism directly affected black students' academic achievement. "It is different being an African American than it is to be white," she said. "My students have the experience of racism, and it has had an impact on how they see themselves. I'm a parent—I'm an African American. My son experienced racism, and it colors the way an individual sees [himself]. And unfortunately, as a parent and as an educator, that has not changed. . . . [W]e were lulled into feeling that . . . things were going to get better. It has not."[19]

Notwithstanding all of these difficulties, educators in the city schools were sure that poor students of color could excel. The consensus among the St. Louis School District principals was that their schools needed principals with the authority to direct curriculum and to hire and fire teachers, within clearly defined rules and limitations.[20] The schools also needed well-trained and well-paid teachers, classes with twenty students or fewer, smaller schools or clusters of students within schools, and clean, safe, and well-furnished facilities. The principals also mentioned early childhood education and parental involvement, and they said that everyone in the educational system ought to hold high expectations for their students.

Principals in St. Louis said the central administrative office sent them teacher applicants, and the principals could do no more than recommend that a certain applicant be hired. According to Terre Johnson, principal of Webster Middle School, this lack of authority was a disadvantage: "[If] they're going to hold me responsible, let me be able to hire or recommend to the superintendent . . . everyone [including] the custodians, the lunchroom assistants. Let me be a part of that with my school-based management team, a council of people, that we should be able to hire."[21]

Doris Carter, principal of Carver Elementary School, said, "Stop having Human Resources just assign teachers here to the schools. Have the principals interview just like businesses do, interview to see if those people will fit in your school climate, your culture, and do they understand what I want."[22]

Steve Warmack, the principal of Roosevelt High School, said, "I need to have the ability to pick and choose the teachers who see the future as I do. There is always room for improvement in terms of budget. The budget is not my big concern. My biggest concern is having a staff willing to go in the classroom and attempt to use some new teaching strategies that teach to the students what the test is testing."[23]

Doris Carter described the way she led her staff and teachers:

> I talk to the staff. What is our vision? What are we trying to do here? Where do we want to go? Then try to instill pride in the children . . . what kind of school do you want? Do you like a school that the walls [are] all marked up, dirty floors, and all of that? Do you want a clean school? How does it make you feel when your school is clean and pretty? What can we do to keep it that way? . . . I'm trying to build pride, that they're proud of being here and what we're trying to do for them.
>
> With the teachers, I tell them, I don't expect to have to watch you. . . . Why are we here? We're here for the children and to teach. Every decision that I make is based upon what is best for the children. I work hard so I expect everybody else to work and do their very best here.[24]

Juanita Doggett, principal of Sherman Elementary School, attended St. Louis City schools from 1944 to 1946 and became a classroom teacher after graduating from Stowe Teachers' College. Principal Doggett said, "I think the principal leads the way. . . . You set the tone for what happens in that school."[25]

Joyce Roberts began teaching in the St. Louis public school system in 1971 in an all-black school. At the time of the interview she had been the principal of LaClede Elementary School for seven years. She described how she actively evaluated teaching performance: "I'm a very visible administrator; I'm in the classrooms on a regular basis, on a daily basis as a matter of fact. And there's a mechanism in place for those teachers who aren't quite measuring up, and my role as instructional leader is to identify that, find the resources and the manpower to help the teacher. And if all else fails, then my recommendation is that they're not working in the best interests of the children."[26]

According to Rosalind Mason, principal of Wilkinson Early Childhood Center, a principal's vision needed to extend beyond the staff. For Mason, both staff and parents were critical for success. Principal Mason explained, "A strong principal has to have vision, and in that vision you have to have high expectations. . . . Make sure that high expectation [lies] not only with your staff but with your parents."[27]

Some principals observed that to get well-qualified committed people to become teachers, teaching had to become an attractive and worthwhile career. High-quality teachers made an obvious difference. Doris Carter, principal at Carver Elementary School, said that her school had a great science teacher who used techniques that helped the children do well in science.

Webster Middle School Principal Terre Johnson said, "You've got to be committed to teach. . . . [I]t's a commitment, a love to work with children in the urban [schools], and that I think is what we need in more people."[28] Principal Doggett agreed. "If a teacher isn't motivated, I don't care how hard you try to motivate your children, you can't motivate them," she said. "You have to first be motivated yourself."[29] To find motivated, qualified teachers, Doggett said, "I actually went and found people, made fliers. I'm looking for [teaching assistants] now, so I went to Harris last week. . . . I'm out working and I work all day and all night."[30]

Some principals tried new ways to attract high-quality staff. Ann Meese, principal of Jefferson Elementary School, said she advertised privately on the Internet and worked with universities that granted education degrees.[31] However, Principal Doggett noted that teacher candidates from some universities knew much more about Missouri test standards than some others did. [32]

"Teachers used to be respected in the community; that's no longer [true]. So we lose all kind of people who would be great teachers," said Carmel Hall. "We've got to attract quality teachers. We've got to provide them with excellent educational opportunities. We've got to find those people maybe who are ready to retire but still have a lot of energy. We've got to find those people and get them into our schools."[33]

Steve Warmack had been the principal of Roosevelt High School for five years at the time of the interview. He said that 35 to 40 percent of Roosevelt students were special education students—a number four times the level of other comprehensive high schools in the city. He said that under increasingly difficult circumstances, teachers educated in the 1970s and before should commit to continuing their own educations. "You can't do lectures with kids anymore. . . . You have to use other activities, other strategies. I think our district is trying to do that."[34]

Principal Johnson agreed. "I would like . . . to have the funds available for teachers who really, really want to understand how to teach today's children to be retrained. Because my teachers who graduated, including me, who graduated in the

'60s and in the '70s, we were not prepared to work with children in the '90s and 2000. A lot of the teachers still want to lecture, want to hand out ditto sheets, and I would like to have monies available that my teachers could be retrained to teach the children of today."[35]

Principal Doggett said that the current system may overload teachers with expectations for continued education, causing "teacher burnout." In her view:

> We are overloaded, and teachers are, too. They have obligations. In order to stay in the program, they have to go to school. They have to take a course or two. And then we have a wonderful professional development and a whole lot of activities going on in our district. Saturdays you go all day long and every evening we go all night long, and it's wonderful to have those opportunities, but what we're finding, at least as an administrator, and I feel guilty, because when I see this, I said they really need this. . . . We're just pushing that button too hard for us to be effective. I'm being very honest. It's killing the school system.[36]

In 1998, the St. Louis School District was a startling 270 teachers short at the start of the school year, and in 1999, it was 200 teachers short. [37] According to Principal Atkinson, many teachers left the system because the work was so demanding. Principal Ludgood said that in September 2000 Vashon High School had sixteen teacher vacancies. "We have had to fight tooth and nail to try to get some people in here," she said.[38]

The principals all said teaching should pay more. Principal Doggett explained, "[W]e must be able to give all persons, administrative and staff alike, a decent salary. I think that is one of the killers—we have not been able to really pay educators."[39] The principals also suggested salary enhancements or other ways of rewarding successful teachers.[40]

Glenn Campbell served as a teacher and a principal in the St. Louis School District as well as executive director of the Desegregation Planning and Monitoring Office. Campbell said:

> Raising salaries might be a good thing to attract people. I think they'd have to be significantly higher than some of the surrounding [districts]. . . . I'm talking about not an across-the-board basis; on the basis of teachers identified as . . . master teachers, people who have really mastered the thing and really know what they're doing and who apply it. Why not a salary differential? You don't raise everybody's salary because McGuire hit seventy home runs; you raise his salary.[41]

Campbell added, "There are some very, very fine teachers in that school district

still, and I know of a lot of them, but I don't think that there are enough top-qual-
ity people to really handle the very difficult job they've got."[42] Based in part on his
experience with the Desegregation Planning and Monitoring Office, Campbell preferred that teachers' contracts be negotiated individually, so that the finest teachers
could be recruited and retained. In his opinion, teachers should be reimbursed for
continuing their educations.[43]

Retaining teachers was a problem also cited by James Irons, principal of Farragut, an all-black elementary school. Irons said that he had lost six teachers in the
previous five years to the county—because of the salary. "[T]hey usually increase
their salary anywhere from nine to ten thousand dollars, " he said, "and we've become, as I see it, . . . a training ground for teachers to learn their craft real well, and
then they're able to put it across the street or across the district."[44]

Even the Riverview Gardens School District, an all-black district located adjacent to the city, managed to recruit a large number of teachers from the city because
Riverview offered better pay. The superintendent of Riverview Gardens said, "We
could pay a whole lot less for teachers, and hire teacher aides, for instance. My
philosophy is you're better [off] having a well-paid, highly prepared, highly trained
teacher and no aide than to have a . . . less-prepared teacher and an aide."[45]

Teacher salaries in the St. Louis School District were lower than in many of the
surrounding school districts, particularly the suburban county schools. Superintendent Hammonds said that the St. Louis School District was "competitive with about
half of the districts as far as salary's concerned, but school systems like Clayton and
Rockwood, Parkway [in St. Louis County] can outbid us for the people who are
available."[46]

Dorothy Ludgood said that some teacher applicants had been so put off by the
appearance of the city's school buildings that they would not even come inside for
an interview.[47]

Several educators said that black children who may struggle with poverty and
family instability could and did succeed in the St. Louis public schools. To encourage greater academic achievement, they said, educators had to expect students to
score well on tests and thrive in a rigorous academic environment. A. Susan Tieber,
principal of Gateway Institute of Technology, a recently established magnet school,
said, "You have to convince the students that they're smart, that they're as good as
everybody else and better, and then you help them to get there to do it."[48]

Glenn Campbell reluctantly acknowledged that some teachers were without
high expectations for city students. "[H]opefully a minority, a very small minority,"
he said. "But to me it's a given: You've got to speak to the child as you expect him to
learn or her to learn, and you've got to express some confidence in that child."[49]

In Campbell's experience, many St. Louis County schoolteachers perceived, cor-
rectly or not, that city teachers expected little from their students:

> There are too many exceptions to that to just blanket the
> district with it, but it's maybe a little easier to hold those high ex-

pectations if you're working with a kid who comes out of a strong, middle-class home, is read to as a child, and listens to music with his parents, and travels, and does all those nice things that build vocabularies. We think with words, so if you've got a decent vocabulary, you think pretty well. A lot of our kids . . . aren't exposed to that in the city, and it does put them at a disadvantage.[50]

LuVerne Cameron, associate director of the Desegregation Monitoring Committee, credited the Effective Schools Program,[51] designed for all-black schools, with encouraging higher expectations. The program "redirected the way the staff viewed themselves, viewed their relationships with their students, and it made a difference, ultimately."[52] Four elementary schools joined the program: Stowe, Hempstead, Arlington, and LaClede, city schools with all-black student bodies. Cameron said that after these schools completed the program "it was just amazing, the confidence with which they spoke, the commitment that they gave in to. They really believed in the principles of the program."[53] Unfortunately, only a few schools bought into the Effective Schools Program, and the district did little to encourage participation in the program or provide the resources necessary to make the program successful. Cameron said the most important thing established was "commitment, caring about every single young person that's in that school. And then, I hasten to say, in large part we saw that, and we documented that time after time—that there were principals and teachers who just went way beyond the call of duty to care for and to nurture the children."[54]

Former Metro High School principal Betty Wheeler also said that along with high expectations teachers and staff should let students "know that somebody knows them, somebody cares about them. . . . I believe in giving students love, caring, letting them know I care."[55]

Chris Wright said that a school with high expectations for students likely also has "a very special climate in that building that is created by both the principal and by a group of teachers who work well together as a team. They're willing to take risks; they're willing to try new things. . . . [T]hey will do whatever it takes to make their children successful."[56] Principals also wanted their staffs to have a unified educational vision, providing a sense of purpose for the entire community: students, their families, and all school employees.

All of the educators acknowledged that the *Liddell* federal court desegregation orders reduced the size of classes in the city's magnet schools and the all-black schools. Principal Joyce Roberts of LaClede Elementary School said that before desegregation LaClede had classes of thirty to thirty-five students.[57] Under the court-ordered desegregation plan, she said, "it was twenty, tops." In the 2000–01 school year, class size at LaClede had increased again, to around twenty-five.[58]

. Principal James Irons reported that when he first came to Farragut Elementary School there were about forty children per classroom.[59] After the court approved the desegregation plan, Farragut's class size was cut to twenty students, which the school could handle because its overall enrollment declined.[60] After the settlement agreement was signed in 1999, class size increased to twenty-seven. Vashon High School principal Dorothy Ludgood said that "[i]f I had my wish list, I would start with enough qualified staff members to reduce this pupil-teacher ratio to 15 to 1."[61]

Smaller classes cost money, as the educators were well aware. Webster Middle School Principal Terre Johnson said that the most effective class size, in her opinion, would be 15 to 1.[62] But, "to say that we need 15 to 1, and then no one gets the money and make it available—that's just a farce."[63] After the desegregation case was settled, in the 1999–2000 school year, Webster's class size rose from twenty to thirty students per classroom.

Educators also said they would prefer to have smaller schools, so that the students could feel as if they were part of a caring community. Principal Tieber of the Gateway Institute of Technology magnet school envisioned "one hundred–person high schools in the future. . . . [I]f you have a small school, everyone is a person, everyone is looked at for what they are: wonderful."[64] Henry Elementary School Principal Lloyd Washington said:

> I'd also like to see some type of equity in the number of students per school. We're up to, like, 426. . . . [If you've got less than 200] students and you've got a lot of programs in your building, such as community education and those types of programs going on in your school, you get a lot of extra help in working with youngsters and getting youngsters' scores up.[65]

Betty Wheeler explained how her smaller school benefited students:

> I knew what the test scores were for almost every child in that school, and I knew every child in that school because I studied them all summer long. And then you have to evaluate where these students are and what they need. And the teachers need to know when they come into their classroom, when the students come in, that these are the things that this student is weak in. Please help this student to accomplish this.[66]

At Gateway Institute of Technology, virtually all of the students graduated from high school and attended college.[67] Part of this success could have been credited to Gateway's dividing its thirteen hundred students into smaller academies, so that the students stayed together with a team of teachers from the ninth grade to the twelfth grade.[68] According to Principal Tieber, the smaller teams allowed for personal attention and for relationships to form. She said, "[T]he most important thing to teenagers is the personal relationships. And if you have those personal relationships, they will do anything; they will be successful."[69]

Riverview Gardens schools received a grant from the Institute for Research and Reform in Education and planned to divide its high school into eight learning academies. Superintendent Wright explained the plan:

> Each learning academy or learning community has a group of teachers who will work with a group of students for four years. They will all stay together the entire time they're in high school. And each adult in the high school has 15 families that they are responsible for four years, so they are responsible for regular contact with the adults in that family. They're responsible for meeting with them, for doing home visits, for really establishing a connection. So the whole idea is that the high school will become much more personal, much more user-friendly to kids and adults, much more focused on individual success for children.[70]

Several educators mentioned early childhood or pre-kindergarten education as a way to boost their students' academic achievement. Another important factor at all levels was parental involvement. Principals at the high school level reported more challenges than did those at the elementary and middle school levels. Dorothy Ludgood said her school had "an active PTO; we have a parent liaison on board to try to keep our parents involved. But the way that this seems to happen on the high school level is that parents seem to begin to separate themselves or allow for a lot more independence on the student's part, and they don't become that involved unless the kid gets in trouble. We might have twenty parents in September, twenty parents in October, but then it's the same parents."[71]

Joyce Roberts, principal at LaClede Elementary School, said that most of the parents of students in her school qualified for public assistance, and that the Welfare-to-Work legislation passed in the 1990s had decreased parental participation. "Prior to that time, we had tremendous support because they [parents] were all at home, and they were available to come to school and serve as volunteers and go on field trips and the like," she said. "With the movement from welfare to work, we've seen those numbers diminish because parents must either be in school or they must be on the job."[72]

Principal Roberts said that because the families continued to be poor the school had to do more than educate the children. "Our parents want their children to be very successful," she said, but many of them worked two jobs, and "that has had a dramatic impact on the number of parents that we see on a regular basis. But . . . [w]e move on and we provide our children with basically everything they need. If they need food, then we find that. If they have been displaced from their home, then we have the resource to help them find that."[73]

At Carver Elementary School, where daily attendance reached an impressive 96.9 percent, Principal Doris Carter reported strong parent involvement. "You'll see a lot of my parents come in to the school," Carter said. "You come at 7:30 in the morning, you'll see them in the lunchroom and they go out on the yard with the teachers. I have a real good situation, and I think it's because I'm a neighborhood school where we can just walk back and forth."[74]

Principal Carter's parent liaison works closely with teachers, administrators, and families to monitor student attendance:

> [S]he goes to every classroom to see who's absent. She reports
> back to me, and my parents know now that if a child is absent,
> they have to call me because otherwise they're going to get a call
> from the parent liaison first. But if . . . we notice a pattern, the
> child is out maybe once every week or coming in late, then I make
> the call. We'll go get them. . . . If they don't come every day, we
> can't teach them. They won't learn as much. So that's my theory,
> and they cooperate, but they know I'll show up at their door.[75]

Principal Carter said parents should make education the child's first priority and should ensure that children do their homework assignments: "Do you ask them, how was your day at school today, what did you learn? What did you do? Tell me something that you learned. Just those simple questions. If they say 'nothing' or 'we didn't do nothing,' and they consistently say that, then you come over and you see what it is."[76]

Rosalind Mason said that strong parental involvement was the reason that the Wilkinson Early Childhood Center was a success. "Our parents are most supportive when it comes to activities in the classroom, school events. . . . [O]ur parents have high expectations. We work together as a team, the school and home."[77]

Dr. Cleveland Hammonds also said that parental involvement was always important, but he added:

> [Y]ou cannot expect that mother to behave like a suburban
> mother. . . . If we can get that . . . mother to set aside a specific
> time for study at home to control the environment and make sure
> that child is in at a certain time, make sure that the company the
> child keeps is a positive group of people, then to me that's the
> kind of parental involvement that we can count on. But to use the
> same model that you want to be room mothers, that you want to
> attend all the PTA meetings, it will not work.[78]

Ashland Elementary School Principal Sandra Wilson said: "[T]hey're not up here with a bake sale and fabulous PTA and all that kind of stuff; no, they're not. But they do cooperate. . . . The parents help us the best way they can."[79]

Tutoring, one principal observed, "particularly for children with reading deficiencies, is critical."[80] Other principals wished for more school nurses and counselors. One principal desperately wanted to update the students' desks from the old-fashioned sloping-surface type to a flat tabletop, to promote cooperative, hands-on learning. Many principals wanted their buildings air-conditioned, technologically up-to-date, and safe.

The current MAP test was part of a broader legislative package passed in 1996 meant to improve Missouri's schools, which included an emphasis on changing curriculum.[81] The educators discussed the MAP tests at length. Many students of color in the St. Louis schools had low test scores. The question was why. In 1997, the Missouri Department of Elementary and Secondary Education explained, "[G]ains have been made in closing this gap, but there remains a significant and unacceptable difference."[82] Dr. Chris Wright said, "To the extent that you have a good match between what is tested and what is taught, you're going to do well on the MAP test, assuming that you have a group of students who read and write well, because writing is critical on the MAP test."[83] Dr. Wright said that there were reasons, having nothing to do with schooling, why some schools returned scores that were lower than expected. "In some of my schools, the mobility rate is as high as 90 percent. . . ."[84]

Dorothy Ludgood believed that the MAP test was an effective, unbiased measuring device. "MAP standards are very comparable to national standards, and I think it's really, really good. . . . I don't think [the test] is culturally biased. . . ."[85]

Dr. Cleveland Hammonds, superintendent of the St. Louis Schools from 1996 to 2003, also saw the MAP test as a valuable tool: "I think the MAP test reflects a more realistic approach to judging students' performance than the previous standardized tests."[86]

Some principals thought the MAP test format was too sophisticated for elementary students. Vera Atkinson said, "It takes children longer to . . . develop the skill required to explain why they can do things."[87]

Others thought the MAP test was culturally biased. Joyce Roberts said, "You can't be successful in something that you haven't been taught. And if it's not in the curriculum, then that creates a discrepancy. There's terminology that our kids haven't been exposed to either that is not a part of their culture; it's not in the curriculum as well."[88] Another educator used as an example a MAP test question that asked about "the habitat of a wild animal," something city students might not be familiar with.[89]

Educably mentally handicapped (EMH) students were required to take the MAP test, and their results, compiled with those of the rest of a school's students, lowered the school's median score and could jeopardize its status in the district. One principal said, "The state says you can't have more than 10 percent of [EMH students] not taking it, otherwise your district will be penalized for not testing those kids. . . ."[90]

Steve Warmack was outraged at the district's lack of foresight when the MAP tests were introduced. "Our district did not prepare our staffs to prepare the children," he said. "You look at the county districts—they immediately started professional development inservice, teaching their teachers how to instruct children to prepare for taking that test. We, for the first two or three years, were nonbelievers until the test scores hit us right between the eyes."[91]

Joyce Roberts said that her school was "redesigning the instruction so that it's correlated with the format of the MAP test, and we're identifying those children who need additional help and providing them with that help."[92]

According to the principals, another problem with the MAP test was that high school students did not believe the test was relevant to their lives. Colleges and universities asked for the students' scores on the SAT test, but not on the MAP test.[93]

The educators who have worked for years in the St. Louis school system made it clear in their interviews that in the twenty-first century providing a high-quality education for the district's poor children of color, while enormously difficult, is imperative for the city's future. Urban schools educate, at the very least, 60 to 70 percent of all school-age children in the United States and are obliged to educate all children. A high-quality education requires well-trained and well-paid teachers, small class sizes, and good facilities, all of which are expensive. But it will be much more costly to the city of St. Louis, the state of Missouri, and indeed, the nation, if all the children of the city are not well educated and prepared to be productive citizens in a multicultural society.

I think it is important and historic to note what has never been said heretofore in an open Court. For many years, the State supported segregation, and that was wrong.

–Missouri Attorney General Jay Nixon[1]

{Chapter Eleven}

The 1999 Settlement Agreement:
The St. Louis Public Schools Are on Their Own

Racism and segregation were an integral element of Missouri and St. Louis society for more than 160 years. Integration of the St. Louis public schools began in earnest in 1984, and then only after federal court decrees overrode the objections of state officials and many Missouri citizens.

The state complied with court orders, and Minnie Liddell's lawsuit produced a significant degree of integration by the mid-1990s. The state, however, never fully embraced the U.S. Supreme Court's thesis that separate education was inherently inferior, nor did it view the court-imposed desegregation plan as one that should be continued indefinitely. Its view, rather, was that the court-ordered programs, particularly the interdistrict program and the various remedial and compensatory programs, should be terminated after seven years.

The cost to the state of the desegregation program, particularly the interdistrict element, was always its principal argument against the 1983 settlement agreement. The state made this argument even though the cost of educating black city students in county schools was less than the cost of educating them in the city. In the 1998–99 school year, the average cost to the state for city black students attending county schools was six thousand dollars per pupil, including transportation costs and home district incentives, while the per-pupil cost of educating students in the city public schools was eight thousand dollars.[2] The cost of the entire program when broken down among all the students who benefited, city and county alike, was less than eight hundred dollars per pupil. The cost, spread over all of the students in the state, was less than forty dollars per pupil.

Underlying the opposition to the St. Louis desegregation plan were continuing racial animosity and a misunderstanding of the details of the plan. Some citizens said that it was wrong to force students to rise very early in the morning to be bused to a school a half-hour or more from their home. This argument ignored the fact that students had a choice to participate in the interdistrict program or to attend school in the city. Others, such as St. Louis Mayor Freeman Bosley, Jr., argued that neighborhood schools were better for parents, students, and the city, and that money would be better spent on improving education in the city rather than on "busing" students and enriching county schools. Ironically, this plea ignored the increased funds that the court-ordered desegregation plan provided for city magnet schools, and remedial and compensatory programs for the remaining all-black schools. Under the 1983 settlement agreement, city schools had twice as much money per student to educate the remaining students than they had before the plan went into effect. Moreover, there was no evidence that the state would reallocate funds from the interdistrict program, should it be terminated, to support the city schools.

The opening salvo in the struggle to end the court-ordered program was fired by the attorney general of Missouri, William Webster. On October 11, 1991, he moved the district court to declare the St. Louis School District "unitary"—meaning, fully compliant with court orders and constitutional law. Therefore desegregation by court order could come to an end. He simultaneously agreed to enter into a consent judgment and decree which would continue state payments to the St. Louis public schools for building construction, magnet schools, transportation, and other programs until the year 2001.[3]

The *Liddell* plaintiffs responded that Webster's motion was premature, arguing that "[i]f the state's request were granted, both the city district and suburbs would suffer resegregation by court order without ever having achieved desegregation in the first place."[4] No reply was filed by the state and no action was taken by the district court.

Seven months later on May 7, 1992, when he was a candidate for governor, Webster filed another motion requesting that the district court declare a partial unitary status.[5] The district court held that the motion was premature, but authorized the state to look into whether the St. Louis public school district achieved partial unitary status.[6] This decision motivated transfer students to organize, and they collected six thousand signatures on a petition asking Judge Gunn and the General Assembly to continue the desegregation program. Scott Tovlov, a sophomore at Parkway South, organized the drive and credited the program with allowing students "to grow up learning that blacks and whites are equal."[7] He explained that eliminating the transfer program "just wouldn't be right" because without it "[a]ll the students would live in their environment only and our problems would just multiply."[8]

On September 29, 1993, the campaign to end court-ordered desegregation escalated when recently elected St. Louis Mayor Freeman Bosley, Jr., the city's first African American mayor, and Attorney General Jay Nixon appeared together before a packed crowd in a Catholic church auditorium in South St. Louis.[9] Nixon told the crowd that within a few weeks he would file a new motion with the district court to release the St. Louis School District from the desegregation order. Bosley pledged to work with Nixon to ask the courts to end their jurisdiction over city schools. He said, "'Kids need to go to school in the neighborhood in which they live. . . . There is no reason we need to be waking up kids at 5:30 in the morning' to catch a school bus."[10]

Bosley, Jr., was one of the first black leaders in St. Louis to publicly oppose the interdistrict student transfer program. As he tells it, his opposition to the desegregation plan began in the late 1980s when he was asked to give a presentation to public-school students at a suburban school. He agreed, but on the day he was to speak, he said that he "started paying attention to the directions and started driving and I realized that I was outside the city and then I was going up to the county. . . . I realized I had probably driven about thirteen, fourteen miles to get out there. It took me more than maybe thirty minutes."[11] Although the suburban school impressed him with its facilities, he was surprised when only six children were present at his talk. Of the six, three lived in Bosley's own neighborhood.

Bosley recalled that the neighborhood where he grew up was a true mixed-race community that had "everything you would need," including "a sporting goods store . . . laundromats, bakeries . . . a Woolworth's, [and] two theaters."[12] But by the early 1970s, Bosley noticed a change: "The white people had left the community. And when they left, all the businesses and all the stores left, too."[13] He went on to say, "I know race did have something to do with it, but I think a lot of it had to do with choices that people were making. I think it was the whites that were making the choices. First, they were looking for better quality housing stock, and then I also think that they were looking for places where they thought their children could get a better education."[14]

As mayor, Bosley said he believed that more money should be put into city schools to bring back the vibrant neighborhoods he remembered. However, it was his view that to achieve true integration in schools, housing issues had to be addressed. As he put it, "If you want black and white people to go to school all together . . . you have to create situations in which they will live together. And in order to do that, you've got to have housing stock and things of that nature that blacks and whites will want to live in regardless of what the race is."[15] The tragedy was that the city, state, and federal governments did very little between 1954 and 2000 to improve either housing or the infrastructure within black neighborhoods.

Further, in Bosley's view, busing students did not result in integration, because "the white kids would be on one side [of the cafeteria] at lunchtime and the black kids would be at another." And he questioned whether students of different races got along, created friendships, and "hung out together in the summertime when school was out."[16] Bosley also disputed what he regarded as the NAACP's view that the only way black children could get a good education was if they were sitting in a classroom with white kids.[17]

Bosley said he thought that "about $70 million per year was being spent on the [interdistrict transfer] program, and meanwhile the [city] schools [were] falling apart and people [were] becoming disconnected from their neighborhoods and their communities."[18] When attorneys, superintendents, and Dr. Susan Uchitelle presented him with the facts, however, Bosley acknowledged that *the all-black city schools under the desegregation plan received twice as much money per pupil as they had received before.* His argument then became that the city schools did not spend this money properly.[19] Bosley said that state money then currently spent on the voluntary inter-district plan and busing could be redirected to the city schools, where it would be spent on improvements. From the evidence, it appeared that there was, in fact, little chance that this would happen.[20]

On November 22, 1993, Missouri Attorney General Jay Nixon filed an amended motion to declare unitary status for the St. Louis schools. At that time, the state withdrew its earlier offer of a consent decree. On February 28, 1995, the district court entered an order stating that a unitary status hearing would begin on September 27, 1995.[21]

On June 12, 1995, the U.S. Supreme Court, in a 5–4 decision authored by Chief Justice Rehnquist in *Jenkins v. State of Missouri* (*Jenkins III*),[22] held that the district court in the Kansas City school desegregation case erred in requiring the state of Missouri to fund Kansas City magnet schools to attract white students from adjacent suburban schools, because no suburban school had discriminated against black students. The Supreme Court said that in the case of Kansas City the district court wrongly provided an interdistrict remedy for an intradistrict violation.

Six months later on January 4, 1996, Attorney General Nixon filed a motion to terminate the voluntary interdistrict transfer program in St. Louis, arguing that the Supreme Court's opinion in *Jenkins III* brought the constitutionality of the St. Louis interdistrict transfer program into question.[23] The plaintiffs and the United States responded and urged the Court to appoint a settlement coordinator to attempt to resolve the litigation, and the City Board requested that action on the state's motion be postponed. Shortly thereafter, the Court again held that the state's motion to end the transfer program was premature.[24] It stated:

> The Court agrees with plaintiffs that the best resolution of this case would be an agreed-upon plan for ending Court supervision of the St. Louis Public Schools. The Court, however is reluctant to continue the hearing. It may well be that the possibility for settlement will be greater following the hearing, at which time the appointment of a Settlement Coordinator would be appropriate and beneficial.[25]

No appeal was made from this decision. On January 19, 1996, the Caldwell and Liddell plaintiffs moved the court to appoint a settlement coordinator. The state opposed the motion.[26]

On March 3, 1996, after several delays, the district court began a three-week unitary status hearing. Participating were the state of Missouri and related state defendants; the Liddell plaintiffs, the Caldwell plaintiffs, and the NAACP; St. Louis Board of Education; the United States; three suburban county school districts—Mehlville, Pattonville, and Ritenour—that had participated in the transfer program;

and Teachers Local No. 420, representing city teachers.[27]

The state argued that it had complied with all prior court orders, had demonstrated its good-faith commitment to desegregate, had eliminated all vestiges of the prior *de jure* segregation to the extent that was practical, and had proposed a transition plan that provided enough money for the St. Louis School District to make the transition from a school district undergoing desegregation to a unitary district. The state said it had spent $1.834 billion between 1980 and 1996, or $115 million per year. Of that sum, $1,300 per pupil was for transportation costs, and the remainder of $4,700 per pupil was the payment to the receiving schools for the full cost of educating the transfer student.

The Caldwell, NAACP, and Liddell plaintiffs asserted that the state failed to allege or prove that St. Louis schools met the legal standards for unitary status. They argued that the state had not fully and satisfactorily complied with the court's decree with respect to magnet schools, interdistrict transfers, and student, faculty, and staff assignments, and that the state had not made a good-faith commitment to ensure that it would not return to its former segregated ways.

The City Board's brief, like the plaintiffs', argued that the court-ordered remedies in the magnet plan, the voluntary interdistrict transfer program, the quality education programs, and the integrated housing initiatives, had not been fully implemented. It asserted that the desegregation plan had not eliminated the vestiges of segregation. An achievement gap remained between black and white students. It also asserted that the state had demonstrated a lack of good faith by consistent efforts to reduce the scope of or eliminate the desegregation remedy, generally opposing desegregation, and interfering with the remedies ordered by the district court. Finally, the City Board in its brief strenuously objected to the state's transition plan, calling it "a recipe for disaster."

The United States argued that the burden was on the state to show that the city school system had achieved unitary status. In particular, it asserted that the state's transition plan was inadequate in that it had not shown that (1) several court orders had been implemented in their entirety; (2) the plan had been in effect for a reasonable period of time and vestiges of segregation had been eliminated to the extent practical; and (3) the state had not demonstrated its good faith in implementing the decrees of the court. The United States also argued that the state's plan was inadequate because it:

> (1) would take place only after a declaration of unitary status by [the district] court, thus eliminating any protections for the class affected by the transition; (2) does not consider desegregative impact in any way; (3) would unnecessarily return students from integrated schools to segregated ones; (4) would phase out the program in too short period of time without sufficient examination as to the ability of the SLPS to handle the increased number of students; and (5) does not preserve successful elements of the

program. While the state's plan may be less expensive than the
other alternatives, "[i]t lacks the human touch."[28]

The county districts did not take a position on whether unitary status had been
achieved. These districts sought to insure that if the transfer program ended, existing
transfer students would "be allowed to continue in the program through high school
graduation, with continuing state funding, transportation and logistical support."[29]
The county districts also argued that any phase-out of the transfer program should
follow the terms of the settlement agreement, which provided that the county
districts' rights could not be diminished or modified without their consent. The
county districts took no position with respect to the details of the phase-out system
except that there should be a lead time before any phase-out began. They said they
had renewed their "commitment to the transfer program and its students—a commitment we have honored for more than an entire generation of students and one
which we will steadfastly continue to honor, in accord with the provisions of the
Settlement Agreement, until such time as the Court determines that the program
should end."[30]

The Teachers' Union stated that before any plan was made to eliminate the
voluntary interdistrict transfer program, it wanted to ensure that the plan provided
adequate financing for quality education for St. Louis public school students.

At the unitary status hearing, each party presented expert witnesses.[31] The state
called Dr. Christine Rossell, a professor of political science at Boston University.[32]
She testified that 60 percent of the white students in St. Louis went to private or
parochial schools.[33] Of the white students remaining in the St. Louis school system,
60 percent were enrolled in magnet schools.[34] Thus, only 16 percent of the white
students living in the city attended traditional public schools. She called the St.
Louis interdistrict transfer program "an extraordinary success."[35]

Dr. David Armor, a research professor at George Mason University's Institute
of Public Policy, was also an expert witness for the state.[36] He said that two-thirds
of the achievement gap between black and white students could be explained by
socioeconomic differences.[37]

Dr. Eric Hanushek, a professor of economics and public policy at the University of Rochester, also testified on behalf of the state.[38] He pointed out that in
the 1994–95 school year, 82 percent of the St. Louis students were eligible for free
lunch as compared to 31 percent in the rest of Missouri.[39] He stated that the quality
of teachers was extraordinarily important in student achievement, more important
than class size.[40] He also noted that at the time of the hearing Missouri ranked forty-
eighth in the nation in per-pupil expenditures for education.[41]

Dr. Kern Alexander, the president of Murray State University, an expert witness for the City Board,[42] disagreed with Dr. Armor. He said that if the class size in
elementary and middle schools could be reduced to fewer than eighteen students per
class, the quality of education would improve.[43] He noted that 64 percent of the students in the St. Louis public schools were eligible for AFDC benefits as compared

with 13.4 percent in the rest of the state,[44] and said that state aid for poor children of color should be one and one-half times that provided for children who are not at risk.[45]

Dr. Alfred Hess, the executive director of the Chicago Panel on School Policy, another expert witness for the City Board,[46] testified that students in the St. Louis public school system were doing much better than in 1980, particularly students in magnet schools;[47] that attendance was dwindling in the middle and high schools;[48] and "[t]he evidence in St. Louis seems to be that white parents would rather put their children anywhere but in the schools" where black students were in the majority.[49] He concluded that it would be devastating if the court-ordered programs were discontinued.[50]

Dr. David Mahan, the superintendent of the St. Louis School District, made two points. As many as 50 percent of students at any school attended more than one school during a single school year. This "mobility rate" made it difficult to provide a high-quality education for such students.[51] He also stated that 15 percent of the students were classified as handicapped and eligible for independent educational services, while in suburban districts the Special Education School District provided such services.[52]

Dr. Leonard Stevens,[53] an expert witness for the United States, testified concerning the limited impact of the voucher program, widely proposed as a solution for improving urban education that was popular among voters and that had been tried in the city of Milwaukee:

> [A] voucher program tends to perhaps unintentionally mask the real problem by opening up opportunities to a very small number of youngsters who can get into a voucher program and get into private schools or non-public schools. But it leaves the vast majority of youngsters still locked into a non-choice system for the most part in the city school district or in the metropolitan area, so I think it is sort of a release valve on a problem but I don't view the voucher program, at least in the Wisconsin version, as a solution to the needs, the educational needs of the children that are in the city of Milwaukee.[54]

He also noted that the St. Louis interdistrict transfer program was more extensive than Milwaukee's. In St. Louis, thirteen thousand out of forty-five thousand students participated; in Milwaukee, only six thousand of ninety-five thousand.[55]

Lois Turner, a teacher in the St. Louis public schools for forty years called by the NAACP, said that most of the classrooms had at least thirty-five to forty students prior to the desegregation program.[56] She added, "I can tell you as a classroom teacher that it makes a difference in the stress level for the teacher, but it also makes a difference as far as the stress level for the students."[57]

Dr. William Trent, associate chancellor and professor at the University of Illinois at Champaign–Urbana, an expert witness for the NAACP,[58] testified that the race of the student accounted for a substantial portion of the variance of achievement test scores.[59] His views were that "tracking," or placing a student in a low-ability group early on, hampered the student's long-term educational opportunities.[60] African American students who participated in desegregated schools were more likely to work in an integrated workplace, attain a somewhat higher occupational ranking, and a somewhat higher income.[61] Graduation rates in the magnet schools were higher than in nonmagnet schools, and transfer students were more likely to graduate when they attended high schools with large numbers of college-bound students.[62]

Dr. Roger Clough, the superintendent of Pattonville School District, a participating county district, testified that the Pattonville Board of Education believed the voluntary interdistrict transfer program was successful and was good for all students. As of the date of the hearing, 20 percent of the students in Pattonville were transfer students.[63]

Dr. Charles Rankin testified as an expert witness for the Teachers' Union.[64] He said that the advantages of an integrated education were unlimited,[65] and that the voluntary interdistrict transfer program was having positive effects.[66]

Dr. Gary Orfield, who had been involved as an expert witness in the *Liddell* case for many years, this time testified as a rebuttal witness for the NAACP.[67] He said:

> [M]y view is that almost no whites who intend to use public schools even consider the possibility of moving into most areas of central cities that have all-black schools. It's not even on their list of possible considerations because of that factor. It's so serious that—and I think that segregated schools have a profound affect [sic], and by the same token, an integrated school can have the consequence of enabling families to stay in the community and to make a long-term investment in the community . . . for the public schools to be genuine community organizations rather than just reflect one racial group in that integrated community. . . .[68]

Orfield stated that the graduation rate for magnet schools was twice as high as that for either the integrated or nonintegrated public schools in St. Louis.[69] He said that very few schools in the nation that have poverty rates of 80 percent have good achievement levels, and intense effort would be necessary to bring achievement levels up substantially.[70] Dr. Orfield also testified that the advantages of desegregated education are clearly much greater when the lower-income children are exposed to predominantly middle-class settings.[71] Finally, he stated that a high school dropout's unemployment rate was much higher, the salary level vastly lower, and prospects of moving out of dead-end jobs were virtually nonexistent. He concluded that an environment that encouraged academic achievement beyond high school was invaluable when the nation's economic gains appeared to be going to families whose breadwinners had had post-secondary education.[72]

On April 23, 1996, one month after the unitary status hearing, the court appointed Dr. William H. Danforth, the former chancellor of Washington University, as settlement coordinator. Danforth had previously chaired a committee that studied the St. Louis public schools. "One of the things that our study showed was that if you were a ninth-grade male in a non-magnet school in the city, in one of the city high schools . . . the chances of your graduating from the St. Louis public schools were under 15 percent," Danforth said in an interview in 2001. "I think that is a clear example that things were not working well."[73]

The court ordered that all components of the 1983 settlement agreement should continue in force until further order. The state appealed the district court's order and sought a stay of the interdistrict desegregation plan pending an appeal. The district court, the Eighth Circuit Court, and Justice Clarence Thomas all denied the motion.[74] The state then filed a petition for rehearing *en banc* with the Eighth Circuit; it was denied. No appeal petition was filed.

Negotiations for the settlement agreement began. "The first goal was to prevent disaster," said Danforth. "Let's say, if the case had come to an end with no settlement agreement, the court had ended it, about twelve thousand kids would have come from the county to the city, the city would have had less money to take care of them than it had before they came, and no facilities," he said. "So the settlement basically continued the good programs instituted under the court order. So it continued the opportunity for kids to go to county schools, it continued the magnet schools, and it provided money, much more money than the school system would otherwise have had."[75]

On March 14, 1997, the state's Attorney General Nixon, again relying on *Jenkins III*, asked the district court for an order that all parties immediately cease efforts to recruit new students into the transfer program and relieve the state of having to pay whatever expenses such students generated. The district court denied the state's motion.[76] This time the state decided to appeal the district court's order. The Eighth Circuit affirmed the district court's decision:

> The State argues that it has expended large sums of money in the twenty years that this program has been in effect, it has done its share, and the time has come to end its responsibilities in the matter. In support of ending its obligations, the State points to the fact that it has initiated a number of programs that have particular benefit to disadvantaged city students and has publicly proposed to settle its obligations by making a lump sum payment to the St. Louis School District.[77]

The court repeated that "the best way to resolve these problems and provide a quality, integrated education to all city students is through good-faith settlement negotiations."

With regard to the *Jenkins III* issue, the court said:

> The State's principal argument is that . . . *Jenkins III* requires
> that the [voluntary interdistrict transfer program] be phased out
> now. We do not agree that *Jenkins III* requires this result. A prem-
> ise of *Jenkins III* was that the trial court specifically found that no
> interdistrict violation had taken place. No such determination has
> been made here. To the contrary, from the beginning the plaintiffs
> asserted interdistrict violations. Rather than contest these allega-
> tions, the County Districts entered into a settlement agreement
> under which they agreed to accept a significant number of transfer
> students and in return were promised judgments relieving them
> from any possible constitutional violations. Under these circum-
> stances, it would be wholly inappropriate for this court to make an
> initial determination with respect to an interdistrict violation.
>
> To require the County Districts to litigate this issue now, after
> voluntarily accepting thousands of city transfer students for twen-
> ty years, would violate their fundamental right to due process. . . .
> Moreover, the fundamental and undisputed fact remains that the
> State has been found to be the primary constitutional violator, and
> this court has consistently held in panel and in *en banc* opinions
> that the State could be required to fund the [voluntary interdis-
> trict transfer program].[78]

Settlement negotiations continued through 1996 and 1997. St. Louis School
Superintendent Cleveland Hammonds, Jr., remembered that programs consistently
ranking low were eliminated. "[That] may be what some of the principals are talking about when they say the resources have been cut back," he said. "Then we took
a program like the college prep that was only in some of the magnet schools, and
. . . redirected that money and gave everybody that same amount so that they could
implement a college prep program."[79]

During the negotiations, it became clear that legislation would be necessary to
facilitate the settlement. Danforth had studied the accounting books and the capital
needs of the public schools. "When we got into the negotiations, it was very clear
that there was not enough money available in the system that was being spent to
settle the case," he said. "[T]here was no incentive at all for the plaintiffs or the St.
Louis public schools or really most of the county school districts, to settle the case.
They had a good deal going, and without sufficient resources, there was very little
chance of getting it settled. So we went to the state legislature to get more resources
and we failed in the first year, went back in the second year, and were successful."[80]

In May 1998, the Missouri General Assembly passed Senate Bill 781, which
provided the funding and laid additional groundwork for a possible settlement
agreement. Like every other stage of the St. Louis desegregation saga, negotiations

over Senate Bill 781 were intensely political; the bill included general provisions regarding educational reform and gave increased funding to many districts around the state in order to ensure its passage.[81]

The bill's supporters saw it as a chance to "take back" the schools from the federal courts and reduce the amount the state would pay to desegregate city schools. The bill set dates when various desegregation remedies would end, and it provided funding for a somewhat limited version of the interdistrict transfer plan and magnet schools. A state senator observed: "There's a federal judge raiding our state treasury, and the reason is, we didn't give these kids a decent education to begin with."[82]

Senate Bill 781 contemplated the end of court supervision. A new corporation was established to implement the voluntary school transfer program in the St. Louis metropolitan area. The corporation was to be governed by a board of directors consisting of one representative from each school district participating in the voluntary transfer program.[83] The bill directed the Board to provide for the transportation of all students. It also provided for state payments to school districts for the education of transfer students.

To carry out its duties, the bill permitted the new corporation to retain the services of a fiscal agent and to hire a consultant, but an obvious retaliatory amendment forbade the corporation from hiring any contractor or employee of the Voluntary Interdistrict Coordinating Council or any other program established by the federal district court.[84] Even with this amendment, Judge Stephen Ehlmann, who had authored the amendment, said that many in the General Assembly "felt betrayed by the final document. Everyone decided to give the school district one more chance. [However,] if we had known that the [existing] School Board would get another chance, we probably would not have voted for the bill."[85]

To address the continuing needs of schools within the city of St. Louis, the bill provided for approximately $40 million in state money each year over and above basic state aids. This was subject to the city voters' approval of a sales tax to raise $20 million each year. This $60 million contribution of state and local money was to replace the $70 million that St. Louis had been receiving each year through court orders.

The bill required ongoing efforts to gauge support for the interdistrict program. Each district in the voluntary transfer program was required to place before the voters in the district a proposal to continue participation in the transfer program. If less than a majority of the voters supported continued participation, the bill required a plan for the phase-out of the district's participation.[86]

The bill contained other important educational reforms. It changed the way the city school board was to be elected, from a seven-person board elected from the city at large to a twelve-member board elected from subdistricts, this change to take effect in 2003.[87] In the meantime, an "overlay" three-member school board would oversee the transition and have the power to run the city's school system if it lost its state accreditation.[88]

The bill allowed the state board to determine which schools in the state were "academically deficient."[89] It gave the state board the power to suspend or terminate teachers' and administrators' contracts at that school and "reconstitute" the school with new teachers and administrative staff.[90] The bill also authorized school districts to develop incentives and rewards systems for teachers.[91] And—the harshest sanction in the bill—if a district failed to meet state standards and the state board revoked its accreditation, the district's elected school board would be dissolved and replaced by a three-member overlay board appointed by the state board of education. The bill for the first time tied student test scores to school accreditation. It created severe penalties, including state takeover of a district if its test scores did not meet the state's expectations.

The 1999 settlement agreement softened the threat of such measures for St. Louis schools, however, by postponing any possibility of a state takeover until the end of the 2001–02 school year. In mid-October 2000, the Missouri Board of Education further delayed the de-accreditation process by granting provisional accreditation status to St. Louis schools through 2004.

Further, the bill allowed for charter schools in St. Louis and Kansas City.[92] These schools were to be managed by a private group using money from the school district. Under the legislation, charter schools had to receive sponsorship from the urban district, a nearby community college, or a four-year college to qualify for state monies. The school funding formulas focused on increasing aid to those districts with high percentages of students receiving free or reduced-priced lunches (considered a reliable and acceptable indicator of poverty), and those where the tax rate was already high.[93] It also included additional funds for poor rural schools.

On June 24, 1998, then-Governor Mel Carnahan signed Senate Bill 781 into law, stating: "It is time for the city of St. Louis to regain control of its schools and get the federal court out of the business of running local schools."[94] Although the bill established the funding and framework for ending court supervision, two conditions still had to be met if the bill was to take effect. First, the parties to the *Liddell* litigation had to accept the legislation by settling the litigation in accordance with the law, and the district court had to approve the settlement. Second, the voters of St. Louis had to pass a referendum to raise the sales tax to partially make up for the loss of state desegregation funds.

Dr. Danforth, the settlement coordinator, now had a framework for ending the litigation. Remarkably, this was the first time that the state was a serious participant in any type of settlement negotiations. Danforth worked for months to get an agreement that all the parties could live with.[95] In mid-January of 1999, at a meeting Minnie Liddell attended, an agreement was announced. Supporting herself on a cane, Mrs. Liddell, who by this time had three grandchildren who were attending schools in St. Louis, told reporters: "[T]his has been a long time coming, yet we have just begun."[96] For the first time, the state apologized for having supported segregated schools for so many decades.[97]

Building on the text of Senate Bill 781, the settlement agreement set the stage for the eventual end of the remedies that had been available under the 1983 court order. But for a transitional period, it left the three basic elements of the previous plan in place, but gave the programs fewer resources. The agreement stated, "The plaintiffs, the United States, and City Board recognize the need for continuing remedial efforts to ensure that the enjoyment of full equality of opportunity by plaintiff schoolchildren is not impaired by the effects of past segregation."[98]

The City Board agreed to maintain all-day kindergarten, summer school, college-preparatory, and preschool programs for ten years at "current levels of enrollment, scope, and quality." *However, the class size, which had been at a ratio of 20 to 1 for all elementary schools under the court-ordered plan could be increased to 25 to 1 for all grades above fourth grade.*[99] The settlement agreement also put in place a new framework for vocational education and increased accountability for test scores.

For the first time, the City Board obligated itself to establish standards for improvement in standardized achievement test scores, attendance, the dropout rate, and career preparation.[100] Under Section 7 of the agreement, the City Board agreed to establish yearly performance standards for all schools, select forty underperforming schools as "schools of opportunity" and slate them for intensive improvement, and reconstitute at least two schools a year.[101] Any student assigned to a "school of opportunity" which failed to improve within two years was allowed to transfer to another public school within the district, with the district paying the transportation costs.[102] The City Board was required to develop a teacher and principal accountability plan "which will specify rewards and sanctions based upon their job performance and student outcomes in their building." To clarify the validity of the standards specified in the settlement agreement, Section 7A stated that the standards adopted in the settlement agreement "do not supersede any State standards including 'Missouri School Improvement Program' standards."

Section 16 of the settlement agreement stated that if the St. Louis School District were to be classified as unaccredited, the state board of education could not take action until after two years. In the meantime, the city and state had to work together to try to improve the district's standing. The section required the commissioner of education to report the district's efforts to the state board, and the City Board was required to comply with any of the commissioner's recommendations.

In August 1999, the *St. Louis Post-Dispatch* reported that many teachers were skeptical of the district administration's ability to keep its accreditation, and of its increased emphasis on student test scores.[103] The Teacher's Union was particularly vocal. The union had sued the St. Louis public schools the last time the district used student test scores to evaluate teacher performance, and in 1988, the district had stopped using such test-based evaluations. The union's president, Sheryl Davenport, asserted that "accountability is a two-way street," and said that administrative support of teachers was crucial to student success: New teachers needed mentoring, school supplies should arrive on time, teaching vacancies should be filled, and teachers' salaries should be increased.[104] The teachers said that increased funding, not draconian measures such as reconstitution, was the best way to improve student achievement.

In October 1999, the teachers' fears were realized when Missouri Education Commissioner Robert Bartman recommended to the state board of education that the St. Louis School District lose its accreditation because the district met state standards in just three of eleven areas in student performance. The district needed to pass four areas for provisional accreditation.[105] Under the terms of the settlement agreement, however, the state board was required to wait until 2002 before revoking the district's accreditation, so St. Louis kept its accreditation despite its low marks.[106] Kansas City, on the other hand, met none of the eleven standards, and lost its accreditation, although no sanctions were immediately imposed against the district.[107]

In response to the St. Louis School District's brush with unaccreditation, Superintendent Hammonds developed a plan which expanded the school year for 23 elementary schools from 174 days to 203 days, reassigned five administrators to new sites, and set aside reward money for schools that made the greatest gains.[108] Hammonds also called for thousands of volunteers and for corporate assistance to support the district's improvements.

In mid-October 2000, the state board of education granted provisional accreditation to the St. Louis public schools because the district had shown some progress in increasing student test scores and attendance, and in reducing the dropout rate. This allowed the district to delay its next review until late 2004.[109] Critics then voiced the opinion that St. Louis had evaded careful examination of its students' performance, and did not deserve even provisional accreditation. Steven Ehlmann, a former state legislator and state court judge, wrote that in 2000 St. Louis had met five out of eleven performance criteria, but only two were related to the students' performance on the MAP test. The district had increased the number of proficient readers in third grade by 6 percent, and in grades 7 and 8 by 3.7 percent.[110] But Ehlmann objected on the grounds that these gains were meaningless, because "for neither of these reading criteria was there a minimum level of proficiency required."[111]

In addition to state legislation and the 1999 settlement agreement, the Missouri Department of Elementary and Secondary Education (DESE) adopted the Missouri School Improvement Program. Under this program, each district had to submit a School Improvement Plan in response to a state evaluation of the district's strengths and weaknesses. Review and accreditation of the 524 school districts followed a five-year cycle, so that each year about 20 percent of the districts underwent reviews. The reviewing body, the Department School Improvement Committee, reported on the districts' resources, progress, and performance. Depending on the committee's recommendation, the state board of education designated districts as "unaccredited," "provisionally accredited," or "accredited," based on the standards set by the Missouri School Improvement Program.

In 2001, the Missouri Department of Elementary and Secondary Education developed thirty-three "top ten" lists. Schools with the highest percentage of students scoring in the "proficient" and "advanced" levels, as well as those schools that made the most progress in advancing students to the "progressing" and "proficient" levels, earned a spot on the lists. In St. Louis, the elementary schools Banneker, Carver,

Columbia, Hodgen, Bryan Hill, Mark Twain, Marshall, Meramec, Hickey, and Fanning, as well as L'Ouverture and Long Middle Schools, were included in the Most Improved Schools Top Ten list because they had moved the highest percentage of students from the "Step 1" level to the "progressing" level.

The agreement provided for magnet school programs to continue for ten years, and the City Board agreed to pursue the court's longtime goal of enrolling fourteen thousand students in magnet schools. The Board could modify individual magnet school enrollments and grade configurations, provided that at least 20 percent of magnet seats would be at the high-school level and an equal percentage at the middle-school level. The racial balance was set at 60 percent black and 40 percent white, plus or minus five percentage points.[112]

The agreement continued the interdistrict program and its state funding, but it downsized the program. Current high school transfer students could finish their education at the schools they had chosen. The county districts, with the exception of Ladue, expressed a good-faith belief that they would continue to accept eligible students for a period of six years at 70 percent of current levels. In a separate agreement with the NAACP, the Liddell plaintiffs, and the United States, the county districts agreed to maintain enrollment within 15 percent of the current number of city transfers.[113] However, the agreement established zones that paired up parts of the city with certain designated suburban districts, a technique designed to reduce transportation costs. This requirement, which restricted a transfer student's options, could reduce the number of students who chose to attend a county transfer school.[114]

The agreement required the state to create a transition fund, totaling $180 million, for capital improvements to city schools. The fund would start at $28.5 million for the first year, and taper down gradually to $9 million ten years later. This would help the city schools accommodate the increased enrollment as fewer students transferred out to the county.[115] The agreement also required the state to provide $40 million per year in state funds if the voters of St. Louis approved a two-thirds-of-a-cent sales tax that would raise $20 million for the city schools each year. On February 2, 1999, the voters approved the tax by a 2-to-1 margin.[116] One voter put it this way: "I vote yes, but I vote incredibly sadly. It's a poor solution to a complex problem. The end of desegregation is very sad."[117] On February 28, 1999, Judge Limbaugh approved the settlement agreement in all respects.[118] The federal court's role in the *Liddell* litigation had ended.[119]

Perhaps the most important difference between the 1983 and 1999 agreements was that the 1999 settlement agreement contained time limits for ending the desegregation programs. Much to the dismay of the state, the 1983 agreement had been open-ended. The 1999 agreement contemplated at most ten years of support for the magnet schools, and only three guaranteed years for the interdistrict transfers (longer, if approved by the county schools).

The second major change was that Senate Bill 781 and the 1999 agreement provided significantly less state money for city schools. Even with the $40 million from the legislation and the $20 million from the sales tax increase, the city schools would lose between $7 million to $10 million each year.

The reasons for settling the litigation are varied and many. The following were among the most important.

First, although the state obeyed every court order either before or after it exhausted its appeals to higher courts, it resisted every step of the way. The state filed numerous appeals to the United States Court of Appeals, and the parties petitioned the U.S. Supreme Court on five occasions.[120] The state argued repeatedly that the court did not have the authority to order the state to fund the interdistrict programs, and that the costs to the state were too high and without precedent. While complaining about the high costs of the desegregation program, the state spent over $8 million pursuing these legal actions.[121]

Second, many state legislators, primarily those from rural areas, strenuously objected to funding the desegregation plan, believing that the desegregation payments to St. Louis and Kansas City would leave the state unable to adequately fund public education in the rest of Missouri.

Third, the 5-to-4 U.S. Supreme Court decision involving the desegregation of the Kansas City schools in the *Jenkins* case inspired a widespread belief that a majority of the Supreme Court would no longer support desegregation plans similar to those in St. Louis. The legal climate had changed between the 1970s and the early 1990s. After Presidents Reagan and Bush made their judicial appointments, the Supreme Court became increasingly conservative and less willing to approve the affirmative remedies used in St. Louis. The *Jenkins* decision added to the perception that the Court would declare the St. Louis School District unitary, if given the chance.

Fourth, a split developed in the black community in St. Louis. The segment led by Mayor Freeman Bosley, Jr., argued that the interdistrict program should end. They held that all resources should be dedicated to improving neighborhood schools, and that integration should no longer be a goal. Others, led by the NAACP, believed that integration remained important and that the interdistrict program, as well as other programs, should continue.

Fifth, three successive state attorneys general—Webster, Ashcroft, and Nixon—and other Missouri officeholders succeeded in politicizing the issue, raising anew segregationist sentiment that had an enduring base in Missouri.

Sixth, the district court, faced with the difficult decision of whether to declare the city district unitary or to continue supervising the city's public schools, decided to put its efforts toward settling the case. Its decision was supported by the court of appeals and the United States Supreme Court. The district court appointed William H. Danforth to be the settlement coordinator, and Dr. Danforth's integrity and his prestige, and his unremitting efforts with the public, the legislature, and the parties to the litigation, led to the settlement agreement.[122]

Finally, those who wanted desegregation to continue had few options. So although the legislation and settlement agreement limited the remedies for black children in city schools, it was better than nothing. The NAACP and other plaintiffs faced the risk that Judge Limbaugh—who again had "inherited" the case after Judge Gunn died in 1998—would end the remedies completely, a considerable risk in light of his enthusiasm for the settlement agreement: "Senate Bill 781 is a remarkable piece of legislation. . . . It appears that the state funding under Senate Bill 781, as well as the provisions of the Agreement, go beyond what can reasonably be expected in the long term from continued litigation and judicial oversight in the case."[123] In an editorial titled, "The Judge's Thunderbolt: 'Take It,'" the *St. Louis Post-Dispatch* told those who wanted more for city schools that this was the best deal they could possibly expect from the legislature and this judge. The editorial also cautioned: "And if the school tax should pass, as it must, let there be no illusions that the problems of our schools are solved. The hardest work lies ahead."[124]

Dr. William Danforth, appointed settlement coordinator, worked for two years to get an acceptable settlement that allowed the program to operate without court supervision.

Some felt that the gains from the *Liddell* case had been tragically compromised in the new agreement. Former Special Master Bruce La Pierre compared the 1999 settlement with the one he had negotiated in 1983. "[W]hen I settled the case in 1983, there wasn't much support for the settlement," he said. "But in 1998, when my good friend—but I don't approve of what he did—Bill Danforth negotiated out of the settlement—he calls it a settlement—they had a party in the Chase Park Plaza to celebrate, and I thought the party was wildly inappropriate, because what we were celebrating was abandoning our commitment rather than staying with the commitment."[125]

According to LuVerne Cameron of the Desegregation Monitoring Committee, some St. Louisans were not aware of all that they might be losing. She said, "Well, I know folks that I talked to, they just had no clue, just had no clue what was going on. And perceptually everybody saw an end to the yellow bus, the yellow bus that's rolling, and never mind that most of the busing that went on in the city was voluntary, had nothing to do with mandatory desegregation, nothing at all."[126]

As expert witnesses testified and as the numbers of interdistrict transfers show, the St. Louis school desegregation program was the largest and most successful choice program in the nation. The program was costly to the state, but those costs were more than reasonable in light of Missouri's 160-year history of slavery and segregation and the state's long history of underfunding education.

The future of St. Louis as a modern city able to compete in the worldwide economy depends on its having a well-trained, well-educated workforce. With the end of the federal court's involvement, it is up to parents, teachers, school administrators, business, labor, and political leaders to make the "Danforth" 1999 settlement agreement work and to provide a quality public education to all students irrespective of their race or economic status.

{Epilogue}

The Struggle Continues

For more than 160 years, black children in the state of Missouri were either denied the opportunity to receive a public education or were required to attend inferior, segregated public schools. Minnie Liddell and other black parents initiated a federal court action in 1972, which led to a court-approved settlement agreement in 1983, which, for the first time, gave thousands of black children an opportunity for a high-quality, integrated education in the St. Louis metropolitan area. Under that agreement, by 1999 nearly thirteen thousand black students from the city were attending county schools as participants in the Voluntary Interdistrict Transfer Program. This program was the largest and most successful choice program in the nation, described by Judge William L. Hungate as the "crown jewel of the desegregation plan" and by Dr. Christine Rossell, a professor of political science at Boston University and an expert witness for the state, as an "extraordinary success."

Enrollment in the integrated city magnet schools reached fourteen thousand students in 1999. By that year, nearly half of the students who lived in St. Louis and attended public schools benefitted from an integrated education either in the magnet school program or through the Voluntary Interdistrict Transfer Program. For many students who remained in the city's all-black schools, remedial and compensatory programs were instituted. These included dramatic reductions in class size, all-day kindergarten, preschool, and summer school programs. The operating budget for these all-black schools nearly doubled, and school facilities underwent significant improvements.

The City Board, the state, and the suburban school districts acted promptly to effectuate the programs and cooperated to ensure their proper implementation. However, neither the State Department of Education nor the City Board focused on whether the programs were improving student achievement as measured by state tests. The state was more interested in *how much money it was spending* rather than whether the money being spent resulted in improved test scores.[1] The City Board was equally lax. In retrospect, the Eighth Circuit undoubtedly erred by not establishing monitoring requirements to ensure that students received the maximum benefit from the changes.

Unfortunately, many of the improvements achieved as a result of the court-ordered 1983 settlement agreement were dismantled by the 1999 settlement agreement. The Voluntary Interdisrict Transfer Program was immediately downsized from 13,262 in 1998–1999 to 10,649 in 2002–2003. As a result, many black students were deprived of an opportunity for a quality, integrated education in a suburban school, the level of segregation in the city schools increased, and the city had to educate more than 2,600 former transfer students with fewer state and local tax dollars. Senselessly, the 1999 settlement agreement put an end to the gathering of data in the county schools regarding suspensions, promotions, retentions, and participation in school extracurricular activities, thus making it impossible to monitor whether the transfer students are being treated equally. Although the state did agree to appropriate $180 million for capital improvements to city schools and many programs remained, the agreement permits class sizes to increase significantly above the levels required by previous court-ordered decrees.[2]

Perhaps the most striking failure of the 1983 settlement agreement was the failure to require annual monitoring of student achievement within the city schools and in the county schools of transfer students. Although students were given state achievement tests during most of the years that the school district was subject to the court decrees, no schools were penalized by the state for failing to meet state achievement standards. The reason is obvious to the authors. If the state, as the primary constitutional violator, complained about poor student achievement, it would be at least jointly responsible for the poor results. In 2002, when the district failed to meet state standards, the district was given a grace period of provisional accreditation until 2004 as provided for in the settlement agreement. Recent test results continue to show that many students perform poorly and that a significant gap in achievement levels between black and white students remains.[3]

Testing is helpful in informing teachers, parents, students, and the public how well or how poorly students are performing, and concomitantly, what skills need to be addressed by the teachers. The experience in St. Louis and similar metropolitan school districts, however, demonstrates that simply imposing penalties on low-achieving schools does little to improve test scores. So the question is: What more needs to be done? The mayor of St. Louis, Francis Slay, spoke to this problem in June 2002:

> The time for excuses in our city school system is over. We live in a world that is getting smaller and more complex each day. We live in a world where the good jobs go to the people with a good education.
>
> Given these basic realities, it is absolutely inexcusable for our city to have a school system that barely qualifies for provisional

accreditation each year—a school system where so many students do not meet Missouri standards.

Make no mistake, this is an issue of survival for our city. If we can't offer good educational options to all of our families, many of them will leave—regardless of how much they may love all of the great things St. Louis has to offer. This is a major reason for the decline of our population, and it absolutely must change if we are going to turn this city around. It's just that simple.[4]

In December 2002, the mayor, acting on his earlier comments, spearheaded the formation of a coalition that included himself, the Danforth Foundation, major St. Louis employers, the Black Leadership Roundtable, and others. The purpose of the coalition was to endorse and elect candidates to the St. Louis Board of Education.[5] On January 16, 2003, after interviewing twenty-two candidates, the coalition selected a racially mixed slate of four for its endorsement: Robert Archibald, president, Missouri Historical Society; M. Darnetta Clinkscale, patient care director, Barnes Jewish Hospital; Ronald L. Jackson, assistant director, Neighborhood Partnership Development, St. Louis For Kids; and Vincent C. Schoemehl, Jr., president and CEO of Grand Center, Inc.[6]

The candidates stated that their goal was a dramatic improvement in the quality of education for children. To achieve that goal, they called for the hiring of an interim superintendent from the business community—"somebody who can galvanize public support and elevate public consciousness on the importance of education,"[7] and who can take a "'chain saw' to cut the budget and trim executive fat. Once some of the dirty work is done, . . . then an educational leader can come in and develop a long-term strategy for the district."[8] No details were given as to how the budget was to be cut or the steps that would be taken to improve student achievement.

The coalition spent $281,000 to elect the slate.[9] The newly elected members gained immediate control of the seven-person School Board. True to its word, the Board promptly hired a "turn-around" management firm, Alvarez and Marsal, at a fee of $5 million, to temporarily perform the duties of school superintendent.[10] Its rationale for this action was that "the school district must function as a business before it can work as a learning institution."[11] Changes designed to improve student achievement were to be postponed until after management of the district was brought under control. In June 2003, William F. Roberti, a partner in the turn-around firm, was named the interim superintendent.[12]

Shortly after Roberti took office, he announced that the school district had a deficit of $90 million.[13] This estimate conflicted with the prior estimate of Dr. Cleveland Hammonds, the departing superintendent, who earlier reported that the deficit was $55 million.[14] An immediate public controversy over the discrepancy followed the report. The governor responded by ordering an audit,[15] which showed a deficit of $73 million.[16] Part of the deficit was undoubtedly caused by a reduction in state aid and by the state's failure to pay that reduced aid in full, as agreed to in the final settlement.[17] Additional causes that would explain the remaining portion of the deficit are being uncovered.[18] To temporarily help cover the deficit, the new management firm quickly negotiated a deal with Missouri Attorney General Jay Nixon to borrow $30 million from the $180 million set aside by the state in the 1999 settlement agreement for future desegregation expenses to be paid back over a period of years.[19] This action was unsuccessfully challenged in court.[20]

In an attempt to save $15 million per year, Roberti recommended, and the Board agreed, to close thirteen elementary schools, two middle schools, and one high school.[21] All but four of the schools were on the north side of St. Louis, where schools had been built to address population growth and avoid integrating schools.[22] In an effort to save an additional $64 million, the Board agreed to lay off 1,463 employees, including 90 administrators, 99 support personnel, 118 secretaries, 102 mechanics, and 164 teaching assistants; to reduce the number of bus routes; to privatize warehouse, janitorial and maintenance services;[23] to create an Internet-based textbook and supply distribution system; and to reduce employee benefits.[24] To achieve additional savings, student/teacher ratios were increased significantly above the levels permitted under either the court-ordered decrees or the settlement agreement to 23 to 1 in kindergarten through grade 2, 26 to 1 in grades 3 through 5, 28 to 1 in grades 6 through 8, and as high as 31 to 1 in grades 9 through 12.[25]

Notwithstanding the personnel cuts, school closings, and higher student/teacher ratios, the acting superintendent, William Roberti, reported in January 2004 that the district needed to reduce its budget by an additional $23 million.[26] He gave no details for the need for the further reduction, in light of the fact that the previous cuts already exceeded the auditor's estimate of a $73 million deficit.

Concurrent with the budget cuts, Roberti entered into a contract with the Council of Great City Schools to review the district's efforts to improve academic performance in the city schools. The Council assembled a team of senior managers from other urban school districts that had, according to the Council, made substantial gains in improving student achievement in their respective districts. However, in spite of the gains made by these school districts, their achievement gaps are still greater than that in the St. Louis public schools, and none of these districts has as many black students or low-income students as St. Louis. The team visited the school district on several occasions and issued its report in May 2004. The report made 85 recommendations, nine of which were related to curriculum and instruction: 1) develop a coherent vision for where the district wants to go academically; 2) set measurable goals for academic improvement; 3) establish a new accountability system for attaining academic goals; 4) standardize districtwide instructional strategies and curriculum; 5) provide uniform districtwide professional development for the implementation and use of the new curriculum; 6) ensure that reforms are implemented at the classroom level; 7) use data to monitor progress and decide on instructional interventions; 8) begin reforms at the elementary level but start reforming high schools; and 9) focus on the district's lowest-performing schools.

Without intending to minimize the thoroughness of the Great Schools study or its recommendations, we are concerned with the report's failure in two respects. First, the report made no mention of the important role that integration has played in improving student achievement. Students in the integrated magnet schools do better than those in the all-black schools. Black students who transfer to predominantly white county schools do better than those who remain in the city schools. More black transfer students graduate, attend college, and do better in state achievement tests.

Second, although the Council makes several recommendations that will cost more money, the report fails to include a recommendation that additional resources are necessary to achieve the plan's goals. Without such a recommendation, the state and the district will not make the needed additional investments in the St. Louis public schools and student achievement will not improve. Roberti recognized the problem in his final meeting with editorial writers of the *St. Louis Post-Dispatch*. He told them, "I'd like to wave a wand and have all your schools up to standards,…but you'd have to spend millions you don't have to do that."[27]

The federal government's efforts to help large urban school districts have fallen short for the same reasons. In December 2001, the U.S. Congress overwhelmingly approved the "No Child Left Behind Act,"[28] which extended the federal government's role in public education. President George W. Bush signed the bill on January 8, 2002. Unfortunately, the sweeping changes were accompanied by very limited additional funding.[29] The act requires annual testing of students in grades 3 through 8, and it sets a twelve-year timetable for closing gaps in achievement between minority and non-minority students. The act, however, provides minimal additional funds to improve reading for younger students, to provide tutoring services for students in chronically failing schools, to allow some students in failing schools to transfer to more successful public schools,[30] or to develop new charter schools.[31]

In advancing his "No Child Left Behind" legislation, President Bush supported holding states, school districts, and individual schools "accountable for ensuring that all students, including disadvantaged students, meet high academic standards."[32] His vision of school reform left the states to determine how to meet the new federal expectations, but he clearly advocated a "tough love" approach by insisting on rigorous standardized testing. The act provided consequences for schools whose students failed to improve and set national standards for teachers. It made no provision, however, for expanding the teaching force, training educators to teach in urban schools having majorities of poor students of color, or increasing teachers' salaries. According to the Act, a school that fails to improve its scores after six years will undergo staff changes, a change in its curriculum, or be converted to a charter school. In some instances, students are given the right to transfer to another school, either in or out of the district. Failure to make these changes will result in the loss of federal aid.

The goal of the recently enacted state and federal accountability standards to improve student achievement by measuring standardized tests, dropout rates, attendance and graduation rates, is a worthy one. Unless these standards are accompanied by policy changes and additional resources, however, the accountability standards will do little or nothing to improve the quality of the education in the public schools in St. Louis. These public schools will continue to have the responsibility of educating most of the students in the city, as most of them simply will not have the opportunity or the desire to attend private, parochial, or charter schools.

Raising student achievement in the St. Louis public schools is a difficult task for several reasons: a 160-year legacy of racial discrimination and an equally long history of underfunding public education in the state of Missouri and in St. Louis, evidenced by the fact that Missouri currently ranks forty-eighth in state funding for public education. Moreover, 83.2 percent of the students qualify for a free or reduced-price lunch, 16 percent are special education students, and as many as 40 percent of the students often move five to six times during an academic year. Finally, at the high school level, many students have lost hope of going to college or finding a good job either before or after college, and thus drop out.

Notwithstanding these difficulties, there are a number of elementary and middle schools in St. Louis and other urban communities where students are doing well. These schools show that improving black students' academic achievement in traditional public schools is an attainable goal. The success stories of strong principals, dedicated and well-trained teachers, and concerned parents demonstrate that poor black students can achieve, even excel, in public schools.

The principals, teachers, and other professionals who have experienced a degree of success in their schools provide a road map for success in improving student achievement in the St. Louis public schools. If we listen to them and implement their policies and practices, then there is hope for the future for the thousands of students of all races who rely on public education to prepare them for a successful life in our great democracy.

These educators say, and we agree, that the following factors are essential to improving black students' academic achievement. Some cost very little, others require increased funding, but *all* are essential if the goal of a quality education for *all* students in St. Louis is to be achieved. No matter how well the school district is organized and no matter how efficiently it is administered, student achievement will not be raised unless the additional resources to accomplish this end are provided by the federal, state, and local governments.

1. *Strong Principals.* Schools need well-trained, experienced principals with the *authority* to hire, discipline, and, if necessary, terminate faculty and staff within well-defined and much simpler procedures than currently exist. Once given authority, principals must be held *responsible* for raising student achievement levels. The principals cannot expect to be exempt from termination if their schools fail to show progress, but they must be treated as valued professionals. They should be rewarded when they are successful, and their salaries must be competitive with those paid by high-performing county schools.

2. *Well-educated, well-trained, well-compensated, dedicated teachers and other professionals.* The best and most dedicated professionals are essential if the achievement

gap is to be closed and the quality of education improved. The nationwide shortage of certified teachers and the challenges that accompany urban education compound the difficulty of retaining excellent teachers in city schools. Recent reports, however, show that very competent teachers are available if they are well paid.[33] In St. Louis, compensation for both principals and teachers must, at the very least, be fully competitive with those paid by high-performing county schools, such as Clayton, Ladue, and Parkway.

Serious questions have been raised with respect to the quality of training for teachers in the St. Louis public schools. It is the responsibility of the State Department of Education to improve and insist that all colleges preparing teachers have strong programs that correlate with state standards for student achievement. Allowing weak or outdated training programs to continue will result in urban students receiving a mediocre education. The state has the responsibility to fairly evaluate all teacher training programs, rank them, and not allow those that do not meet minimum standards to continue. The state must provide enough qualified teachers, certified in the subjects they teach, so that every school can hire and assign the full complement of teachers needed by the opening of school in September.[34]

3. *High expectations.* Every teacher, administrator, and parent or guardian must understand that every child can learn. Low expectations for any student must not be tolerated. Every student must attend school regularly, work hard, and graduate. We recognize that parental involvement is an important factor in student achievement, but only a few principals have been able to secure the active cooperation from parents or guardians necessary to improve their children's performance. We must follow the lead of those principals and teachers who have established a relationship with the community in which they are located and with the parent or parents or guardians whose children attend the school.

Lack of parental involvement, however, can never be used as an excuse for not doing everything possible in schools to improve student achievement. Many students are being raised by someone other than their father or mother—by a grandparent, an aunt, or another relative. The schools can make up, in part, what the students do not receive at home. School staff must visit homes to encourage student attendance and understand the home environment.

Schools also have an obligation to encourage the community to discontinue labeling African American students. As noted by Charles Bean, a graduate of the Voluntary Interdistrict Transfer Program and a transitional specialist at Vashon High School, "A student can have a 4.0 grade-point average, but if he wears baggy pants and a big shirt, there is a perception that he must be a gang member." He also stated:

> At Vashon, we have after-school programs, but if the student does not have respect for the adults in the school system, he will not participate in the programs. Moreover, often when we establish a program it is discontinued because of lack of funding. One

day you have federal money and the next day you lose the money
so the program is dropped.[35]

Among the programs that have been dropped at Vashon for lack of funding are
the latchkey program and the 21st Century Program, which included after-school
tutoring.

Above all, students must have hope that there is an alternative to securing a
minimum-wage job or becoming a gang member after leaving high school. They
must have a reasonable expectation that they can pursue a post-high school education. The whole community must participate in giving hope to these students.[36]
Every vestige of racism and discrimination must be eliminated and every student
must believe that he or she will have an equal opportunity for a home, an education,
and a good job.[37]

4. *Small classes and smaller schools.* Kindergarten through fifth grade classes
ideally should not exceed fifteen students, but certainly never more than twenty.
Classes in middle school should not exceed twenty students, and high school classes
should not exceed twenty-five students. In addition to small class sizes, schools
need to be smaller so that principals, teachers, and counselors know the students,
and the students know that someone cares about them and expects them to excel.
Metro High School has demonstrated that schools need to be smaller. City students,
some of whom are not doing well on standardized state tests, need more individual
attention, including tutoring and mentoring, if they are to succeed. It is expensive
to have smaller classes and smaller schools and the school district must have state
and federal assistance to make the reductions, but the changes are necessary if city
students are to meet the new state and federal standards for student achievement.

5. *Continuity in a single school for at least a full school year.* Every study on the
topic of student achievement acknowledges that student performance suffers when
students do not stay in the same school for a full school year. We recognize that it is
expensive to provide the transportation necessary to dramatically reduce the mobility rate in the schools, but it is extremely difficult to improve student achievement
as long as students have to attend multiple schools in the same school year.[38] Parents
move several times a year, and each time their children have to change schools. Contrary to the Great Schools Report, the Voluntary Interdistrict Transfer Program does
not present a mobility problem. Students enrolled in the program usually stay in the
same school even if their parent or parents move.

6. *Parental involvement.* Admittedly, it is difficult for single parents to fully participate in their children's education, particularly for those single parents who must
work full time. Some of these parents overcome the difficulties and others must,
and it is society's obligation to help them do so. There are new and creative ways
to engage parents that must be tried. Some principals in St. Louis and elsewhere
have developed programs that have succeeded in getting parents involved in their
children's education. These programs must be implemented in all city schools.[39]

7. *Early childhood education.* Early childhood education for every child is neces-

sary to promote and accelerate black students' early literacy and cognitive skills. The 1999 settlement agreement requires the city schools to enroll five hundred additional preschool children by 2003. Certainly no number less than this can be tolerated.

8. *A curriculum that prepares students to succeed not only on standardized tests but also in post–high school education and in life.* Given the fact that achievement test scores are to be given such a high priority in determining whether a school or a school district is providing a quality education for its students, there is no alternative but to make sure that the curricula are designed to teach the students the subject matter covered by the standardized achievement test. Efforts also must be made to ensure that students understand the techniques of test taking and, more importantly, the importance of doing well on the test. This must be done, however, without detracting from the larger goal of educating students to be productive citizens.[40]

9. *Student- and parent-friendly buildings equipped with technology to prepare students for the twenty-first century.* One reason given by many parents for sending their children to magnet or county schools is that the school facilities in the traditional city schools are, for the most part, older two-story structures without air conditioning,[41] while the facilities in the county schools are modern, airy, and air conditioned. Some progress has been made in improving facilities, but city schools still lag far behind the county schools with which they compete. Even though $180 million has been made available under the settlement agreement for school construction, it is clear that this sum will not be sufficient to bring the school buildings in the St. Louis district up to the level of those in the county. We believe that the federal and state governments must participate in the costs of modernizing school buildings and grounds if all schools in St. Louis are to be successful.

As part of the modernizing process, schools must be equipped with the technology necessary to prepare students for the twenty-first century. Equally important, teachers must be trained to use this technology on an ongoing basis. Moreover, books and school supplies must be made available on a timely basis. There is also a continuing need to provide state-of-the-art computers and other equipment in every school and to make sure that each school is connected to the Internet.

10. *High school and post–high school education.* The task of educating poor students of color is most difficult at the high school level. Our experience suggests that there are several reasons for this. Many current high school students are products of unsuccessful elementary and middle school programs. Some students drop out of school because they must support themselves, their mothers, and their siblings. Other students do not believe that they have a good chance of securing a post–high school education, either because they are not informed about the possibilities or, more likely, because they do not have the resources to pay the tuition and to meet other financial responsibilities.

In our conversations with Vashon High School's Charles Bean, he has highlighted additional difficulties unique to the high schools:

> Our young males do not have the positive role models. . . .

Fathers [are not] like they used to be. More African American males are behind bars. You cannot be a father to a young male when you are behind bars....

The positive role models I had were police, firemen, doctors. However, teenagers today do not trust these people like I did. . . . The media and movies show crooked doctors and cops . . . and the young males say, I want to be just like them.

Our young males, and now our young females, are doing the things they are doing for attention. They are doing it to reach someone. They want love. Most of them are not getting love at home. Most are raising themselves. . . . Young men and women need attention 24/7. If they cannot get that attention from the home and if they cannot get it from the school, they will turn toward the street. It is the lack of hope. "If I cannot get it anywhere, what is the use? The only person who will respect me is the drug dealer." Once a young man or woman loses hope and faith, he will go to the street.[42]

11. *Continue the Voluntary Interdistrict Transfer Program.* For nineteen years, St. Louis has had the largest and most successful choice program in the nation. As many as 13,000 black city students transferred to county schools yearly. The choice to participate in the city-to-county transfer program was a realistic one for students because the State was required to pay the transportation costs for students. Furthermore, the county school districts chose to participate in the program because they were reimbursed by the state for the full cost of educating the students they received. Without those provisions, most black students would not have been able to participate in the interdistrict program. They could not afford the transportation costs, which averaged about $1,500 per year. Moreover, it now appears that most county districts will not receive full funding for transfer students beginning in the 2004–05 school year, giving districts the opportunity to opt out of the program. With fewer black students transferring to the county for their educations, segregation in the city schools will inevitably grow worse.

A major success of the Voluntary Interdistrict Transfer Program was a significant increase in the number of students who graduated from high school and then enrolled in a two-year college, four-year college, or post–high school technical school. This phenomenon is attributed to encouragement from faculty, administrators, and peers as well as high standards and expectations. Most upper-class resident county students plan to go to college and talk about it among themselves and with city transfer students. For them, going on to college is the norm rather than the exception. This shared expectation in integrated county schools, more than any other factor, appears to have encouraged city transfer students to go to college in larger numbers.

This increase in the number of students attending college and other post-secondary programs must be replicated in the city schools. In addition to adopting high expectations for all students, teachers, administrators, and policymakers around the country must expand on existing programs to keep poor students from dropping out of high school, including internship programs and work study programs under which high school students are paid a minimum wage to work in schools or in the community for ten hours per week. Furthermore, high school students attending neighborhood schools must be made aware of post–high school educational opportunities and the various scholarship and loan programs available. They must be constantly encouraged to further their education and be repeatedly reminded of the economic benefit of doing so. In addition, there must be an immediate and substantial increase in both state and federal financial aid for poor students to attend college.

The state of Missouri insisted on an agreement to significantly reduce the number of city-to-county transfers. That position was adopted in the 1999 settlement agreement. During the sixteen years that the court-ordered interdistrict program was in effect, the state consistently opposed it because, as the primary constitutional violator, it was required to bear the full cost of the program. Moreover, many state officeholders did not support the goal of providing an integrated education for thousands of city and county students. They were for student choice as long as the cost to the state was limited and integration was not a goal.

12. *Continue magnet schools.* Magnet schools offer another choice for city and county students. Fortunately, the 1999 settlement agreement required the St. Louis City Board to maintain the existing magnet school program for at least ten years and to continue to pursue the goal of enrolling at least 14,000 students. As of June 30, 1999, 12,441 students were enrolled in the magnet schools, about 1,200 of whom were from the county. Of the enrolled students, 3,500 were high school students, 3,000 were middle school students, and the remaining 6,000 students were elementary and preschool students.

13. *Alternative choices.* In addition to the public choice programs, parents have long had other choices, including sending their children to religious or private schools. This option has been extensively exercised by white parents in St. Louis. In fact, 85 percent of all white students who live in St. Louis attend private or religious schools. This historical pattern of enrollment has contributed, in part, to the lack of support for public schools in St. Louis. Most of the private schools are segregated, not as a matter of policy but because of the location of the school and the tuition and transportation costs involved in attending the school.

Recently, policymakers have suggested providing state-funded school vouchers to help poor students bear the cost of attending private and parochial schools. On June 27, 2002, the U.S. Supreme Court, in a 5-4 decision,[43] upheld the constitutionality of Ohio's Pilot Project Scholarship Program,[44] which provides 3,700 below-poverty-level elementary students with tuition vouchers to attend private or parochial schools in Cleveland, Ohio. Following this ruling, there will undoubtedly be strong pressure to institute a similar voucher program in St. Louis. Policymakers, however, must realize that fewer than 5 percent of Cleveland's 75,000 public school students currently benefit from the voucher program. In St. Louis, as in Cleveland, the public schools will retain the obligation of educating at least 95 percent of the poor students of color who do not participate in the interdistrict transfer program, even with an opt-out benefit of a voucher plan.

Unless additional resources are provided to the St. Louis public schools, they will fail, leading to a demand by some parents for alternative educational opportunities. As in Ohio, parents and others interested in the privatization of public education will mount pressure for the implementation of voucher programs that will enable their children to go to private or parochial schools. If not a voucher program, parents may demand more charter or other alternative schools.

Even though there is no evidence that these alternatives will provide a superior educational opportunity to the students, the parental demands will in all probability give rise to a diversion of funds away from public schools to the various privatization programs. This may benefit a few students, but the problem of providing a quality education to most students will remain, and the public schools will worsen because their already limited budgets will be cut even further to fund the alternative education programs.

Conclusion

Excellent public schools are essential in a democracy. Experience has demonstrated that urban city schools educate and will continue to educate most school-age children. Moreover, public schools have an obligation to educate all children—rich and poor, black, brown, and white, gifted or special. Unless children are well educated and well trained, they will be unable to take their place as full participants in our vibrant democracy.

Segregated housing, a long history of discrimination in education and employment, and the historic lack of opportunity for African Americans to participate fully and equally in all aspects of life make the task ahead a challenging one. Although throughout the litigation the state of Missouri especially fought provisions that would increase costs, we have learned that a quality education requires quality teachers, small class sizes, and quality facilities. Even though providing a good education is expensive, we agree with Mayor Slay that it will be much more costly to the city of St. Louis, the state of Missouri, and indeed, the nation if all the children of the city are not well educated and prepared to be productive citizens. We cannot afford to deprive thousands of young people the opportunity for an equal education, which they are entitled to under the Equal Protection Clause of the Fourteenth Amendment to the U.S. Constitution. To meet the goal of providing a quality education to *all* students, the nation, the state, and the St. Louis School Board must provide the additional resources necessary to close the achievement gap between city and county schools, as well as the gap between black and white students, wherever they are educated. Moreover, the Voluntary Interdistrict Transfer Program and the magnet school program must be continued to provide students with a realistic choice to attend an integrated school.

The new Board of Education has taken steps to eliminate "executive fat" and to make the schools as efficient as possible. But this is only the first step. The Board must now act to improve student achievement and to eliminate the achievement gap between black and white students. Successful educators in the St. Louis school system have outlined a blueprint for success. By following their advice, we, as a society, can fulfill our obligation to provide *all* children with the quality, free public education they need and deserve.

End Notes

Chapter 1

1. Minnie Liddell, interview by author, St. Louis, 15 June 1999.
2. *Brown v. Board of Education*, 347 U.S. 483, 495 (1954) (*Brown I*).
3. "Complete Integration Due by September 5th Under 3-Step Program Starting This Fall," *St. Louis Post-Dispatch*, 23 June 1954.
4. *Liddell v. Board of Education*, 469 F. Supp. at 1315 (E.D. Mo. 1979).
5. "Complete Integration."
6. Amy Stuart Wells and Robert L. Crain, *Stepping Over the Color Line* (New Haven: Yale University Press, 1997), 85.
7. *Liddell*, 469 F. Supp. at 1315.
8. Ibid., 1304, 1315.
9. "The 'Big Wheels' of Justice Have Spoken: May 17—Unanimous! Segregation Unconstitutional," *St. Louis American*, 20 May 1954.
10. Howard B. Woods, "Nine Distinguished Jurists," *St. Louis Argus*, 21 May 1954.
11. J. Benjamin Horton, Jr., "Integration is Inevitable and Eminent *[sic]*–Asserts NPHC Panel," *St. Louis American*, 27 May 1954.
12. Editorial, *St. Louis Post-Dispatch*, 19 May 1954.
13. Daniel L. Schlafly, *Twenty-Eight Years on the St. Louis School Board: 1955–1981* (St. Louis, 1995), 156–57.
14. Ibid., 157–58.
15. References to race were made once again in student records starting in 1962.

16. *Liddell*, 469 F. Supp. at 1316.
17. Ibid., 1317.
18. Schlafly, *Twenty-Eight Years on the St. Louis School Board*, 159.
19. Ibid.
20. Wells, *Stepping Over the Color Line*, 86.
21. Ibid.
22. Dr. George Hyram, interview by author, St. Louis, 11 January 2001.
23. Doris Carter, interview by author, St. Louis, 13 November 2000.
24. Ibid.
25. Juanita Doggett, interview by author, St. Louis, 17 February 2000.
26. James DeClue, interview by author, St. Louis, 13 December 1999.
27. Doggett, interview.
28. Ibid.
29. Hyram, interview.
30. Sandra Wilson, interview by author, St. Louis, 11 May 2000.
31. *Brown v. Board of Education*, 349 U.S. 294, 301(1955) (*Brown II*).
32. Ibid., 299. *Brown I* involved the following school districts: Topeka, Kansas; Clarendon County, South Carolina, Prince Edward County, Virginia; and New Castle County, Delaware. In *Brown II*, all states requiring or permitting racial discrimination in public education were invited to present their views. The states of Florida, North Carolina, Arkansas, Oklahoma, Maryland, and Texas responded to the invitation, filed briefs, and participated in oral argument.
33. Ibid., 300.
34. Liddell, interview.

35. This area was declared blighted in 1953 and razed in preparation for a new housing development.

36. Dale Singer, "Mother on the March," *St. Louis Post-Dispatch*, 31 May 1998.

37. Ibid.

38. Liddell, interview.

39. Singer, "Mother on the March."

40. Craton became a named plaintiff in the St. Louis school case.

41. Craton attended Ashland Elementary School for kindergarten, and Wallbridge Elementary School for first, second, and third grades. Singer, "Mother on the March."

42. Liddell, interview.

43. Ibid.

44. Ibid.

45. Ibid.

46. Ibid.

47. As early as 1956, Morris Henderson, chapter president of the NAACP, warned that segregated housing was "a genuine stumbling block" in the implementation of school integration. *St. Louis School News*, December 1956.

48. *Liddell*, 469 F. Supp. at 1324.

49. Ibid., 1318.

50. Ibid., 1319.

51. Ibid.

52. Ibid.

53. Ibid.

54. Lorenzo J. Greene, Gary L. Kremer, and Antonio F. Holland, *Missouri's Black Heritage* (Columbia: University of Missouri Press, 1993), 214. Another source reports that 33,000 dwellings targeted for urban renewal were destroyed between 1950 and 1969. George R. LaNoue and Bruce L. R. Smith, *The Politics of School Decentralization* (Lexington, MA: Lexington Books 1973), 215.

55. *Liddell*, 469 F. Supp. at 1324

56. "Urban League Director Presents Facts on Status of Minorities in Area," *St. Louis American*, 27 November 1958, 5.

57. Ibid.

58. Greene, *Missouri's Black Heritage*, 216.

59. Ibid.

60. Wells, *Stepping Over the Color Line*, 56.

61. Ibid., 57 (citations omitted).

62. Ibid.

63. Ibid., 58.

64. "In Need of Funds: Growing Population Impedes Progress of Public Schools," *St. Louis American,* 9 September 1965.

65. Integration experts have reported that stable integration is achieved only when the percentage of black students remains less than 50 percent of the school's enrollment. Once the percentage of black students exceeds 50 percent, what was integrated enrollment becomes an all-black or virtually all-black enrollment. *Liddell*, 469 F. Supp. at 1327.

66. Wells, *Stepping Over the Color Line*, 86.

67. Ibid., 37.

68. Liddell, interview.

69. Ibid.

70. Ibid.

71. Ibid.

72. Wells, *Stepping Over the Color Line*, 90.

73. Singer, "Mother on the March."

74. Minnie Liddell, Barbara Goldsby, Samuel Yarber, Louise Moore, and Lois LeGrand brought the action on behalf of their children, who were also named in the complaint. On February 12, 1972, Minnie Liddell, as president of Concerned Parents, wrote to the NAACP advising that an action would be filed, but the NAACP did not initially join the suit. Liddell, interview.

75. *Liddell v. Caldwell*, 546 F.2d 768, 772 n.9 (8th Cir.1976) (citing Complaint).

Chapter 2

1. *Dred Scott v. Sandford*, 60 U.S. 393, 410 (1857) (quoting The Declaration of Independence).
2. E. M. Violette, "The Black Code in Missouri," *Proceeding of the Mississippi Valley Historical Association for the Year 1912–1913* (1913), 287–301.
3. Ibid., 289–90.
4. Ibid., 291.
5. Ibid., 292–93.
6. Ibid., 292.
7. Ibid., 294.
8. Ibid., 295–96.
9. Ibid., 299.
10. For an extended discussion of the criminal code for slaves in Virginia, see Philip J. Schwartz, "Forgetting the Shackles: The Development of Virginia's Criminal Code for Slaves," in *Ambivalent Legacy: A Legal History of the South*, eds. David J. Bodenhamer and James W. Ely, Jr. (Jackson: University Press of Mississippi, 1984), 125.
11. Violette, "The Black Code in Missouri," 300.
12. Ibid.
13. Ibid., 309–10.
14. Act of June 4, 1812, ch. 95, § 14, 12th Cong., 1st Sess.
15. The Mason-Dixon Line is a name popularly used to designate the line dividing the free states from the slave states during the debates in Congress over the Missouri Compromise in 1820. It generally runs along the 36°30' parallel, with the exception of Missouri.
16. E. M. Violette, *A History of Missouri* (Cape Girardeau: Ramfre Press, 1951), 105.
17. T.A. Parker, *Report of the Superintendent of the Public Schools of the State of Missouri, to the Twenty-Fifth General Assembly* (1869) 28.
18. Ibid.
19. This clause meant slavery was prohibited in Kansas and Colorado and all other states north of Missouri.
20. Donnie D. Bellamy, "Free Blacks in Antebellum Missouri, 1820–1860," *Missouri Historical Review* 67 (1973): 198–99.
21. Ibid., 198. The delegates narrowly failed to pass another clause providing that an "emancipated slave shall depart from the state; and give security that he will never thereafter return thereto." Ibid. The anti-black nature of the convention was applauded by the newspapers and corresponded with the tenor of public sentiment. One delegate stated that he had been called an "emancipator" and that this was "the worst name that can be given in the state of Missouri." Ibid.
22. Ibid.
23. The Missouri Compromise was found to be unconstitutional in *Dred Scott v. Sandford*, 60 U.S. 393 (1857). Chief Justice Roger B. Taney, writing for the majority, ruled that the Missouri Compromise of 1820, which forbade slavery in that part of the Louisiana Purchase (except Missouri), was an unconstitutional exercise of constitutional power. Justices Benjamin R. Curtis and John McLean dissented, reasoning that Congress was authorized by the Constitution to forbid slavery in the territory, and thus the Missouri Compromise was not unconstitutional. President Abraham Lincoln, reacting to the case, suggested that the Supreme Court was planning to force slavery into the North. He stated:

> We shall lie down pleasantly dreaming that the people of Missouri are on the verge of making their state free; and we shall awake to the reality,

instead, that the Supreme Court has made Illinois a slave state.

Paul M. Angle, ed., *Created Equal? The Complete Lincoln-Douglas Debates of 1858* (Chicago: University of Chicago Press, 1985), 7. For a comprehensive discussion of the Dred Scott case, *see* Eric T. Dean, Jr., *Reassessing Dred Scott: The Possibilities of Federal Power in the Antebellum Context*, 60 University of Cincinnati L. Rev. 713 (Winter 1992); and John S. Vishneski, *What the Court Decided in* Dred Scott v. Sandford, 32 Am J. Legal His. 373 (1988).

24. Parker, 25 (quoting Organic Act of 1812).
25. Claude A. Phillips, *A History of Education in Missouri* (Jefferson City, Mo.: Hugh Stevens Printing Co., 1911, revised 1912), 7. In 1869, T.A. Parker, who was then the state superintendent of schools, estimated that the federal grant of land amounted to more than 1.2 million acres. He stated: "A moderate estimate of the income which should be now available, is $546,476, an amount sufficient to pay ninety percent of the expenditures necessary to maintain the public schools." Parker, 25. Unfortunately, because of imprudent administration of the public land, much less than 90 percent of the expenditures had actually been provided for schools.
26. Ibid., 28–9.
27. Ibid., 32.
28. Ibid., 33.
29. Violette, *A History of Missouri*, 43.
30. Phillips, 8.
31. Ibid., 9.
32. Ibid..
33. Parker, 38.
34. Ibid., 9.
35. Parker, 43.
36. Parker, 45.
37. Parker, 49.

38. Selwyn K. Troen, *The Public and the Schools: Shaping the St. Louis System, 1838–1920*, (Columbia: University of Missouri Press, 1975) 11, 12.
39. Parker, 50.
40. Troen, *Shaping the St. Louis System*, 18.
41. Parker, 51.
42. Troen, *Shaping the St. Louis System*, 16.
43. Parker, 54.
44. Donnie D. Bellamy, "The Education of Blacks in Missouri Prior to 1861," *Journal of Negro Education* 59 (April 1974): 149.
45. Parker, 46–7.
46. Bellamy, "The Education of Blacks," 143, 146.
47. Ibid.
48. Ibid., 148.
49. Ibid.
50. Ibid., 149.
51. Ibid.
52. Ibid.
53. Ibid.
54. Ibid., 147.
55. Ibid., 146.
56. Violette, "The Black Code in Missouri," 305.
57. Ibid.
58. Ibid., 306.
59. Ibid., 310.
60. Ibid.
61. Lorenzo J. Greene, Gary R. Kremer, and Antonio F. Holland, *Missouri's Black Heritage*, rev. ed. (Columbia: University of Missouri Press, 1993), 42.
62. Violette, "The Black Code in Missouri," 312.
63. Ibid.
64. Bellamy, "Free Blacks," 204.
65. Ibid., 205.
66. Violette, "The Black Code in Missouri," 312.
67. Ibid., 313.
68. Ibid.

69. *Laws of the State of Missouri, Fourteenth General Assembly, First Session* (Jefferson City: James Lusk, 1847), 104.

70. Violette, "The Black Code in Missouri," 313.

71. Ibid., 312.

72. *Laws of the State of Missouri*, 104.

73. Bellamy, "The Education of Blacks," 150.

74. Ibid., 151.

75. Ibid., 152.

76. Greene, *Missouri's Black Heritage*, 68.

77. Bellamy, "The Education of Blacks," 156.

78. The paradox of collecting property taxes from free blacks while failing to provide educational access is cited as a motivating factor in the decision to operate these schools. Elinor Mondale Gersman, "The Development of Public Education for Blacks in Nineteenth Century St. Louis, Missouri," *The Journal for Negro Education* 41 (1972): 35–47. Free blacks paid taxes in St. Louis throughout the slavery period. Bellamy, "Free Blacks," 217. The wealth of the free black community in St. Louis was estimated at several million dollars. Ibid., 216. In 1850, free blacks in St. Louis paid taxes on real estate valued at approximately $3 million.

79. Bellamy, "Free Blacks," 223.

80. Ibid.

81. Ibid., 224.

82. Ibid.

83. Bruce was the first black to serve a full term in the U.S. Senate. Although Hiram Revels served in the U.S. Senate before Bruce, Revels served only a partial term.

84. The 1847 law was not a dead letter, however. In addition to the fact that schools could not operate openly, at least one school was shut down. Reverend Meachum's school was closed by officials and the teachers arrested. Lawyers were able to obtain acquittals for the teachers, and Meachum moved his school to a steamboat on the Mississippi River. Bellamy, "Free Blacks," 224.

85. Horace Mann Bond, *The Education of the Negro in the American Social Order* (New York: Octagon Books, 1966), 21.

86. Harrison Anthony Trexler, *Slavery in Missouri, 1804–1865* (Baltimore: Johns Hopkins Press, 1914), 83.

87. The cost savings were arrived at by multiplying the average number of school-age black children for each decade by the average annual dollar expenditure statewide for white schoolchildren from the entire period of 1820 to 1860. The average yearly black population for each decennial period was arrived at by simply dividing by two the populations reported by each respective census. In order to approximate the number of school-aged children for each census period, we extrapolated from data contained in the 1850 census, the only census during the relevant time period to break down the population of racial categories by age group. Among free and enslaved blacks, the proportion of the population aged five to fourteen was 30.3 percent. We used that figure throughout the period of 1820 to 1860. While this is necessarily an estimate, there is no reason to suppose that the percentage deviated greatly during this time period. The average annual expenditure per student, approximately ten dollars, was arrived at by examining the county reports in the annual reports of the Missouri Department of Education. Of course, this figure varied widely by school district. This figure was multiplied by a factor of fifteen to convert to 1998 dollars. The factor was arrived at by averaging the change in the consumer price index in 1998 dollars for the years 1825, 1835, 1845, 1855, and 1865. The

consumer price index for 1825–1865 was obtained from *Historical Statistics of the United States* (USGPO, 1975). The 1998 data is from the annual *Statistical Abstracts of the United States*.

Chapter 3

1. Walt Whitman, "O Captain! My Captain!" *Leaves of Grass* (Philadelphia: David McKay, 1891–92).
2. *Report of the State School Superintendent to the General Assembly* (1867), 240–41.
3. Ibid., 239.
4. Ibid., 185.
5. Ibid., 247.
6. Ibid., 204.
7. Ibid., 220.
8. Ibid., 242.
9. William E. Parrish, *A History of Missouri, Vol. III* (Columbia: University of Missouri Press, 1971), 1–10; E. M. Violette. *A History of Missouri* (Cape Girardeau: Ramfre Press, 1951), 322–33.
10. Parrish, *A History of Missouri*, 10–25.
11. Ibid., 30–58.
12. Ibid., 87–97.
13. Ibid., 101–17.
14. Lorenzo J. Greene, Gary R. Kremer, and Antonio F. Holland, *Missouri's Black Heritage*, rev. ed. (Columbia: University of Missouri Press, 1993), 88.
15. 12 Stat. 589 (1862); 12 Stat. 319 (1861).
16. Violette, *History of Missouri*, 393–406.
17. Parrish, *A History of Missouri*, 158–59; James Neal Primm, *Lion of the Valley: St. Louis, Missouri 1764–1980*, 3d ed. (St. Louis: Missouri Historical Society Press, 1998), 318.
18. Parrish, *A History of Missouri*, 159; Primm, *Lion of the Valley*, 318.
19. Parrish, *A History of Missouri*, 159.

20. George L. Mann, "The Development of Public Education for Negroes in St. Louis, Missouri" (Ph.D. diss., Indiana University, 1949), 107.
21. Parrish, *A History of Missouri*, 160.
22. Mann. "The Development of Public Education for Negroes in St. Louis," 107 (quoting *Eleventh Annual Report of the Board of Directors, for the Year Ending August 1, 1865*, 26).
23. Primm, *Lion of the Valley*, 318.
24. 1865 Missouri State Constitution, Art. IX, §1 (1865).
25. Ibid., § 5.
26. Ibid., § 2.
27. General Statutes of the State of Missouri (1866), Chapt. 48, sec. 20.
28. Ibid.
29. Ibid., sec. 9.
30. W. Sherman Savage, "The Legal Provisions for Negro Schools in Missouri from 1865–1890," *The Journal of Negro History* 26 (1931): 310–11; Henry S. Williams, "The Developments of the Negro Public School System in Missouri," *The Journal of Negro History* 5 (1920): 137, 142, 146.
31. Williams, "The Developments of the Negro Public School System in Missouri," 142.
32. Parrish, *A History of Missouri*, 160–61. In March 1866, of the thirty-four black schools in the state only two were located in counties in which Southern sympathizers predominated. Williams, "The Developments of the Negro Public School System in Missouri," 141.
33. J. W. Evans, "A Brief Sketch of the Development of Negro Education in St. Louis Missouri," *The Journal of Negro Education* 8 (1938): 548–51.
34. Selwyn K. Troen. *The Public and the Schools: Shaping the St. Louis System, 1838–1920* (Columbia: University of Missouri Press, 1975), 83–85.

35. Elinor Mondale Gersman, "The Development of Public Education for Blacks in Nineteenth Century St. Louis, Missouri," *The Journal for Negro Education* 41 (1972): 35–47.

36. Gersman, "The Devleopment of Public Education," 36; Parrish, *A History of Missouri,* 162.

37. Troen, *Shaping the St. Louis System*, 85.

38. Ibid.

39. Parrish, *A History of Missouri*, 163–64.

40. Troen, *Shaping the St. Louis System*, 21.

41. Ibid., 22.

42. Ibid., 24.

43. Ibid., 28–29.

44. Ibid., 30.

45. Williams, "The Developments of the Negro Public School System in Missouri," 143.

46. Parrish, *A History of Missouri,* 163.

47. *Report of the Superintendent of Public Schools* (1867), 186.

48. Ibid., 188.

49. Ibid., 205.

50. Ibid., 217.

51. Ibid., 229.

52. Ibid., 191, 194.

53. Ibid., 210.

54. Ibid., 209.

55. Ibid., 213.

56. Ibid., 220.

57. Ibid., 221.

58. Ibid., 251.

59. T. A. Parker, *Fourth Report of the Superintendent of Public Schools to the Adjourned Session of the Twenty-Fifth General Assembly* (1870), 182.

60. Ibid., 186.

61. Ibid., 226.

62. Ibid., 196.

63. Ibid., 254.

64. Ibid., 202.

65. Parrish, *A History of Missouri,* 172.

66. *Sixteenth Annual Report of the Board of Directors of the St. Louis Public Schools, for the Year Ending August 1, 1870* (1871), Table II. In 1870, a bill was introduced in the legislature proposing a voucher plan under which each child would receive ten dollars from the school tax that could be applied to any school that the state approved. Rural legislators from the largely Protestant area outside St. Louis joined with those city representatives sympathetic to the state board of education to defeat the legislation. Troen, *Shaping the St. Louis System,* 44–45.

67. *Sixteenth Annual Report of the Board of Directors of the St. Louis Public Schools, for the Year Ending August 1, 1870* (1871), Table II.

68. Ibid, Table VI.

69. Parrish, *A History of Missouri*, 163.

70. Ibid.

71. Missouri Laws sec. 86 (1869); Missouri Laws sec. 164 (1874).

72. Parrish, *A History of Missouri,* 165.

73. Mo. Rev. Stat. § 7054 (1875).

74. Williams, "The Developments of the Negro Public School System in Missouri," 145; Parrish, *A History of Missouri*, 165.

75. Parrish, *A History of Missouri,* 165.

76. Williams, "The Developments of the Negro Public School System in Missouri," 147. Parrish, *A History of Missouri*, 165. As late as 1876, the state superintendent of education complained that, in many cases through ignorance of the law and in other cases through willful disobedience of the law, schools for blacks had not been established. Williams, "The Developments of the Negro Public School System in Missouri," 142.

77. Williams, "The Developments of the Negro Public School System in Missouri," 152; Parrish, *A History of Missouri*, 166.

78. Parrish, *A History of Missouri,* 159.

79. Troen, *Shaping the St. Louis System*, 89–92.
80. Gersman, "The Development of Public Education," 40.
81. Williams, "The Developments of the Negro Public School System in Missouri," 152.
82. Ibid.
83. Greene, *Missouri's Black Heritage*, 100; Parrish, *A History of Missouri*, 166.
84. T. A. Parker, *Fourth Report of the Superintendent of Public Schools* (1870), 36.
85. Ibid.
86. Williams, "The Developments of the Negro Public School System in Missouri," 151.
87. Gersman, "The Development of Public Education," 37; Mann, "The Development of Public Education for Negroes in St. Louis," 147.
88. *History of Sumner* available at http://www.umsl.edu/~s805376/History_of_Sumner.htm.
89. Mann, "The Development of Public Education for Negroes in St. Louis," 148.
90. Troen, *Shaping the St. Louis System*, 87.
91. William E. Parrish, *Missouri Under Radical Rule* (Columbia: University of Missouri Press, 1965), 268–326; Parrish, *A History of Missouri*, 174–75; Williams, "The Developments of the Negro Public School System in Missouri," 155–56.
92. Williams, "The Developments of the Negro Public School System in Missouri," 156–57.
93. Mo Const., Art IX, § 3 (1875).

Chapter 4

1. Selwyn K. Troen, *The Public and the Schools: Shaping the St. Louis System, 1838–1920* (Columbia: University of Missouri Press, 1975), 79.
2. Gerald W. Heaney, "Busing, Timetables, Goals, and Ratios: Touchstones of Equal Opportunity," *Minnesota Law Review* 69 (1985): 735, 745.
3. Edward Franklin Frazier, *The Negro in the United States* (New York: MacMillan, 1957), 426–27.
4. Horace Mann Bond, *The Education of the Negro in the American Social Order* (New York: Octagon Books, 1966), 92–115; *see also* Frazier, *The Negro in the United States*, 426. ("The demagogic leaders of the poor whites attributed their inadequate schools to the fact that money had been wasted in the education of the Negro.")
5. 83 U.S. (16 Wall.) 36 (1872).
6. Ibid., 74. Justice Field, joined by Chief Justice Chase and Justices Swayne and Bradley, dissented. Ibid., 83. Justice Bradley and Justice Swayne also wrote long and vigorous separate dissents.
7. 92 U.S. 542 (1875).
8. Ibid., 548; see Civil Rights Act of 1870, ch. 114, Sec. 6, 16 Stat. 140–41 (codified as amended at 18 U.S.C. Sec. 241 [1982]); *United States v. Williams*, 341 U.S. 70, 72–82 (1951) (tracing history and discussing scope of 18 U.S.C. Sec. 241).
9. *See* Cruickshank, 92 U.S. at 554–55. The Court also concluded that all sixteen counts "lack[ed] the certainty and precision required by the established rules of criminal procedure." Ibid., 559.
10. Rev. St. Sec. 5519 (1878), reprinted in 3 U.S.Comp. St. § 5519 (1901) (repealed 1909).
11. 106 U.S. 629, 635–44 (1882); *see* Heaney, *Touchstones of Equal Opportunity*, 745–48.
12. 109 U.S. 3 (1883).
13. Ibid., 8–11. The Court also held that the enforcement powers of Section 5 of the Fourteenth Amendment reached no further than the state action limits of Section 1. Ibid., 19.
14. Ibid., 20.
15. Ibid., 24–25.

16. Ibid., 25–26.

17. Ibid., 34, 36, 43, 62.

18. 19 S.W. 1109 (1892); *see also* 35 Central L.J. 269 (1892) (containing annotation discussing similar cases).

19. Younger, 19 S.W. at 1110.

20. Ibid., 1111.

21. 163 U.S. 537 (1896).

22. Ibid., 538.

23. Ibid., 551.

24. Ibid.

25. Ibid., 559.

26. Ibid., 560. Eighty-five years later, the Supreme Court in *Jones v. Mayer*, 392 U.S. 409 (1968), upholding the constitutionality of an Act of Congress providing all citizens with the right to inherit, purchase, sell, hold, or convey property noted:

   Whatever the present validity of the position taken by the majority [in *The Civil Rights Cases*]—a question rendered largely academic by Title II of the Civil Rights Act of 1964—we note that the entire Court agreed upon at least one proposition: The Thirteenth Amendment authorizes Congress . . . to eradicate the last vestiges and incidents of a society half slave and half free, by securing to all citizens, of every race and color, " the same right to make and enforce contracts, to sue, be parties, give evidence, and to inherit, purchase, lease, sell and convey property, as is enjoyed by white citizens."

Ibid., 443, n.78 (citations omitted). Justice Douglas concurred. Quoting from Frederick Douglass, he wrote:

   Of all the races and varieties of men which have suffered from this feeling, the colored people of [this] country have endured most. . . . They are Negroes–and that is enough, in the eye of this unreasoning prejudice, to justify indignity and violence. In nearly every department of American life they are confronted by this insidious influence. It fills the air. It meets them at the workshop and factory, when they apply for work. It meets them at the church, at the hotel, at the ballot-box, and worst of all, it meets them in the jurybox. . . .

Ibid., 446–47. We note that a grandson of the first Justice Harlan, Justice John Marshall Harlan, II, departed from the position of his grandfather and wrote a dissenting opinion, saying that in his view the Court erred in holding that a seller's racially motivated refusal to sell blacks a home entitled them to judicial relief on statutory and constitutional grounds. Ibid., 449.

27. 175 U.S. 528 (1899).

28. Ibid., 532. Justice Harlan assumed as valid the state court finding that the termination was not rooted in racial animus and concluded that because the establishment of high schools is purely discretionary and because the plaintiffs had elected the wrong remedy in requesting an injunction to close the white schools, the funding disparity was not a violation. Ibid., 544–45.

29. Ibid, 531.

30. Ibid., 545.

31. 211 U.S. 45 (1908).

32. Justices Harlan and Day dissented.

33. 211 U.S. at 53–55.

34. Ibid., 67.

35. Professors Reams and Wilson discuss the school segregation laws and selective other segregation laws in thirty-seven states,

including all of the present Eighth Circuit states except North and South Dakota. Bernard D. Reams, Jr., and Paul E. Wilson, *Segregation and the Fourteenth Amendment in the States: A Survey of State Segregation Laws, 1865–1953* (Buffalo: W.S. Hein, 1975).

36. Ibid., 9, 27, 41–42, 78–71, 90, 115, 186, 202, 262, 295–99, 335, 351, 493, 564–66, 604, 630–31, 690, 703. The eighteen states were: Alabama, Arkansas, California, Delaware, Florida, Georgia, Indiana, Kansas, Kentucky, Maryland, Michigan, Mississippi, North Carolina, South Carolina, Tennessee, Texas, Virginia, and West Virginia.

37. Bureau of Education, Department of Interior, "Negro Education: A Study of the Private and Higher Schools for Colored People in the United States" (Bulletin Nos. 38–39, 1916 [2 vols.]) Hereinafter cited as 1916 Bureau of Educ. Study.

38. Ibid., Vol. 1, 24.

39. Ibid., Vol. 1, 1–7; Vol. 2, 9–11, 24. Others have documented how separate education was indeed unequal. In 1939–1940, the former slave states spent $58.69 on schooling for each white child but only $18.82 for each black child. Frazier, *The Negro in the United States*, 437. Black school facilities were worth, on average, one-fourth the value of white facilities. Henry Allen Bullock, *A History of Negro Education in the South* (Cambridge: Harvard University Press, 1967), 182. In 1929, teachers in black schools earned about two-thirds as much as teachers in white schools; by 1950, the proportion had risen to 85 percent. Ibid., 181. In 1939–1940, the average school term for blacks was 156 days; for whites it was 173.5 days. Frazier, *The Negro in the United States*, 447. In 1930, 16.3 percent of blacks aged 10 and above were

illiterate, whereas only 1.8 percent of native-born whites were illiterate. Bureau of the Census, *15th Census of the United States: 1930 Population,* 1219 and table 1 (1933).

40. 250 S.W.2d 137 (Mo. 1952).

41. Ibid., 138.

42. Ibid., 139–40.

43. Ibid., 141.

44. Ibid.

45. 360 Mo. 671, 230 S.W.2d 724 (1950).

46. Ibid., 680, 230 S.W.2d at 730. In *Bluford v. Canada,* 32 F. Supp. 707 (W.D. Mo. 1940), *appeal dismissed,* 119 F.2d 779 (8th Cir. 1941), state officials refused to admit a black female applicant to Missouri's journalism school graduate program. Although the state had not provided comparable programs for black students, the court held that it would sustain the state's motion to dismiss unless the petitioner amended her petition to allege that she had requested a graduate journalism program at the state's black university and that the black university had had time to develop such a program. 32 F. Supp. at 710–11. Although the state court followed the Supreme Court's analysis set out in *Missouri ex rel. Gaines v. Canada,* 305 U.S. 337, 346–51 (1938), the practical result would have been no black journalism school at all or a one-woman black program.

47. In St. Louis for example, voters passed a referendum in 1916 requiring city blocks to remain segregated. Roland G. Usher, "Negro Segregation in St. Louis," *New Republic* 6 (March 18, 1916): 176–77. The Missouri General Assembly also enacted laws requiring segregation. *See* Mo. Rev. Stat. Sects. 3361, 4651 (1939) (miscegenation a penal offense); Mo. Rev. Stat. Sec. 9390 (1939) (segregation in colony for feebleminded); Mo. Rev. Stat. Sec. 10474 (1939) (local authorities may

segregate races at playgrounds, libraries, and public parks); Mo. Rev. Stat. Sec. 10632 (1939) (segregated teachers' institute); Mo Rev. Stat. Sec. 9477 (1929) (same).

48. *See Frank v. Herring*, 240 Mo. App. 425, 434, 208 S.W.2d 783, 788 (1948).

49. Troen, *Shaping the St. Louis System*, 82.

50. Richard S. Kirkendall, *A History of Missouri, Vol. 5* (Columbia: University of Missouri Press, 1986), 158.

51. Henry Sullivan Williams, "The Development of the Negro Public School System in Missouri," (Ph.D. diss., University of Chicago, 1917), 29.

52. Elinor Mondale Gersman, "The Development of Public Education for Blacks in Nineteenth Century St. Louis, Missouri," *The Journal for Negro Education* 41 (1972): 38.

53. Troen, *Shaping the St. Louis System*, 94.

54. Ibid., 95.

55. Ibid., 96. "Historians . . . have written that, during Reconstruction, freedmen in the South were possessed by an almost mystical enthusiasm and faith in the value and power of schooling. . . . Blacks had well-developed ideas about the kind of instruction they wanted, and only when basic conditions were met did they commit their children to the schools." Ibid.

56. Ibid., 122.

57. Ibid., 126.

58. Ibid., 121. One scholar noted: [T]he patterns of school attendance and employment that emerge from the St. Louis census and school records in 1880, when placed together with data from early twentieth-century studies conducted by the system and outside sources, suggest a broad continuum of practice and attitudes. Only during the 1910s was significant progress made in retaining teenagers, due to the popularization of the high school,

the introduction of vocational and commercial courses, and effective compulsory attendance laws. Ibid., 130–31. What was true in the 1880s remains largely true today. The drop-out rate for poor, male children of high school age, most of whom are black, remains unacceptably high. Now, as then, these students drop out because they need to provide for themselves or their families, or because they have lost hope for their future.

59. Ibid., 157.

60. Lorenzo J. Greene, Gary R. Kremer, and Antonio F. Holland, *Missouri's Black Heritage*, rev. ed. (Columbia: University of Missouri Press, 1993), 107.

61. *See Lehew v. Brummell*, 15 S.W. 765 (Mo. 1891).

62. W. Sherman Savage, "The Legal Provisions for Negro Schools in Missouri From 1865–1890," *The Journal of Negro History* 26 (July 1931): 319.

63. *Lehew v. Brummell*, 15 S.W. 765 (Mo. 1891).

64. Savage, "The Legal Provisions for Negro Schools in Missouri," 318, 319.

65. Ibid., 319.

66. Williams, "The Development of the Negro Public School System in Missouri," 35–36.

67. Ibid.

68. Kirkendall, *A History of Missouri*, 99.

69. In 1889, the shortage of black teachers was aided by the establishment of a normal department at Sumner High School (the program later would become Stowe Teachers' College). By 1923, nearly one-quarter of all of the teachers in Missouri (white and black) had not had four years of high school. Kirkendall, *A History of Missouri*, 102.

70. Greene, *Missouri's Black Heritage*, 146–47.

71. Robert Irving Brigham, "The Education of the Negro in Missouri" (Ph.D. diss.,

University of Missouri, 1946), 131;
Kirkendall, *A History of Missouri*, 106.

72. Ibid.

73. Kirkendall, *A History of Missouri*, 106.

74. Greene, *Missouri's Black Heritage*, 147.

75. Ibid.

76. Brigham, "The Education of the Negro in Missouri," 130.

77. Ibid., 135.

78. Kirkendall, *A History of Missouri*, 102.

79. Ibid., 106.

80. Ibid.

81. Brigham, "The Education of the Negro in Missouri," 142.

82. Missouri Advisory Committee, *Report to the United States Commission on Civil Rights on Desegregation of Schools in Missouri* (July, 1959), 19.

83. Ibid., 18.

84. Kirkendall, *A History of Missouri*, 110.

85. Ibid.

86. Brigham, "The Education of the Negro in Missouri," 140.

87. Kirkendall, *A History of Missouri*, 147.

88. Ibid.,155.

89. Ibid., 156.

90. Dr. George Hyram, interview by author, St. Louis, 11 January 2001.

91. Chas A. Lee, *Eighty-First Report of the Public Schools of the State of Missouri, School Year Ending June 30, 1930* (1930); *Report of the Superintendent of Public Schools of the State of Missouri* (1945).

92. Ibid.

93. Kirkendall, *A History of Missouri*, 189.

94. Ibid.

95. *Report of the United States Commission on Civil Rights on Desegregation of Schools in Missouri*, 23.

96. Missouri Constitution, art. 9, sec. 1(a). This section was amended on August 3, 1976, to delete the provisions with respect to the maintenance of separate schools for black

and white children.

97. Minnie Liddell, interview by author, St. Louis, 15 June 1999.

98. Hubert Wheeler, *One Hundred and First Report of the Public Schools of the State of Missouri, School Year Ending June 30, 1950* (1950), 201.

99. Ibid.

100. Kirkendall, *A History of Missouri*, 185.

101. Ibid.

102. Ibid.

103. This was a well-founded fear. Before the separation, the legislature had the authority to alter the functions and power of St. Louis city government and had exercised that power in almost every legislative session, usually in response to an interest group request. James Neal Primm, *Lion of the Valley*, 3d ed. (St. Louis: Missouri Historical Society Press, 1998), 298.

104. John Kincaid, *Regulatory Regionalism in Metropolitan Areas: Voter Resistance and Reform Persistence*, 13 Pace Law Review 499 (1993). In 1867, the legislature transferred the power to assess and collect city taxes to the county court. St. Louis Mayor James Thomas complained that the state had not only deprived the city of the right to tax, but also "it had authorized a foreign body to do so for us as if we were infants." Primm, *Lion of the Valley*, 299.

105. Kincaid, *Regulatory Regionalism*, 457.

106. William Barnaby Faherty, *St. Louis—A Concise History* (St. Louis: St. Louis Convention and Visitor Commission, 1991), 65.

107. Primm, *Lion of the Valley*, 308–9.

108. Ibid., 307.

109. Kincaid, *Regulatory Regionalism*, 457.

110. Amy Stuart Wells and Robert L. Crain, *Stepping Over the Color Line* (New Haven: Yale University Press, 1997), 35.

111. Ibid.

112. Troen, *Shaping the St. Louis System*, 81. After the Civil War, the vast majority of black Americans were concentrated in Southern states, largely in cotton- and tobacco-growing states, and were involved in agriculture, usually as sharecroppers. By 1970, however, only 53 percent of blacks still lived in the South, and in 1981, just 1 percent of American blacks still worked in farming. St. Louis, because of its duality as both a Southern and Northern city, was in the middle of the Great Migration. Wells, *Stepping Over the Color Line*, 29.

113. Wells, *Stepping Over the Color Line*, 31–36.

114. Primm, *Lion of the Valley*, 416.

115. Wells, *Stepping Over the Color Line*, 30.

116. Ibid., 37–38.

117. 245 U.S. 60 (1917).

118. Ibid., 80–81.

119. Douglas S. Massey and Nancy A. Denton, *American Apartheid: Segregation and the Making of the Underclass* (Cambridge: Harvard University Press, 1993), 35–36.

120. Ibid., 38.

121. Ibid., 35, 42.

122. Wells, *Stepping Over the Color Line*, 36.

123. Ibid., 46.

124. Massey, *American Apartheid*, 42–57.

125. *Kraemer v. Shelley*, 355 Mo. 814, 198 S.W.2d 679 (1946).

126. Ibid., 683.

127. Ibid., 823–24 (citations omitted).

128. *Shelley v. Kraemer*, 334 U.S. 1, 22 (1948).

Chapter 5

1. *Brown v. Board of Education*, 347 U.S. 483, 495 (1954), 493 *(Brown I)*.

2. Ibid., 493.

3. Ibid., 495.

4. *Brown v. Board of Education*, 349 U.S. 294, 301 (1955) *(Brown II)*.

5. Ibid., 300.

6. "Protest Committee Urges Quick Elimination of School Jim Crow," *St. Louis American*, 29 July 1954, 1, 16.

7. "Plan for Integration," *St. Louis Post-Dispatch*, 24 June 1954, 2C.

8. Ibid.

9. Howard B. Woods, "Integration Now!" *St. Louis Argus*, 18 June 1954, 14.

10. A. B. Mizell, Letters From the People, "Integration: How Soon?" *St. Louis Post-Dispatch*, 28 June 1954, 2C.

11. Henry Winfield Wheeler, Letters From the People, "Integration: How Soon?" *St. Louis Post-Dispatch*, 28 June 1954.

12. *Liddell*, 469 F. Supp. at 1316.

13. "Attorney General Rules That Schools Can Integrate Now," *St. Louis American*, 8 July 1954, 1.

14. *Liddell*, 469 F. Supp. at 1313.

15. "Race Designation Removed from Missouri School Law," *St. Louis American*, 23 May 1957.

16. Ibid.

17. Mo. Rev. Stat. Secs. 213, 296, 314.

18. Mo. Const. art. IX, § 1(a).

19. Otis N. Thompson, "Report Shows Teachers Fully Qualified as to College Semester Hours," *St. Louis Argus*, 17 September 1954, 1.

20. Amy Stuart Wells and Robert L. Crain, *Stepping Over the Color Line* (New Haven: Yale University Press, 1997), 86.

21. Thompson, "Report Shows Teachers Fully Qualified as to College Semester Hours."

22. "Tide of Integration," *St. Louis Argus*, 1 October 1954.

23. "Integration Success Rests Heavily on Teachers, Asserts Supt. Hickey," *St. Louis American*, 9 September 1954, 13.

24. "Harris College Moves Ahead Under Program," *St. Louis Argus*, 15 October 1954, 1.

25. Ibid.

26. *St. Louis School News*, December 1956.

27. Ibid.

28. Ibid.

29. Ibid.

30. Ibid.

31. Jewell Smith, "Open Letter to the Children of Dixie," *St. Louis American,* 12 September 1957, 5.

32. Civic Progress Earns St. Louis National Award," *St. Louis American,* 3 January 1957.

33. Wells, *Stepping Over the Color Line*, 85–6.

34. Ibid., 81.

35. "Commitee of 3 to Study School Racial Problems," *St. Louis American*, 9 November 1961.

36. Ibid.

37. Sandra Wilson, interview by author, 11 May 2000.

38. Juanita Doggett, interview by author, 17 February 2000.

39. Craton Liddell attended Ashland Elementary School for kindergarten, and Walbridge Elementary School for first, second, and third grades. Dale Singer, "Mother on the March," *St. Louis Post-Dispatch,* 31 May 1998.

40. "School Integration Here Worse Than Seven Years Ago: Housing Bias, Distribution of Teachers Are Blamed," *St. Louis American,* 6 December 1962, 1.

41. U.S. Commission on Civil Rights, *Civil Rights U.S.A.: Public Schools Cities in the North and West* (New York: Greenwood Press, 1962), 268–69.

42. Ibid., 277.

43. Ibid. Many black leaders and parents continued to support neighborhood schools, as opposed to the interdistrict transportation of black students, well into the 1990s. Although many black parents strongly supported the interdistrict transfer program developed in the *Liddell* litigation, as evidenced by the fact that more than eleven thousand black students each year opted to participate in the program, the division in the black community may well have been a factor that contributed to the support for the ultimate settlement of the St. Louis desegregation case.

44. Ibid., 278, n.63.

45. Ibid., 297. These observations materialized in 1984 when the comprehensive program to desegregate the schools was approved by the federal district court. *See* Chapter 6 *infra.*

46. "Teachers Fear Loss of Jobs at Harris College: School Locations May Create More Segregation Here," *St. Louis American*, 8 November 1962, 1.

47. Ibid.

48. Ibid., 12.

49. Ibid.

50. Ibid.

51. Daniel L. Schlafly, *Twenty-Eight Years on the St. Louis School Board: 1953–1981* (St. Louis, 1995), 67.

52. Ibid., 68.

53. "Conditions Are Getting Worse: Investigation in Charges of School Resegregation," *St. Louis American*, 21 March 1963, 2B.

54. Ibid.

55. Schlafly, *Twenty-Eight Years on the St. Louis School Board*, 68.

56. "Supt. Philip Hickey to Answer Charges of Resegregation: Full Scale Inquiry to Follow," *St. Louis American*, 4 April 1963, 1."

57. Schlafly, *Twenty-Eight Years on the St. Louis School Board*, 69.

58. "Vashon, Harris Proposals Heard by School Board Members and Special Committee: 'Resegregation' Charges Unanswered," *St. Louis American*, 11 April 1993; *Civil Rights U.S.A.*, 298.

59. "Vashon, Harris Proposals," 9.

60. "Parents Urge Students to Boycott Public School Buses," *St. Louis American*, 13 June 1963.

61. Ibid.

62. Ibid.

63. Ibid., 12.

64. Wells, *Stepping Over the Color Line*, 128.

65. "Public School Integration Plan Given to Hickey for 'Study,'" *St. Louis American*, 27 June 1963, 5.

66. "Schlafly Appoints Committee to Draft Integration Plan," *St. Louis American,* 4 July 1963, 7.

67. "School Board Adopts Hickey Report; May Face Law Suit," *St. Louis American,* 1 August 1963, 1.

68. *Civil Rights U.S.A.*, 273.

69. "School Board Adopts Hickey Report," 12.

70. Ibid.

71. Ibid.

72. Ibid.

73. Ibid.

74. "School Board Seeks Supreme Court Junction [sic] to Protect Bus and Neighborhood Jim Crow Policies," *St. Louis American*, 15 August 1963, 8.

75. Ibid.

76. *See* "Dr. Kottmeyer Picked Up Fumble and Ran Out-of-Bounds," *St. Louis American*, 29 August 1963, 8.

77. Ibid., 12.

78. *See Davis v. Board of Education*, 216 F. Supp. 295 (E.D. Mo. 1963).

79. Ibid., 300.

80. Wells, *Stepping Over the Color Line*, 87. Portable classroom units were also used to relieve overcrowding, particularly in 14 all-black or predominantly black districts. *Civil Rights U.S.A.*, 274.

81. Wells, *Stepping Over the Color Line*, 87.

82. "Parents Organize, Want Total Equality in Education Here," *St. Louis American*, 15 July 1965, 7.

83. Ibid.

84. W. K. Wyant, "Study Praises City Schools' Desegregation," *St. Louis Post-Dispatch*, 15 September 1966.

85. Ibid.

86. Ibid.

87. Ibid.

88. Ibid.

89. Ibid.

90. Wells, *Stepping Over the Color Line*, 88.

91. Minnie Liddell, Barbara Goldsby, Samuel Yarber, Louise Moore, and Lois LeGrand brought the action on behalf of their children, who were also named in the complaint. On February 12, 1972, Minnie Liddell, as president of Concerned Parents, wrote to the NAACP advising that an action would be filed, but the NAACP did not initially join the suit. Minnie Liddell, interview by author, St. Louis, 15 June 1999.

92. Ibid.

93. Ibid.

Chapter 6

1. The attorneys were subsequently awarded their fees by the court for their services in the matter.

2. Minnie Liddell, interview by author, St. Louis, Mo., 15 June 1999.

3. See the following cases for a discussion of the use of restrictive covenants to enforce racial segregation in Missouri: *Dolan v. Richardson*, 181 S.W.2d 997 (St. L. App. 1944); *Shelley v. Kraemer*, 355 Mo. 814, 198 S.W.2d 679 (Mo. en banc 1946), *rev'd* 334 U.S. 1 (1947); *Jones v. Alfred H. Mayer Co.*, 255 F. Supp. 115 (E.D. Mo. 1966), *aff'd* 379 F.2d 33 (8th Cir. 1967), *rev'd* 392 U.S. 409 (1968).

4. *Liddell*, 469 F. Supp. at 1387–90.

5. *Liddell*, 469 F. Supp. at 1390.

6. Liddell, interview.

7. The court required the plaintiffs to publish a notice in the *St. Louis Daily Record* setting forth the text of the consent judgment and decree and giving notice to all the prospective members of the class and other interested parties that anyone objecting to the court's approval of the consent decree file with the court a statement of their objections in writing.

8. *Liddell*, 469 F. Supp. at 310.

9. James DeClue, interview by author, St. Louis, Mo., 13 December 13, 1999.

10. Liddell, interview.

11. Ibid.

12. On May 23, 1976, Chief Judge Meredith entered an order requiring the City Board to pay attorneys' fees in the sum of $62,675 to Russell and to reimburse him for the money paid to Dr. Field.

13. D.C. Order, *Liddell v. Board of Educ.*, No. 72C 100 (E.D. Mo., Jan. 23, 1976).

14. *Liddell v. Caldwell*, 546 F.2d 768, 769–70 (8th Cir. 1976).

15. Ibid., 774.

16. Judge Lay wrote: "The Supreme Court decision in *Milliken v. Bradley*, 418 U.S. 717 (1974), seemingly deters the merger of two school districts unless racially discriminatory acts of one or more school districts caused racial segregation in an adjacent district, or unless district lines have been deliberately drawn on the basis of race. However, investigation into the voluntary cooperation of the county in accepting minority transfers should not be overlooked." Ibid. (citations omitted).

17. Ibid.

18. *Liddell v. United States*, 430 U.S. 906 (1977).

19. The Concerned Parents for Neighborhood Schools was a group of white South St. Louis parents who intervened in the action on behalf of their school-aged children and themselves. Their goal was to maintain the largely segregated white schools in South St. Louis. The principal plaintiffs were Jerrianne Adams, Catherine M. Neel, and Horace Edington. [hereinafter "Adams plaintiffs"].

20. In its motion to intervene, the United States gave as its reasons for wanting to intervene: "paramount governmental interest in school desegregation and the public interest in obtaining compliance with the 14th Amendment." D.C. Order H187182 (1982).

21. *Liddell v. Board of Educ.*, 469 F. Supp. 1304 (1979).

22. The court's observation obviously had merit. There were, however, practical reasons why the district court ultimately made the decision not to include housing discrimination as an issue in the school desegregation case. First, it would have meant that the United States would have become a defendant, at least on the housing issue, which may have affected its position as a supporter of the efforts to desegregate the St. Louis schools. Second, it would have brought the city into the case as a defendant on the housing aspects of the case. Third, including housing discrimination as an issue would have unduly complicated the litigation and made settlement efforts more difficult than they already were. There can be no doubt, however, that massive efforts must be made by national, state, and city authorities to improve housing in North and Central St. Louis and to develop integrated neighborhoods and housing projects.

23. Ibid., 1364.

24. Ibid., 1365.

25. Ibid.

26. *Adams v. United States*, 620 F.2d 1277 (8th Cir.), *cert. denied*, 449 U.S. 826 (1980). The City Board decided not to petition the Supreme Court for certiorari, and it drafted a plan to desegregate the city schools within the sixty-day time limit set by the court. On May 13, 1980, the Adams plaintiffs, representing the Concerned Parents for Neighborhood Schools, filed a petition for certiorari with the United States Supreme Court. The petition was denied on October 6, 1980.

27. Ibid., 1287.

28. Ibid., 1287–88.

29. Ibid., 1291.

30. Ibid., 1294.

31. Sally Bixby Defty, "County Districts' Pupil-Swap Role Urged," *St. Louis Post-Dispatch*, 4 May 1980.

32. *Adams*, 620 F.2d at 1295.

33. Ibid., 1294, n.27.

34. In early March 1980 in an effort to obtain funds for the desegregation efforts, the superintendent of schools for St. Louis, Robert E. Wentz, met with the state education commissioner. After the meeting, Wentz stated he thought that the commissioner would provide whatever resources were available to him. T. Flach and R. Stoff, "Wentz Makes Pitch for Integration Aid," *St. Louis Globe-Democrat*, 6 March 1980.

35. Katy Gurley and Charles E. Burgess, "County School Officials Want No Part of Busing Plan," *St. Louis Globe-Democrat*, 4 March 1980.

36. Ibid.

37. G. Schneider, "Desegregation Shock Waves Ripple Through City," *South Side Journal*, 12 March 1980.

38. Bill Smith and Tim Poor, "Integration Order May Bring City-County Busing," *St. Louis Globe-Democrat*, 4 March 1980.

The record indicates that white students had been leaving the school system for several years. For example, for the school years 1971–72 through 1978–79, the enrollment of white students declined from 35,000 to 18,000. *Liddell*, 469 F. Supp. at 1323. There is no evidence that the rate of withdrawal increased after the Eighth Circuit entered its order. Rather, the evidence is that the white population stabilized at approximately 16 percent of the student body.

39. "Catholic Schools Reject City Transfer Requests," *St. Louis Post-Dispatch*, 5 March 1980.

40. George Henry, interview by author, 10 January 2001.

41. M. Shirk, "Integration Starts Smoothly," *St. Louis Post-Dispatch*, 3 September 1980.

42. M. Lerner and L. Lockhart, "Board Approves Desegregation Plan," *St. Louis Post-Dispatch*, 29 April 1980.

43. L. Lockhart and M. Lerner, "School Plan Outlined, Not Everybody Is Happy," *St. Louis Post-Dispatch*, 29 April 1980.

44. Ibid.

45. Ibid.

46. *Liddell v. Board of Educ.*, 491 F. Supp. 351, 359–60 (E.D. Mo. 1980) (quoting *United States v. Missouri*, 363 F. Supp. 739, 748 (E.D. Mo. 1973)), *aff'd in relevant part*, 515 F.2d 1365 (8th Cir. 1975), *cert. denied*, 423 U.S. 951 (1975)).

47. *Liddell v. Board of Educ.*, 667 F.2d 643, 648 (8th Cir.), *cert. denied*, 454 U.S. 1081, and *cert. denied*, 454 U.S. 1091 (1981) (*Liddell II*).

48. This book does not discuss the separate vocational educational programs referred to in this section.

49. *Liddell*, 491 F. Supp. at 353–54.

50. One parent called the deputy school superintendent and demanded to know

"[w]hat in the world were ministers doing riding the school buses. What had happened to separation of church and state? How did the school district know that the ministers were not taking advantage of a truly captive audience to deliver sermons?" Sally Bixby Defty, "Rolling Right Along," *St. Louis Post-Dispatch*, 10 September 1980.

51. Edward T. Foote, Chairman, Desegregation Monitoring & Advisory Committee, *Report No. 3* (October 23, 1980), 5.

52. Ibid., 8–10.

53. Ibid., 11–12.

54. Ibid., 13–16.

55. James E. Adams, "High Absenteeism Is Reported In Many of City's 118 Public Schools," *St. Louis Post-Dispatch*, 4 September 1980.

56. Maura Lerner, "2nd-day Attendance Up In City Schools," *St. Louis Post-Dispatch*, 5 September 1980.

57. Despite the opposition of white parents to the City Board's integration plan, enrollment in private and parochial schools remained steady with forty elementary and eight Catholic high schools in St. Louis enrolling 17,113 students at the beginning of the 1980–81 school year, 12 Missouri Synod Lutheran schools with an enrollment of 2,300 students, the Tower Grove Christian School enrolling 610 students, and Gateway Christian schools enrolling 800 students. James E. Adams, "Little Rise In Rolls of Non-Public Schools," *St. Louis Post-Dispatch*, 7 September 1980.

58. L. Eardley, "Start of Integration Is Called Successful Despite Some Flaws," *St. Louis Post-Dispatch*, 21 September 1980.

59. Edward T. Foote, Chairman, Desegregation Monitoring & Advisory Committee, *Report No. 1* (August 29, 1980), 7.

60. Edward T. Foote, Chairman, Desegregation Monitoring & Advisory Committee, *Report No. 4* (November 19, 1980), 17.

61. Juanita Doggett, interview by author, St. Louis, Mo. 17 February 2000.

62. Georgia Nicolaison, interview by author, St. Louis, Mo., 11 September 2000.

63. Edward T. Foote, Chairman, Desegregation Monitoring & Advisory Committee, Report No. 2 (September 19, 1980), 20.

64. George E. Curry, "Cleveland High School Ends Day On Peaceful Note," *St. Louis Post-Dispatch*, 6 September 1980.

65. Nicolaison, interview.

66. In the fall of 1999, Cleveland NJROTC enrolled 1,050 students, 59 percent of whom were white and the remainder of whom were black. "Gateway Guide to Missouri Schools," *St. Louis Post-Dispatch*, 13 March 2000.

67. In *Swann*, the United States Supreme Court stated, "The importance of bus transportation as a normal and accepted tool of educational policy is readily discernable. . . . Desegregation plans can't be limited to walk-in schools." *Swann v. Charlotte-Mecklenburg Board of Educ.*, 401 U.S. 1, 29–30 (1971).

68. Veronica L. Banks, "Parents Vow Resistance To Plan," *St. Louis Argus*, 4 September 1980.

69. "Founder of Anti-busing Group Ends Protests–At Least Temporarily," *St. Louis Globe-Democrat*, 4 September 1980.

70. See *Liddell v. Board of Educ.*, 508 F. Supp. 101 (E.D. Mo. 1980).

71. Ibid., 105.

72. Ibid.

73. *Liddell v. Board of Educ.*, 667 F.2d 643 (8th Cir. 1981), *cert. denied*, 454 U.S. 1081 (1981).

74. Ibid., 648.

75. Ibid., 651.

76. Ibid., 654.

77. D.C. Order, *Liddell v. Board of Educ.*, No.

72 100C (E.D. Mo. Dec. 30, 1982).

78. Ibid.

79. Statement of U.S. Position, *Liddell v. Board of Educ.*, No. 72 100C (E.D. Mo. Jan. 10, 1983).

80. G. Schneider, "Court Makes It Clear: Area-Wide Busing Coming," *South Side Journal,* 18 February 1981.

81. Sue Littel, "Anti-busing Petition Presented to U.S. State Legislators," *South County Journal,* 18 February 1981, 3.

82. Sue Littel, "NANS Presents Anti-Busing Petitions To Legislators," *South Side Journal,* 18 February 1981, 3.

83. Ibid.

84. Ibid.

85. Nancy Solomon, "NANS Reacts to Desegregation Decision," *South Side Journal,* 18 February 1981.

86. Charles E. Burgess, "School Case Is Step Closer to U.S. Top Court," *St. Louis Globe-Democrat,* 20 February 1981.

87. *Caldwell v. Missouri*, 454 U.S. 1081 (1981).

88. W. Freivogel, "Court Won't Delay School Plan," *St. Louis Post-Dispatch*, 20 April 1981.

89. Editorial, "No More Room For Delay," *St. Louis Post-Dispatch*, 20 April 1981.

Chapter 7

1. *Liddell v. Board of Education,* 567 F.Supp 1037, 1054 (E.D. Mo. 1983) (quoting Congressman Emanuel Celler).

2. The Honorable William L. Hungate, interview by author, St. Louis.

3. E. H. Kohn, "Consider Giving Up Case, Hungate Asked," *St. Louis Post-Dispatch*, 13 February 1981.

4. Ibid.

5. E. H. Kohn, "Judge Demands Action on School Plan," *St. Louis Post-Dispatch*, 5

March 1981.

6. "Text of Order On School Plan," *St. Louis Post-Dispatch*, 5 March 1981.

7. Ibid.

8. Edward T. Foote, An Educational Plan for Voluntary, Cooperative Desegregation at 4, *Liddell v. Board of Education*, No. 72-100C(4) (E.D. Mo. order entered March 4, 1981) (filed March 27, 1981).

9. Bruce LaPierre, interview by author, 11 July 2001.

10. The plan, as finally approved by the court, did not have an expiration date.

11. Gary Orfield, The Voluntary Metropolitan Plan: An Analysis of Edward T. Foote's Proposal, *Liddell v. Board of Education*, No. 72-100C(4) (E.D. Mo. order entered March 4, 1981) (filed April 5, 1981).

12. The Supreme Court denied this request. *Liddell v. Board of Education*, 667 F.2d 643 (8th Cir. 1981), *cert. denied*, 454 U.S. 1081 (1981).

13. State Defendants' Plan for Voluntary Transfer of Students in the St. Louis Metropolitan Area Filed Pursuant to Paragraph 12(a) of the Court's Order of May 21, 1980, as Amended at 10, *Liddell v. Board of Education*, No. 72-100C(4) (E.D. Mo. order entered March 4, 1981) (filed May 4, 1981).

14. The Adams plaintiffs, although not ordered to do so, submitted their own proposal for metropolitan desegregation. They proposed a regional school district, embracing St. Louis, St. Charles, and Jefferson Counties and the city of St. Louis, with several local school units. An elected board would govern the regional school district and local school units with authority over education in the metropolitan area. The regional school district would levy an equalized tax for education throughout the area and distribute the tax money to the

boards of local school units.

15. *Liddell v. Board of Education*, No. 72-100C(4) (E.D. Mo. July 2, 1981).

16. Ibid.

17. The Eighth Circuit stated, "Lest there be any misunderstanding, . . . we make it clear that for Budget Year Two (1981–1982) and succeeding budget years, the state is required to pay one-half of the total actual costs of implementing and operating the [intradistrict aspects of the] desegregation plan." This would hold true whether the state received contributions or grants from the city school board or any other source. *Liddell v. Board of Education*, 677 F.2d 626, 631 (8th Cir. 1982) (*Liddell III*).

18. Initially, the court also ordered the United States to develop a plan, but the court relieved the United States of these responsibilities in an order dated September 21, 1981, noting that the United States was not a defendant but rather a plaintiff-intervenor, and no party had alleged that it engaged in discriminatory practices in education.

19. On October 9, 1981, after meeting with the parties, the district court accelerated from February 1, 1982, to November 16, 1981, the date on which the state and the City Board were to submit feasibility plans for interdistrict school desegregation involving the St. Louis School District and suburban school districts located in St. Louis County. The plans were to be limited only by consideration of feasibility and practicality, including reasonableness of transportation, times, and distances. The reports of three court-appointed experts, David L. Colton, professor of education at Washington University; Robert A. Dentler of Boston University; and Lonnie R. Wagstaff, professor at Ohio State, were to be submitted on the same date. The plans were

submitted on November 16, 1981.

20. G. B. Freeman, "'Volunteer' Districts Delighted with Hungate's Decision," *St. Louis Post-Dispatch*, 25 August 1981.

21. M. Plott and L. Eardley, "State Official 'Can't Believe He Did That," *St. Louis Post-Dispatch*, 25 August 1981.

22. H. S. Goller, "McNary Vows To Fight Mandatory School Plan," *St. Louis Post-Dispatch*, 29 August 1981.

23. Ibid.

24. Editorial, "Mr. McNary to the barricades?" *St. Louis Post-Dispatch*, 2 September 1981.

25. Charles Burgess and A. J. Thompson, "U.S. Urges Hungate to Relent," *St. Louis Post-Dispatch*, 4 September 1981.

26. Ibid.

27. E. H. Kohn, "12 Districts Ask Judge Hungate To Disqualify Himself," *St. Louis Post-Dispatch* (quoting Charles E. Sweeney, president of Hazelwood School Board) 10 September 1981.

28. *Liddell III* at 643.

29. Ibid.

30. Ibid., 644.

31. Ibid., 629 (emphasis added).

32. The Eighth Circuit stated, "We held in *Adams* [*v. United States*, 620 F.2d 2377 (8th Cir. 1980) (en banc), cert. denied, 499 U.S. 826 (1980)] that the state had substantially contributed to the segregation of the public schools of the City of St. Louis. No appeal was taken from that decision *by the state*. That decision has been settled and will not be reopened." Moreover, the Eighth Circuit noted that the court's order regarding a voluntary interdistrict transfer plan to be funded by the state of Missouri (paragraph 12(a)) in its February 13, 1981, opinion (*Liddell II*) would stand, and the Supreme Court had refused to review of that decision in November 1981. Ibid., 641–42.

33. Hungate, interview.

34. Ibid.

35. Ibid.

36. Ibid.

37. Ibid.

38. Ibid.

39. Ibid.

40. Interim Order for Mandatory Interdistrict Desegregation, H(1183)82 (August 6, 1982) (quoted in D. Bruce LaPierre, "Voluntary Interdistrict School Desegregation in St. Louis: The Special Master's Tale," 1987 *Wis. L. Rev.* (1987) n. 72: 971, 992).

41. Hungate, interview.

42. Laszlo K. Domjan, "Hungate Accused of Using Threats On School Merger," *St. Louis Post-Dispatch*, 8 August 1982.

43. Charles E. Burgess, "Hungate Reveals His Guidelines For Mandatory Desegregation," *St. Louis Globe-Democrat*, 7–8 August 1982.

44. Domjan, "Hungate Accused of Using Threats on School Merger," *St. Louis-Post Dispatch*, 8 August 1982.

45. Hungate, interview.

46. Hungate, interview.

47. *See* LaPierre, "Voluntary Interdistrict School Desegregation in St. Louis."

48. In describing Gianoulakis, Professor LaPierre said that he was "the toughest advocate of his client you could possibly be. John understood that the best interests of his suburban school district was to see what their school districts needed in a sense of what would serve the broader public interest." LaPierre, interview.

49. LaPierre, interview.

50. Kathryn Rogers, "Second School Settlement Unlikely, Lawyers Told," *St. Louis Post-Dispatch*, 8 December 1983.

51. LaPierre, interview.

52. Ibid.

53. See Chapter 8.

54. Henry Menghini, interview by author, St. Louis, 5 March 2001.

55. Ibid.

56. Ibid.

57. Robert P. Baine, Jr., interview by author, St. Louis, 8 March 2001.

58. Ibid.

59. Earl Hobbs, interview by author, St. Louis, 6 March 2001.

60. Ibid.

61. Ibid.

62. Ibid.

63. Ibid.

64. Ibid.

65. Jay Moody, interview by author, St. Louis, 5 March 2001.

66. Ibid.

67. Ibid.

68. Jan Paul, "University City Joins Plan for Integration," *St. Louis Post-Dispatch*, 2 June 1983.

69. On appeal, the Eighth Circuit declined to approve the county magnets and increased the enrollment goal of city magnets to fourteen thousand. *See Liddell v. Board of Education*, 731 F.2d 1294, 1298 (8th Cir. 1984) (en banc).

70. Settlement Agreement at A-98, *Liddell v. Board of Education*, 567 F. Supp. 1037 (E.D. Mo. 1983) (No. 72-100C(3)).

71. These ambitious goals were never fully realized.

72. Settlement Agreement at A-99.

73. Ibid. at A-106.

74. This goal of the settlement agreement was also never fully realized.

75. Howard S. Goller, "Judge's Big Question in Schools Case: Who Pays?" *St. Louis Post-Dispatch*, 2 June 1983.

76. *Liddell v. Board of Education*, 567 F. Supp. 1037, 1042 (E.D. Mo.1983).

77. Ibid., 1051.

78. Ibid.

79. Ibid., 1052.

80. Ibid.

81. Howard S. Goller, "Ruling on State's Bid to Halt Desegregation Expected Soon," *St. Louis Post-Dispatch*, 4 September 1983.

82. "Tea Party Held for Hungate," *St. Louis Post-Dispatch*, 5 October 1983.

83. Jan Paul and Martha Shirk, "Give Desegregation A Chance," *St. Louis Post-Dispatch*, 15 September 1983.

84. Margaret Gillerman, "Mehlville Schools Welcome Black Transfer Students Warmly," *St. Louis Post-Dispatch*, 7 September 1983.

85. *Liddell*, 731 F.2d at 1298.

86. Ibid., 1323–24.

87. Ibid., 1309.

88. Ibid., 1314.

89. Ibid.

90. Ibid., 1297.

91. William Freivogel, "State Is Rejected On Desegregation," *St. Louis Post-Dispatch*, 2 October 1984.

92. 469 U.S. 816 (1984).

93. William Freivogel, "State Is Rejected On Desegregation."

Chapter 8

1. Dr. Christine Rossell, an expert witness called by the state to testify at the hearing on the state's motion for unitary status, stated that the voluntary interdistrict transfer program was the largest interdistrict program in the nation. Transcript of Unitary Status Hearing, Vo. 1-A at 48, *Liddell v. Board of Education*, No. 72-100-C(6), (March 3–22, 1996). Thirty percent of the black students in St. Louis were enrolled in the voluntary interdistrict transfer program, compared to 8 percent in Milwaukee, 2 percent in Hartford, and 4 percent in Boston. Ibid., 49. The St. Louis public schools have surpassed all other school districts in the number of white county transfer students coming in, the number of black voluntary interdistrict transfers going out, and the number of students enrolled in magnet schools. Ibid., 49.

2. In 1993, VICC commissioned a study from the Public Policy Research Center at the University of Missouri–St. Louis ("focus group study"). They interviewed five groups of city students who attended county schools (one group of ninth graders and four groups of eleventh graders); two groups of city students who attended city schools, both regular and magnet schools; one group of African American county resident students; one group of white county resident students; and two groups of parents of ninth- and eleventh-grade transfer students. Voluntary Interdistrict Coordinating Council, *Perceptions of the Transfer Program: Focus Group Transcription*, "Parents of Ninth Grade Transfer Students," 17 February 1993, 2–3.

3. *Perceptions of the Transfer Program,* "Parents of Eleventh Grade Transfer Students," 10 February 1993, 10. *See also* Bill Smith, "Youth Gangs Out of Hand in City, School Official Says," *St. Louis Post-Dispatch,* 26 April 1989.

4. Charles D. McKenna and Susan Uchitelle, Voluntary Interdistrict Coordinating Council for the Settlement Agreement, Report No. 1, Submitted to the Federal District Court, Eastern District of Missouri (July 31, 1984) (VICC Report).

5. *Liddell v. State of Missouri*, 717 F.2d 1180, 1183 (8th Cir. 1983) (en banc), *cert. denied*, 469 U.S. 816 (1984). The State of Missouri and St. Louis County filed applications for a stay pending appeal in opposition to the voluntary desegregation program approved on July 5, 1983 by the district court for the

St. Louis area schools. *See Liddell v. Board of Education*, 567 F. Supp. 1037 (E.D. Mo. 1983). They raised two objections: (1) the plan imposed an interdistrict remedy based on violations within only one district, the city of St. Louis, and (2) the plan called for the district court to exercise authority over school tax rates under certain contingencies. The Eighth Circuit denied the request for a stay with the exception that the city and suburban school districts temporarily cease further recruiting and not accept interdistrict transfer students other than those who had indicated an intention to transfer prior to the date of the issuance of the court's opinion.

6. *Liddell v. Board of Education*, 731 F.2d 1294, 1297 (8th Cir. 1984) (en banc).

7. The total enrollment statistics for the sixteen-year program are set forth in Appendix A.

8. Junious Williams, an expert witness for the NAACP at the unitary status hearing, testified that he studied discipline in the county schools. The suspension rate in one suburban district for transfer students was 21.1 percent and for white students it was 6.6 percent. Transcript of Unitary Status Hearing, Vol. 11 at 104. He attributed this difference to the manner in which schools dealt with insubordination and disruptive conduct, which accounted for 80 percent of the suspensions of transfer students. Ibid., 120. He pointed out that among a diverse student body and a diverse staff, what constitutes insubordination reflects personal judgment and experience and varies from teacher to teacher and classroom to classroom. Ibid., 122. He recommended that standards be created so that subjective offenses were judged uniformly. Ibid., 124. He noted that students lose instructional time through suspension and that

suspensions are frequently the beginning of a pattern that is called being "pushed out of school." Ibid., 129.

9. VICC Report (August 15, 1988), 18.

10. Observations about the VICC process are based on Dr. Susan Uchitelle's experiences as the VICC Director.

11. VICC Report (July 31, 1995), Appendix A.

12. VICC's budget for the school year 1985–86 was $498,000; for 1988–89, $949,000; and for 1998–99, $1,409,000. Approximately 60 percent of the budget was devoted to staff salaries and 10 percent to recruitment expenses. The costs for VICC were consistently less than 2 percent of the cost of the fiscal incentives to participating school districts.

13. VICC Report (July 31, 1985), 48.

14. VICC Report (January 1998), 95.

15. *See* VICC, 3-B Minutes, October 5, 1983.

16. *See, e.g.,* VICC Report (January 1999).

17. *See* Appendix B (describing the racial composition of county school districts).

18. Ibid.

19. Susan Uchitelle and Bruce Ellerman, Voluntary Interdistrict Choice Corporation, 1998–1999 School Year, Summary Report, 6.

20. Transcript of Unitary Status Hearing, Vol. 1 at 108.

21. The average per-pupil cost in St. Louis in the school year 2000–01 was $10,289. See St. Louis Public Schools, *School District and Accountability: An Annual Report to the Community* (2001–02), 2.

22. Ibid., 66.

23. In May 1998, the VICC office sent surveys to the 670 enrolled twelfth grade city-to-county transfer students and received a response from 616 of them. Only 25 of the 670 students did not graduate. Of the 616 graduate surveys completed, 77 percent stated that they planned to attend a four- or

two-year college, 48 percent planned to attend a four-year college, and 29 percent planned to attend a two-year college. Of the 475 graduates who reported that they were going to college, 20 percent said that they had received one or more scholarship offers, 13 percent of the graduates reported that they planned to attend a vocational or trade school, 8 percent planned to enlist in the military, and 5 percent said that they would be employed in full-time jobs after graduation. Seventy-five percent of the 616 students surveyed reported that they had participated in at least one extracurricular activity, and 25 percent reported receiving one or more types of honors or awards while in high school. 1998 VICC Survey.

24. Fourteen thousand of these students attended magnet schools in the city, and thirteen thousand black city students attended county schools, along with at least fifty-nine thousand white county students.

25. Charles Rankin, an expert witness for the St. Louis Teachers Union, Local 420, AFL-CIO, testified at the unitary status hearing that the interdistrict transfer program had a positive effect on students. All data show that interacting with people of different races is beneficial to the students, not only as an educational experience but also as preparation for their lives as adults. Students who have this experience tend to seek positions of integrated work, they go to integrated colleges, and they live in integrated neighborhoods once they get married and graduate from school. Transcript of Unitary Status Hearing, Vol. 11 at 17. Rankin also testified:

> In a diverse society, like the American society, these boys and girls of today need to understand each other, they need to come in

contact. We see it in sports, we see it in all other activities of American society. . . . It's just that simple. Any time that people perceive that they're not receiving quality education in one setting versus another setting it is germane to their particular self-esteem, their whole self-worth. Ibid., 25–26.

26. Transfer Students, interview by authors, St. Louis, June 1999.

27. Ibid.

28. Ibid.

29. Derrick Brooks, interview by author, St. Louis, 25 February 1999.

30. Ibid.

31. Ibid.

32. Ibid.

33. Ibid.

34. Ibid.

35. Ibid.

36. Ibid.

37. Ibid.

38. Ibid.

39. Ibid.

40. Ibid.

41. Ibid.

42. "Fulfilling the Dream," VICC pamphlet, fall 1994.

43. "Fulfilling the Dream," VICC pamphlet, spring 1995.

44. Examples include Shunted Abernathy, who was honored with an Academic Recognition Award for a 3.5 grade point average in Valley Park High School in the fall of 1991; Sharpen Loma, who participated in a program called Partners in Achievement and went on to attend Central Missouri State at Warrensburg, studying to be a nurse; Gideon Gravette, who ranked 19 out of 340 at Ritenour High School with a grade point average of 3.69 and was selected

to attend the Missouri Scholars Academy and Missouri Boys' State, where he was named Supreme Court Justice and was a member of the National Honor Society. Richard Cornell, a Pattonville transfer student won the Horatio Alger Scholarship, a nationwide honor awarded to students who have become successful and overcome difficulties. Christy Gregory, a Rockwood High School student, received a scholarship to Purdue. She attributes her ability to go to a university with a very small African American population to the "challenging curriculum and diversity of people in Rockwood schools." *Parent Link*, April 1995.

45. Ibid.

46. *In Their Voices*, VICC pamphlet, winter 1998.

47. VICC Report to the Community, "Making a Difference," 1998–1999.

48. "Fulfilling the Dream," VICC pamphlet, fall 1994.

49. *Perceptions of the Transfer Program:* "Ninth Grade Transfer Students," 17 February 1993, 6.

50. Ibid.

51. *Perceptions of the Transfer Program*: "Eleventh Grade White Students of County School," 23 February 1993, 34.

52. Ibid.

53. Ibid., 23.

54. Ibid., 35.

55. Ibid., 33.

56. Ibid., 29.

57. Ibid., 36.

58. *Perceptions of the Transfer Program:* "Eleventh Grade African American Students Who Are Resident Students of County School," 18 February 1993, 23.

59. Ibid., 26.

60. Ibid., 22.

61. Ibid., 23.

62. Ibid., 27.

63. Vera Atkinson, interview by author, St. Louis, 15 March 2000.

64. Principals, interview by authors, St. Louis, 16 November 2000.

65. Terre Johnson, interview by author, St. Louis, 16 March 2000.

66. Principals, interview.

67. Ibid., 38.

68. Joyce Roberts, interview by author, St. Louis, 10 May 2000.

69. Sandra Wilson, interview by author, St. Louis, 11 May 2000.

70. Emma Cannon, interview by author, St. Louis, 16 November 2000.

71. Ibid.

72. Jimmy Irons, interview by author, St. Louis, 14 September 2000. The Voluntary Interdistrict Choice Corporation's budget for recruitment for the 1998–99 school year was $147,000. In addition, they had a printing and publishing budget of $45,000. (Voluntary Interdistrict Choice Corporation, 1998–99, 17.)

73. Irons, interview. Any and all transferring teachers, whether city or county, received a $2,500 bonus for one year. If they chose to teach in their transfer school for another year, they did so without additional pay over their full salary. This was the policy in the VICC Policies and Procedures Handbook.

74. Johnson, interview.

75. Luverne Cameron, interview by author, St. Louis, September 1999.

76. The study, "Perceptions of Participants in the Voluntary Interdistrict Transfer Program: A Descriptive Analysis of First-Year Desegregation Effects," interviewed white students and parents who lived in those suburban school districts accepting transfer students, talked with educators in both city and county schools, met with community groups, and then summarized

the findings. The researchers talked with students transferring to the suburbs and students from the suburbs transferring to city schools.

77. Ibid., 123.

78. "2,555 Pupils, Parents, Teachers Interviewed," Desegregation Fifth Year Report, *St. Louis Post-Dispatch*, 21–28 February 1988, 11.

79. "Blacks Hail Program, While Whites Are Unsure of its Benefits," Desegregation Fifth Year Report, *St. Louis Post-Dispatch*, 21–28 February 1988, 9.

80. Sixty-one percent of African American students said that they called white students on the telephone each week, whereas only 16 percent of white students said that they had called a black student. Finally, 64 percent of African American students said that they had visited a white student's home at least once in the past year, whereas only 20 percent of white students stated that they had visited the home of a black student. The same differences in perspective were evident in response to other statements attempting to gauge the amount of interaction among black and white students. Ibid.

81. Ibid.

82. Ibid.

83. "Teachers' Views," Desegregation Fifth Year Report, 21–28 February 1988, *St. Louis Post-Dispatch*, 10.

84. Ibid.

85. Trial Transcript, Volume 12 at 55, *Liddell v. Board of Education*, No. 72-100C (6), (E.D. Mo. March 22, 1996) (testimony of Dr. Gary Orfield) (hereinafter "Orfield"). Dr. Orfield was appointed by the district court as its expert during the earliest stages of the litigation to integrate the St. Louis schools, and he subsequently served as a witness for the NAACP at the unitary status hearing.

86. Orfield, 38. A study of the St. Louis schools sponsored by the VICC and performed by Robert Lissitz of the University of Maryland confirms a higher graduation rate among transfer students than their peers who remained in the traditional city schools. The study found that 76 percent of the black students who graduated from county schools attended college, 75 percent of these students earned a degree, and only 15 percent left college before graduating. A January 1995 study indicated that 76 percent of the black transfer students graduating from county schools attended college, and of that number 75 percent earned a degree. Robert W. Lissitz, *Assessment of Student Performance and Attitude, Year IV—1994*, D.C. Document No. G(1442)95, ii. The response rate for this study was low—only 15.6 percent—and the VICC lacked the necessary resources to continue follow-up studies. Other studies, however, also demonstrate high graduation rates. See *supra* endnote 23.

Chapter 9

1. 20 F.3d 326, 329 (8th Cir. 1994).

2. Betty Wheeler, interview by author, St. Louis, 14 February 2000.

3. Ibid.

4. Ibid.

5. Ibid.

6. Ibid.

7. "Racial Disparity Report Card," *Black Pages, 14th Anniversary Edition*, 2001–2002, 40–41.

8. Wheeler, interview.

9. Ibid.

10. Ibid.

11. *Liddell v. Board of Education*, No. 72-100C (E.D. Mo. Dec. 24, 1975) (order).

12. *See Liddell v. Board of Education*, 469 F. Supp. 1304, 1311 (E.D. Mo. 1979).

13. Ibid., 1383.

14. Ibid., 1353.

15. Ibid., 1354.

16. *Adams v. United States*, 620 F.2d 1277, 1294, n.26 (8th Cir. 1980).

17. Ibid., 1297.

18. Ibid., 1296. Unfortunately, the federal government's participation in financing any elements of the desegregation program was short-lived.

19. In *Milliken v. Bradley*, 433 U.S. 267 (1977), the U.S. Supreme Court approved the use of remedial and compensatory programs as a tool to desegregate school systems, including magnet schools. It also held that states could be required to share in the cost of these programs.

20. The six proposed magnet schools were the Academic and Athletic Academy, grades 6–8, emphasis on physical skills as well as academics; Center for Expressive and Receptive Arts, K–8; Classical Junior Academy, grades 3–8, a program for gifted students; Montessori School, K–3; Center for Business Management and Finance, grades 9–12, emphasis on business, finance, office management, commercial advertising, merchandising, hotel management, and food service; and Health Careers Center, grades 10–12. Eardley, "Plan Would Delay Start of Magnet School," *St. Louis Post-Dispatch,* 4 May 1980.

21. "Summary of School Board's Desegregation Plan," *St. Louis Globe-Democrat,* 5 May 1980.

22. "Percentage of White Pupils Rises," *St. Louis Globe-Democrat,* 1 November 1983.

23. *Liddell v. State of Missouri*, 731 F.2d 1294 (8th Cir. 1984).

24. Judge Lay wrote: "Magnet schools are a single element of the panoply of remedies approved by this Court and the district court. . . . [T]hey are 'part of a complex and many-faceted' plan. . . . Magnet schools . . . will be distinguished by . . . individualized teaching, a low pupil-teacher ratio, specialized programs tailored to students' interests, enriched resources and active recruitment. . . . While we approve magnet schools and affirm the district court's decision concerning their funding, we see merit in the State's argument that careful study and planning must precede replication or expansion of magnets." Ibid., 1311–12 (quoting *Hart v. Cmty. School Board. of Education*, 512 F.2d 37, 54 (2d Cir. 1975)).

25. Ibid.

26. The guidelines for admission to magnet schools were set forth in the settlement agreement as follows:

> All students whose race is in the majority in their assigned school and district . . . shall be eligible for acceptance into a magnet school in a district in which their race is in the minority if: (a) their home district signs a statement attesting to no record of recent disruptive behavior; (b) if any identified special needs are diagnosed as no more severe than Phase I; (c) they meet such qualification requirements as may have been approved by the Magnet Review Committee as specifically appropriate to some magnet themes; (d) in addition to the above (i) white students in the City of St. Louis are eligible to attend City magnets if they are enrolled in a school in which the white enrollment is either 0–10 percent or over 50 percent

and (ii) black students in majority black districts are eligible to attend magnets hosted in other majority black districts if all host district black students who have applied have been accepted and slots for black students remain in said school. (Settlement Agreement at 84.)

27. Glenn Campbell, interview by author, St. Louis, 14 December 1999.
28. Charles E. Burgess, "Percentage of White Pupils Rise," *St. Louis Globe-Democrat*, 1 November 1983.
29. The projected cost was $40.9 million. The state paid one-half of this cost, because it viewed the school as an intradistrict magnet school. The state paid the full cost of interdistrict magnet schools. Ibid.
30. *Liddell v. Board of Education*, No 72-100C (E.D. Mo. April 2, 1984) (order).
31. "Less Than Half of Amount Sought Is Recommended For Desegregation," *St. Louis Post-Dispatch*, 22 May 1984.
32. "Judge Cuts 'Magnet' Expansion," *St. Louis Post-Dispatch*, 12 July 1984.
33. *Liddell v. Board of Education*, 758 F.2d 290 (8th Cir. 1985).
34. The state would have to pay the full capital and operating costs of magnets established under the settlement agreement. The state was also required to pay its share of the "reasonable" capital and operating expenses of these magnet school programs without an arbitrary dollar limit on these costs. Ibid., 298–299.
35. Ibid., 303–304.
36. *Liddell v. Board of Education*, 801 F.2d 278 (8th Cir. 1986).
37. Ibid., 280.
38. Ibid., 282.
39. Ibid.
40. Ibid., 280, 284.

41. "Judge Scraps Magnet Plan, Orders Study," *St. Louis Post-Dispatch*, 18 March 1987.
42. Ibid.
43. Ibid.
44. "Experts Picked to Develop Magnet Plan," *St. Louis Post-Dispatch*, 14 May 1987.
45. *Liddell v. Board of Education*, 823 F.2d 1252 (8th Cir. 1987).
46. Ibid., 1256.
47. Ibid.
48. "Plan Would Revamp Magnet Schools," *St. Louis Post-Dispatch*, 1 September 1987.
49. "Magnet Plan Is Attractive," *South County Journal*, 4 September 1987 (editorial).
50. *Liddell v. Board of Education*, 696 F. Supp. 444, 451 (E.D. Mo. 1988).
51. Ibid., 460.
52. Ibid., 461–62.
53. Ibid., 463.
54. Ibid., 454.
55. *Liddell v. Board of Education*, 696 F. Supp. 444, 460 (E.D. Mo. 1988).
56. Ibid., 460.
57. "First Lottery Held for Magnet Schools," *St. Louis Post-Dispatch*, 16 March 1990.
58. In 1980, the Missouri Department of Elementary and Secondary Education published the *Handbook for Classification and Accreditation of Public School Districts in Missouri*, which set forth the requirements for accreditation for elementary and secondary schools. Accreditation was divided into two categories: Class AAA and Class AA. Class AAA status was more prestigious because it mandated more stringent standards for administrative and teaching experience among educators, libraries, class size, pupil personnel services, and curriculum.
59. *Liddell v. Board of Education*, No. 72-100C(5), 1990 WL 58060 at *4 (E.D. Mo. Mar. 2, 1990).
60. *Liddell v. Board of Education*, No. 72-100C

(E.D. Mo. April 20, 1990) (order expanding magnet programs).

61. "St. Louis Schools Rebuked," *Kansas City Star*, 27 April 1990.

62. In November 1990, plans for the Gateway Schools were placed on hold because of the failure of a city bonding issue. The school as planned would be home to more than 1,200 elementary and middle students and was to include programs in math, science and technology. "Magnet School Plan Thrown Into Limbo," *St. Louis Post-Dispatch*, 23 November 1990.

63. "School Board Cites Court in Magnet School Delays," *St. Louis Post-Dispatch*, 1 May 1990.

64. "St. Louis Magnet Schools Fill Fast; No Room for 3,200 Students," *St. Louis Post-Dispatch*, 24 March 1991.

65. *Liddell v. Board of Education*, 771 F. Supp. 1503 (E.D. Mo. 1991).

66. *Liddell v. Board of Education*, 771 F. Supp. 1493, 1495 (E.D. Mo. 1991).

67. *Liddell v. Board of Education*, 967 F.2d 1241, 1244 (8th Cir. 1992).

68. Ibid., 1245.

69. *Liddell v. Board of Education*, No. 72-100C(5), 1991WL 177702 at *8 (E.D. Mo. Sept. 4, 1991).

70. Judge Gunn served in the Navy during World War II. He received his law degree from Washington University in 1955 and privately practiced law for several years. He served on the Missouri Court of Appeals from 1973 through 1982 and the Missouri Supreme Court from 1982 through 1985. Judge Gunn took senior status in 1996 and was a member of the court until his death on May 20, 1998.

71. *Liddell v. Board of Education*, 795 F. Supp. 927, 929 (E.D. Mo. 1992).

72. "Schools Ordered to Pay 'Hard-to-Come-By' Cash," *St. Louis Post-Dispatch*, 30 March 1994.

73. *Liddell v. Board of Education*, 20 F.3d 326, 328 (8th Cir. 1994) (citations omitted).

74. Ibid., 329–330.

75. *Liddell v. Board of Education*, 126 F.3d 1049, 1056 (8th Cir. 1997).

76. Annual Report to the Community, St. Louis Monitoring and Support Task Force, at 63 (May 20, 2002).

77. Ibid., 62.

78. As the following table shows, the achievement gap between black and white students, as measured by test results of students in the third and fourth grade, ranges from approximately 15 percent to 18 percent in the magnet schools. The gap is wider for St. Louis schools as a whole, especially in Communication Arts, although the figures for St. Louis schools include the magnet schools as well as all other schools. The figures in each column represent the percentage of students who achieved the nearing proficiency, proficient, and advanced levels of the MAP tests. The number in parentheses in the first column indicates the grade level tested.

Magnet Schools

Subject	Black	White	Gap
Mathematics (4)	66.13	84.69	18.56
Communication Arts (3)	59.20	76.36	17.16
Science (3)	76.36	91.32	14.96
Social Studies(4)	56.33	73.75	17.42

MAP Results—Spring 2001, data provided by Larry Hutchins, St. Louis School District.

St. Louis

Subject	Black	White	Gap
Mathematics (4)	56	71	15
Communication Arts (3)	46	60	26
Science (3)	58	73	15
Social Studies(4)	45	60	15

MAP Disaggregate Report, District, All Subjects, 2000–2001 School Year, 19 October 2001. Figures include magnet schools. Obviously the gap would be somewhat larger if the magnet schools were excluded from these figures.

79. Minnie Liddell, interview by author, St. Louis, 15 June 1999.

80. *Liddell v. Board of Education*, 567 F. Supp. 1037, 1043, 1049 (E.D. Mo. 1983).

81. Ibid., 1056.

82. *Liddell v. State of Missouri*, 717 F.2d 1180, 1181 (8th Cir. 1983) (en banc).

83. Ibid., 1184.

84. *Liddell v. State of Missouri*, 731 F.2d 1180 (8th Cir.) (en banc), *cert. denied*, 469 U.S. 816 (1984). Judge John R. Gibson concurred in part and dissented in part with the Court's majority opinion. He disagreed insofar as the findings did not support the interdistrict aspect of the desegregation program, the requirement that the state provide funding for capital improvements in the physical plant of the city schools, and the inappropriateness of a federal court ordering state and local taxing authorities to impose tax increases. Ibid., 1326–1332. Judge Pasco Bowman joined in Judge Gibson's dissent and also dissented from other aspects of the majority's opinion. Ibid., 1332–1336.

85. Ibid., 1316–1317.

86. Ibid., 1319.

87. Ibid.

88. Ibid., 1323.

89. *See* Orders in *Liddell v. Board of Education*, No. 72-100C, (E.D. Mo. filed July 11, 1984) Doc. Nos. H(3218)84, H(3220)84, H(3221)84, and H(3222)84; and Doc. No. H(3356)84, filed August 29, 1984; Doc. No. H(3368)84, filed September 10, 1984; Doc. No. H(3380)84, filed September 19, 1984; Doc. No. H(3393)84, filed September 24, 1984; Doc. No. H(3448)84, filed November 7, 1984; and Doc. No. H(3485)84, filed November 21, 1984.

90. *Liddell v. Board of Education*, 758 F.2d 290, 294 (8th Cir. 1985). The Eighth Circuit stated:

> We acknowledge that *Liddell VII* is not entirely clear on this subject. We now clarify that opinion and hold that the state can be required to pay one-half the cost of those programs in the "A" series which were *in effect* in the nonintegrated schools at the time of our *en banc* opinion.

91. Ibid., 302.

92. *Liddell v. Board of Education*, 801 F.2d 278, 280–81 (8th Cir. 1986). The district court defined the state's responsibilities with respect to the nursing program, elementary art, vocal music, and physical education. The City Board objected to the district court order, contending that the proposed budget did not permit integrated schools to meet AAA standards in these areas. The Eighth Circuit affirmed the district court with respect to the nursing program, ibid., 285–286; but remanded the question with respect to the funding of the other programs for additional hearings. Ibid., 286–287.

93. *Liddell v. Board of Education*, 830 F.2d 823, 826 (8th Cir. 1987).

94. Ibid., 827.

95. Kathryn Rogers, "Appeals Court Orders

City School Improvements," *St. Louis Post-Dispatch*, 18 September 1987.

96. *Liddell v. Board of Education*, 674 F.Supp 687, 692 (E.D. Mo. 1987).
97. Ibid., 696.
98. Ibid., 714.
99. Ibid., 721.
100. Ibid., 727. Virginia Hick, "Board Backs Judge on School Closings," *St. Louis Post-Dispatch*, 10 September 1987.
101. "Vote Yes for City Schools," *St. Louis Post-Dispatch*, 1 June 1988.
102. Lisha Gayle and Tim O'Neil, "Vote on School Taxes Followed Racial Lines," *St. Louis Post-Dispatch*, 9 June 1988.
103. Lisha Gayle, "Schools Striving to Meet Judge's Classroom Ratio," *St. Louis Post-Dispatch*, 28 August 1988.
104. Editorial, "Words To The Wise," *St. Louis Post-Dispatch*, 11 June 1989.
105. *See* 1999 Settlement Agreement, ¶ 3d, *Liddell v. Board of Education*, No. 72C100, Doc. No. L(167)99.
106. Liddell, interview.
107. According to an article entitled "St. Louis Post-Dispatch Gateway Guide to Public Schools," *St. Louis Post-Dispatch*, 15 May 2003, there are 102 elementary and secondary schools in the St. Louis public school system, of which 57 have an enrollment of 90 percent or more black students.
108. LuVerne Cameron, interview by author, St. Louis, September 1999.
109. Ibid.
110. Ibid.
111. Ibid.
112. Ibid.
113. Ibid.
114. Ibid.
115. Ibid.
116. Ibid.
117. Campbell, interview.
118. Ibid.
119. Ibid.
120. Ibid.

Chapter 10

1. Chris L. Wright, superintendent of Riverview Gardens School District, interview by author, 13 July 2001.
2. The BEST test was administered to all eighth-grade students, including those in St. Louis, through 1987, when the BEST test was suspended. Although the test was simple, only 27.7 percent of St. Louis eighth graders passed in 1981. By 1987, however, 83.4 percent of the city's eighth-graders passed the test. *Liddell v. Board of Education*, No. 72-100C (E.D. Mo. March 14, 1996), Transcript of Trial, Testimony of Dr. G. Alfred Hess, Jr., Volume 7, 7–163.
3. The MMAT was phased in beginning with the 1987 school year, when the MMAT was administered to representative samples of Missouri students in grades 3, 6, 8, and 10. The next year, samples of students in grades 2, 4, 5, 6, 7, and 9 took the test. It measured student achievement in reading, math, science, and social studies. Although MMAT was more comprehensive than the BEST, it was not administered to all students, and its use for accreditation purposes was discontinued in 1998. Correspondence with Dr. Sharon Ford Schattgen, coordinator of Curriculum and Assessment, Missouri Department of Elementary and Secondary Education, November 5, 2001.
4. The CAT was administered in the St. Louis public schools from 1982 through 1988. The CAT test measured achievement in reading, language, and math. In 1987, the St. Louis school district's composite scores

in all three subjects on the CAT test exceeded the national average in grades 1–8 but fell below the national average at the high school level. Linda Eardley, "St. Louis Schools Are Allowed Only Vital Purchases," *St. Louis Post-Dispatch*, 20 May 1987. There is no evidence that any negative consequences befell schools that did poorly on the CAT tests, nor that these schools received resources to improve achievement levels.

5. Wright, interview.
6. Interview of principals, interview by author, 16 November 2000. In addition to the individual interviews conducted with the principals, the authors invited many of them to a dinner on November 16, 2000, and had a roundtable discussion of the educational issues that had been raised in the individual interviews.
7. Emma Cannon, interview by author, 16 November 2000.
8. Cleveland Hammonds, Jr., interview by author, 12 March 2001.
9. Ibid.
10. Wright, interview.
11. Interview of principals, 6.
12. Dorothy Ludgood, interview by author, 14 February 2001.
13. Wright, interview.
14. Ibid.
15. Ibid. In our view, this is a misguided policy. Students cannot be expected to learn if they move from one school to another more than once during a school year. If the school district expects the children to learn, they must have a policy that permits a student to remain in the school during the full school year and provide the transportation necessary to implement that policy.
16. Ludgood, interview.
17. Cannon, interview.
18. Barbara Kohn, interview by author, 11 July 2001.
19. Carmel Hall, interview by author, 14 March 2001.
20. Not many years ago most principals lacked the authority to run their schools. In recent years, however, the principals generally agree that their authority has been enhanced. If principals have authority, they must be held accountable for the achievement of their students.
21. Terre Johnson, interview by author, 16 March 2000.
22. Doris Carter, interview by author, 13 November 2000.
23. Steve Warmack, interview by author, 13 March 2000.
24. Carter, interview.
25. Interview of principals.
26. Joyce Roberts, interview by author, 10 May 2000.
27. Rosalind Mason, interview by author, 15 February 2000.
28. Johnson, interview.
29. Ibid.
30. Juanita Doggett, interview by author, 17 February 2000.
31. Ann Meese, interview by author, 14 November 2000.
32. Interview of principals, 14.
33. Hall, interview.
34. Ibid.
35. Johnson, interview.
36. Ibid.
37. "City School Officials Are Trying to Persuade Some Retired Teachers to Return to Classrooms. District is Struggling to Fill 200 Faculty Vacancies," *St. Louis Post-Dispatch*, 17 August 1999.
38. Ludgood, interview.
39. Doggett, interview.
40. According to a recent newspaper article, the availability of teachers is closely related to the salaries paid by the school districts:

Education analysts often say the nation faces a looming teacher shortage. . . . But this year in New York City, the shortage mostly disappeared, despite the difficult conditions in many urban schools. Qualified teachers flocked to New York for starting salaries of $39,000 a year, up from $32,000 in 2001. Those with experience elsewhere started as high as $61,000. Certified teachers left parochial schools, the suburbs and other professions to work for the city. . . .

Teachers in middle-class areas will move to disadvantaged schools if salaries in poor neighborhoods rise above suburban rates. The differential has to be big enough to compensate for the greater skill and dedication required. . . .

New York City teachers can get a 15 percent bonus for work at the most difficult schools. The state has a program that provides an added $3,400 a year for such assignments. Richard Rothstein, "Teacher Shortages Vanish When the Price Is Right," *New York Times*, 25 September 2002.

41. Glenn Campbell, interview by author, 14 December 1999.

42. Ibid.

43. Ibid.

44. Jimmy Irons, interview by author, 1 September 2000.

45. Wright, interview.

46. Hammonds, interview.

47. Ludgood, interview.

48. Ibid.

49. Campbell, interview.

50. Ibid.

51. The 1983 settlement agreement provided that an effective schools model be adopted as the major emphasis for all St. Louis public schools. The model identified the following five characteristics as essential to an effective school: strong administrative leadership, high teacher expectations, positive school climate, emphasis on basic skills, and ongoing student assessment. Settlement Agreement, *Liddell v. Board of Education*, No. 72 100C (E.D. Mo. Aug. 18, 1983), Sec. IV, Subd. 3.

52. LuVerne Cameron, interview by author, September 1999.

53. Ibid.

54. Ibid.

55. Betty Wheeler, interview by author, 14 February 2000.

56. Wright, interview.

57. Roberts, interview.

58. Ibid.

59. Irons, interview.

60. Ibid.

61. Ibid.

62. Ludgood, interview.

63. Johnson, interview.

64. Ibid.

65. A. Susan Tieber, interview by author, 16 February 2000.

66. Lloyd Washington, interview by author, 16 March 2000.

67. Wheeler, interview.

68. Tieber, interview.

69. Ibid.

70. Ibid.

71. Wright, interview.

72. Ludgood, interview.

73. Roberts, interview.

74. Ibid.

75. Carter, interview.

76. Ibid.

77. Ibid.

78. Rosalind Mason, interview by author, 15 February 2000.

79. Hammonds, interview.
80. Wilson, interview.
81. Wright, interview.
82. *See* Mo. Ann. Stat. Section 160.514 (1993). In 1993, the Missouri Legislature established student performance standards through the Outstanding Schools Act. Mo. Ann. Stat. Section 160.500. The act also provided for reduced class sizes, accountability, grants for secondary schools to increase student achievement, and more funds for early childhood development, teacher training, and vocational and technical education. Missouri created MAP to comply with the Outstanding Schools Act.
83. "Raising the Bar—Closing the Gap: Recommendations for Improving the Academic Achievement of African American Students in Missouri," Robert Bartman, Commissioner of Education, Missouri Department of Elementary and Secondary Education, December, 1997. www.dese.state.mo.us/news/academicreport.htm.
84. Wright, interview.
85. Ibid. The same strategy is used for students performing poorly in math.
86. Ludgood, interview.
87. Hammonds, interview.
88. Vera Atkinson, interview by author, 15 March 2000.
89. Roberts, interview.
90. Washington, interview.
91. Atkinson, interview.
92. Interview of Principals.
93. Roberts, interview.
94. Interview of Principals.

Chapter 11

1. Rick Pierce and Diane Toroian, "Final Pleas are Made on Desegregation Deal," *St. Louis Post-Dispatch,* 10 March 1999.
2. *See* www.dese.state.mo.us/schooldata/four/115115/finanone.html.
3. Motion for Declaration of Unitary Status, *Liddell v. Board of Education,* 72-100C(6) (E.D. Mo. Oct. 11, 1991).
4. Linda Eardley, "Desegregation Ease Facing Crossroads," *St. Louis Post-Dispatch,* 22 December 1991.
5. Motion for Declaration of Unitary Status, *Liddell v. Board of Education,* 72–100C(6) (E.D. Mo. May 7, 1992).
6. *Liddell v. Board of Education,* 105 F.3d 1208, 1211 (8th Cir. 1997).
7. Virginia Hick, "Parkway Students Move to Keep Desegregation," *St. Louis Post-Dispatch,* 19 May 1992.
8. Ibid.
9. Freeman Bosley, Jr. was born in St. Louis in 1954, and attended an all-black elementary school. He later graduated from the St. Louis University Law School. He served as mayor of St. Louis from 1993 to 1997. His father had long served on the City's Board of Aldermen. Bosley Jr. ran for re-election twice and was defeated.
10. Jo Mannies and Linda Eardley, "Bosley Remains Firm on Anti-Busing Stance, NAACP Leaders Vow to Fight to Keep Program," *St. Louis Post-Dispatch,* 29 September 1993.
11. Freeman Bosley, Jr., interview by author 9 January 2001.
12. Ibid.
13. Ibid.
14. Ibid.
15. Ibid.
16. Ibid.
17. The NAACP's view is based on the unanimous decision of the United States Supreme Court in *Brown v. Board of Education,* 347 U.S. 483, 495 (1954), where

the Court concluded:

> [I]n the field of public education
> the doctrine of "separate but equal"
> has no place. Separate educational
> facilities are inherently unequal.
> Therefore, we hold that the plaintiffs
> and others similarly situated for
> whom the actions have been brought
> are, by reason of the segregation
> complained of, deprived of the equal
> protection of the laws guaranteed by
> the Fourteenth Amendment.

In the view of Dr. James DeClue,
Chairman of the St. Louis NAACP,
opposition to the voluntary interdistrict
transfer program developed in the black
community because Mayor Bosley was
very vocal. He was certain Mayor Bosley
was not opting for separate but equal
schools, even though that's what it may have
sounded like. Dr. James DeClue, interview
by author, 13 December 1999.

18. Ibid.

19. Ibid.

20. Governor Mel Carnahan was quoted as
saying that Bosley's "suggestion is one whose
time has come. . . . The mayor's suggestion
is an important one for this group to
consider." The article then notes that
"Carnahan is counting on savings on
desegregation to help finance his education
package." In response, William Clay, Sr., a
long-time black leader, stated: "We cannot
abandon the concept that separate schools
are inherently unequal. Whites who are
opposed to busing have vehemently
opposed all other issues of advancement of
race." Bryant Lindecke, "Busing Issue
'Comes Down to Money,' Judge Says,"
St. Louis Post-Dispatch, 28 September 1993.

21. Memorandum and Order, *Liddell v. Board*

of Education, No. 72-100C (E.D. Mo. filed
Feb. 28, 1995).

22. 515 U.S. 70 (1995).

23. *Liddell v. Board of Education*, 105 F.3d at
1211.

24. Ibid.

25. Ibid. The judge believed that an attempt
should be made to settle the case out of
court to avoid further lengthy court
proceedings.

26. Ibid.

27. The following St. Louis County school
districts also joined in the brief: Bayless
School District, Clayton School District,
Hancock Place School District, Hazelwood
School District, Kirkwood R-7 School
District, Ladue School District, Brentwood
School District, Parkway School District,
Rockwood School District, Valley Park
School District, Webster Groves School
District, Affton School District, and
Lindbergh School District.

28. Brief of the United States in *Liddell v. Board
of Education*, No. 72-100C, Doc. No.
G(1978)96, filed 2/23/96 at 42–43, quoting
Liddell v. Board of Education, 718 F. Supp.
1434, 1436 (E.D. Mo. 1989).

29. County Districts' Hearing Brief, *Liddell v.
Board of Education*, No. 72-100C, Doc. No.
G(1950)96, filed 2/23/96 at 1–2.

30. Ibid., 7.

31. Dr. Christine Rossell, Dr. David Armor,
Dr. William Clark, and Dr. Eric Alan
Hanushek appeared on behalf of the state;
Dr. Kern Alexander, Dr. G. Alfred Hess, Jr.,
and Dr. Charles L. Leven appeared on
behalf of the City Board; Dr. Leonard
Stevens appeared on behalf of the United
States; Dr. Samuel Coburn Stringfield,
Dr. William Thomas Trent, Michael Puma,
Dr. Dennis Judd, Junious Williams, and
Dr. Gary Orfield appeared on behalf of the
Liddell plaintiffs, the Caldwell plaintiffs and

the NAACP; and Dr. Charles Rankin appeared on behalf of Teachers Local 420.

32. Dr. Rossell had extensive experience researching school desegregation plans and their effect on communities. Tr. of Unitary Status Hr'g, Vol. 1, 202, *Liddell v. Board of Education*, No. 72-100C (E.D. Mo. Mar. 4–21, 1996). During her 20 years at Boston University, she taught courses in school desegregation, research methods, program evaluation, and public policy analysis. Ibid., 204. She published three books on school desegregation and 45 articles on the topic. Ibid., 205. She also received a number of grants from the United States Department of Education. Ibid., 207.

33. Ibid., Vol. 1-A, 14.

34. Ibid., 26.

35. Ibid., 90.

36. Dr. Armor served on the Los Angeles School Board for three years. Ibid., 210. He served as a consultant for the Department of Education on the Coleman Study Ibid., 212. He served as a consultant for the United States Commission on Civil Rights. Dr. Armor published several articles and served as an expert in thirty desegregation cases. Ibid., 217.

37. Ibid., 100.

38. Dr. Hanushek's thesis for his doctorate degree from M.I.T. was entitled, "The Education of Negroes and Whites." Ibid., Vol. 4, 3. He has published in the areas of school finance and funding. Ibid., 5. He testified in a number of cases with respect to school financing. Ibid., 6.

39. Vol. 4, 18.

40. Ibid., 87.

41. Ibid., 49–50.

42. Dr. Alexander was an elementary school teacher and was employed at the Kentucky Department of Education and in the United States Department of Education. He served

as the director of the Institute for Educational Finance at the University of Florida and had published extensively in that area. Ibid., Vol. 5, 81, 82.

43. Vol. 5, 99.

44. Ibid., 114–15.

45. Ibid., 164.

46. Dr. Hess received his Ph.D. in educational anthropology from Northwestern University. He is the executive director of the Chicago Panel on School Policy, a research and advocacy organization that studies public issues in Chicago and the Midwest. Ibid., Vol. 7, 147–148. He testified that he studied the school systems in Milwaukee, Cleveland, and St. Louis. Ibid., 149.

47. Vol. 7, 164.

48. Ibid., 170.

49. Ibid., 181.

50. Ibid., 189.

51. Ibid., Vol. 8, 8.

52. Ibid., 31.

53. Dr. Stevens received his Ph.D. from the University of Massachusetts. Ibid., Vol. 9, 4. He served as a federal court monitor for school desegregation in Cleveland from 1978 through 1988, and as chief executive of a consortium in Milwaukee, Wisconsin that supported an interdistrict choice program for students. Ibid., 7. He worked on school desegregation cases in Yonkers, New York; Fort Wayne, Indiana; Muscogee County, Georgia; Hillsborough County, Florida; and Topeka, Kansas. Ibid. 11.

54. Ibid., 33.

55. Ibid., 86.

56. Ibid., Vol. 9, 141.

57. Ibid., 160.

58. Dr. Trent received his Ph.D. in sociology from the University of North Carolina at Chapel Hill. Ibid., Vol. A, 37. He served as a member of a national panel on school

desegregation. Ibid., 40. He served as an expert witness in desegregation cases, including the Cleveland case. Ibid., 42.

59. Vol. 10-A, 65.

60. Ibid., 71, 76.

61. Ibid., 85–86.

62. Ibid., 91, 93.

63. Ibid., Vol. 10-B, 75.

64. Dr. Rankin received his degree in urban education. Ibid., Vol. 11, 5. He served as an elementary teacher in the Wichita public schools for three years. Ibid., 6. He served as a director of a general assistance center at the University of Missouri at Columbia from 1973 to 1978. The purpose of the center was to assist school desegregation with the implementation of school desegregation orders. Ibid., 8. He had responsibility for several county schools and St. Louis city schools. Ibid., 9. At the time of his testimony, he was the director of the Midwest Desegregation Assistance Center. Ibid, 10.

65. Ibid., 25.

66. Ibid., 17.

67. Dr. Orfield, a professor of education and social policy at Harvard, directed the Harvard Project on School Desegregation. Ibid., Vol. 12, 7. Dr. Orfield was first retained by the Justice Department as an expert witness in 1978. Thereafter, he was retained by the court as a court-appointed expert. Until the May 21, 1980 order was issued, the state officials were very cooperative. Vol. 12, 66–69. After that order was issued, his communications in his role representing the court were cut off. Commissioner Arthur Mallory told him it was not his choice. He had been ordered by Ashcroft not to provide information. Sometime after the May 21st order, Attorney General Ashcroft directed Commissioner Mallory not to talk to

Orfield anymore. Ibid., 71.

68. Vol. 12, 20–21.

69. Ibid., 36.

70. Ibid., 45.

71. Ibid., 46.

72. Ibid., 47.

73. Dr. William H. Danforth, interview by author, July 12, 2001.

74. Memorandum and Order, *Liddell v. Board of Education*, 72-100C (E.D. Mo. April 23, 1996).

75. Danforth, interview.

76. *See Liddell v. Board of Education*, 126 F.3d 1049, 1055 n.6 (8th Cir. 1997).

77. Ibid., 1051, 1057–58 (citation omitted).

78. Ibid., 1058.

79. Cleveland Hammonds, interview by author, 12 March 2001.

80. Danforth, interview.

81. Virginia Young, "Senate Panel Oks Bill to Ease End of Desegregation," *St. Louis Post-Dispatch*, 19 February 1998.

82. Ibid.

83. The vote of each member was to be weighed proportionately to the percentage of the total number of transfer students who attended school in the member's district.

84. Judge Steven Ehlmann, who served in the Missouri Senate at the time Senate Bill 781 was enacted, was the author of this amendment. He stated that he did not know the people personally, but they were perceived to be part of the failed regime, even though they may have done an excellent job regarding the goals of the court. *See* Telephone Interview of Judge Steven Ehlmann, Oct. 17, 2001. It appears to the authors that this provision was simply a protest over the success of the interdistrict program. The VICC's only areas of responsibility were recruitment of magnet school students and the interdistrict programs, both of which were successful,

not only in terms of the numbers participating, but also in the academic achievements of the students involved.

85. Judge Stephen Ehlmann, interview by author, 17 October 2001.

86. Virginia Young, "Legislature Oks Bill that Could Close Desegregation Case," *St. Louis Post-Dispatch*, 16 May 1998.

87. Marcia L. Koenig, "Law Driving Desegregation Talks Imposes Several Reforms," *St. Louis Post-Dispatch*, 3 January 1999.

88. The board would consist of three residents of the district, one to be appointed by the governing body of the district, one by the mayor of the city of St. Louis, and one by the president of the board of aldermen of the city. In the event the school district was declared unaccredited, the governing board of the district was to be replaced by a chief executive officer nominated by the state board of education and appointed by the governor with the advice and consent of the senate. This provision effectively gave the governor the power to run the school district once it was declared unaccredited if the governor chose to follow that alternative. Susan C. Thomson, "Desegregation Bill Mandates Many Changes in City Schools," *St. Louis Post-Dispatch*, 5 July 1998.

89. "Academically deficient" schools were to be determined based upon the MAP assessment system. Mo. Stat. Ann. Sections 160.518 and 160.538 (1993).

90. Mo. Ann. Stat. Section 160.538 (1993).

91. Mo. Ann. Stat. Section 160.540 (1998).

92. According to Judge Steven Ehlmann, who served in the Missouri Senate at the time Senate Bill 781 was enacted, the motive behind limiting the charter school provisions to St. Louis and Kansas City simply was a matter of practical politics.

There was no way the public would allow charter schools everywhere. Their theme was that if they were going to spend the money, they wanted to give it to someone who would get the job done. They viewed the desegregation program as having spent a lot of money. Maybe the schools achieved some things in terms of desegregation, but that was not the legislature's concern. With regard to better test scores, it was a waste of money.

93. The funding change stood to help many of the black suburbs that largely had been left out of the 1983 settlement agreement because of the agreement's focus on the desegregation of the city schools rather than those in the suburbs.

94. Bill Bell, Jr., "Carnahan Signs Bill for Ending Desegregation Case," *St. Louis Post-Dispatch*, 24 June 1998.

95. Rick Pierce, "Deadline is Extended for Desegregation Deal," *St. Louis Post-Dispatch*, 5 January 1999.

96. Pierce, "Settlement is Reached in Desegregation Case," *St. Louis Post-Dispatch*, 7 January 1999.

97. Rick Pierce and Diane Toroian, "Final Pleas are Made on Desegregation Deal," *St. Louis Post-Dispatch*, 10 March 1999.

98. *Liddell v. Board of Education*, No. 4: 72CV100 SNL, Doc. No. L(167)99 Settlement Agreement at 2 (E.D. Mo. filed Feb. 23, 1999).

99. Ibid., 5.

100. Ibid., 6–8.

101. Ibid., 9. Reconstitution involved sweeping changes in administration, faculty, staff, and programs.

102. The Elementary and Secondary Education Act was passed by Congress in December 2001. It provides a similar option to students in failing schools to transfer to other schools in their district with better

academic records. Interviews with educators suggest that most successful urban schools are already at capacity or over. Thus, there will be no practical alternative for students. *New York Times*, Dec. 22, 2001. It is difficult to understand the rationale for this provision in light of the fact that the settlement agreement limited the opportunity of city students attending "academically deficient" schools to transfer to a county school. The provision can only be explained by the state's determination to limit its financial responsibility.

103. Pierce "St. Louis Schools Are Crafting Plan to Hold Teachers Accountable," *St. Louis Post-Dispatch*, 26 August 1999.

104. Ibid. In 1999, St. Louis teachers' salaries ranked 73rd out of 76 school districts in the "bi-state" area. Ibid.

105. Pierce, "School Board Quizzes State Official About Accreditation," *St. Louis Post-Dispatch*, 20 October 1999. The eight St. Louis schools that met the state student-performance standards included: Metro High, Busch Academy, Ashland Elementary, Baden, Farragut, Kennard, Shaw, and Wyman. Pierce, "St. Louis Schools Get 2-Year Reprieve While Kansas City Loses Accreditation," *St. Louis Post-Dispatch*, 22 October 1999.

106. Ibid.

107. Ibid.

108. Matthew Franck, "St. Louis School Chief Says New Plan Will Help Regain Partial Accreditation," *St. Louis Post-Dispatch*, 21 November 1999.

109. Steve Ehlmann, "City Schools Show It Doesn't Take Much to Gain Provisional Accreditation," *St. Louis Post-Dispatch*, 31 October 2000.

110. Ibid.

111. Ibid.

112. Ibid., 24.

113. Ibid., 69, Appendix E.

114. Ibid., 8.

115. Ibid.12.

116. Dale Singer, "City Voters Support Tax Hike to End Desegregation," *St. Louis Post-Dispatch*, 3 February 1999.

117. Ibid.

118. Memorandum and Order, *Liddell v. Board of Education*, Nol 72-100C (E.D. Mo. filed Feb. 28, 1999).

119. In the event of a dispute between the state, the City Board, and the suburban districts concerning their contractual obligation, the agreement states that the matter be adjudicated only in state court with venue being determined by whoever brings the action.

120. *See Missouri v. Rockwood Sch. Dist.*, 488 U.S. 825 (1988); *Missouri v. Liddell*, 469 U.S. 816 (1984); *Missouri v. Liddell*, 459 U.S. 877 (1982); *Missouri v. Liddell*, 454 U.S. 1091 (1981); *St. Louis Board of Education v. Caldwell*, 433 U.S. 914 (1977).

121. Carl Peterson Florissant, "Don't Blame Desegregation," *St. Louis Post-Dispatch*, 29 August 1992.

122. Dr. Danforth's brother, former U.S. Senator John Danforth (R-Missouri), worked closely with him to secure passage of the necessary legislation in the Missouri Legislature.

123. "The Judge's Thunderbolt: 'Take It,'" *St. Louis Post-Dispatch*, 30 January 1999.

124. Ibid.

125. Bruce LaPierre, interview by author, 11 July 2001.

126. LuVerne Cameron, interview by author, September 1999.

Epilogue

1.   Historically, Missouri has been among the states that spend less per student attending

public schools than most other states. For the school year 2000–2001, the average amount spent per student in the United States was $7,284, while in Missouri it was $6,593, making Missouri number 30 in per student spending. Lori Horvitz, "Florida Drops to 41st in School Spending," *Orlando Sentinel*, 12 March 2003.

2. Memorandum and Order, *Liddell v. Board of Educ.*, 72-100C (E.D. Mo. April 23, 1996), 5. *See also* Missouri Department of Elementary and Secondary Education, Accreditation Standards for Public School Districts in Missouri, July 1, 2001, § 2.1.

3. *See Black Pages*, 15th Ed., 2003–2004, 40–49. The Missouri fourth-grade average math test scores in 2003 were slightly above the national average: 235 compared to 234. The fourth-grade average reading test scores in 2003 were also slightly above the national average: 222 compared to 216. National Center for Education Statistics, *The Nation's Report Card*, 2003.

To be fair, this racial gap exists throughout the state of Missouri and the nation. One would expect that the gap would be smaller in the county schools that perform very well on state and national tests. The reverse is true, however. Test scores of black students are higher in the county schools, but so are those of the white students. Black students do well in some city schools. The test scores at several all-black city elementary schools, including Ashland, Baden, Banneker, Bryan Hill, Columbia, Dewey, Emerson, Farragut, Kennard, LaClede, LaFayette, Lyon Academy, Mullanphy, and Mitchell, are higher than both the state and St. Louis averages. *Black Pages*, 15th Ed., 2003–2004, 43.

As expected, the students in the integrated elementary, middle, and high schools that enroll gifted students perform better than

the state or the St. Louis average. *Ibid.* A prime example is Metro High School. Its test scores are the highest in the state, not only for white students, but for black students as well. Another example is Kennard Elementary School. There 80 percent of the black students score higher than the national norm in math and 81 percent score higher than the national norm in communication arts. The scores for the white students are 91 percent and 83 percent, respectively. *Black Pages*, 15th Ed., 2003–2004, 40–49.

With few exceptions, there does not appear to be a significant difference between the performance of black students in St. Louis and those in the rest of the region and the state. The same is true with respect to the achievement gap between black and white students at the elementary level. However, the achievement gap is significantly higher for middle and high school students in the region. This appears to be the case because white students do significantly better in suburban school districts than they do in St. Louis.

Students' Average National Percentiles for MAP
Tests—Math

District	Elementary Grade 4			Middle School Grade 8			High School Grade 10		
	B	W	Gap	B	W	Gap	B	W	Gap
State	40	62	18	34	61	27	42	67	35
City of St. Louis	39	56	19	30	50	20	41	60	19
St. Louis Area	40	69	29	34	67	33	42	72	30
Clayton	47	81	34	39	79	40	49	88	39
Parkway	40	71	21	37	75	28	49	81	32
Rockwood	34	75	41	33	72	39	41	78	37

What is true for students taking the math
test is equally true for students taking the
communications arts test.

Communications Arts

District	Elementary Grade 4			Middle School Grade 8			High School Grade 10		
	B	W	Gap	B	W	Gap	B	W	Gap
State	43	62	19	41	61	20	44	62	18
City of St. Louis	39	54	15	36	51	15	43	59	16
St. Louis Area	44	40	4	41	66	25	44	67	23
Clayton	52	78	26	42	80	38	47	71	24
Parkway	41	72	31	41	72	31	52	73	21
Rockwood	37	72	35	39	67	28	42	69	27

Test results showed that black students in
some schools in suburban St. Louis,
including Brentwood, Hazelwood, Ladue,
Parkway, and Pattonville, performed
substantially better than black students in
the St. Louis public schools, while black
students in other suburban schools
performed at the same or lower levels as the
black students in the city. *Black Pages,* 15th
Ed., 2003–2004, 70–74.

4. Mayor's Speeches, "Presentation of the
St. Louis Community Monitoring &
Support Task Force Annual Report," 25
June 2002.

5. Press Release, Mayor's Office, city of
St. Louis, 21 December 2002.

6. Press Release, Mayor's Office, city of
St. Louis, 16 January 2003.

7. Jake Wagman, "Picking Superintendent Is
Key Issue; Candidates Split Over
Qualifications for St. Louis Schools Chief,"
St. Louis Post-Dispatch, 31 March 2003.

8. Ibid.

9. Jo Mannies, "Companies Are Investing in
Election; Coalition That Supports Four
Candidates Raised $235,000 in March,"
St. Louis Post-Dispatch, 1 April 2003.

10. Jake Wagman, "Private Management
Company Will Take Over St. Louis Public
Schools in 'Turnaround' Plan," *St. Louis*

Post-Dispatch, 31 May 2003.

11. Wagman, "School Board Seeks Help of 'Turnaround' Firm," *St. Louis Post-Dispatch*, 4 May 2003.

12. Wagman, "Private Management Company Will Take Over St. Louis Public Schools in 'Turnaround' Plan."

13. Bill McClellan, "Money is Only Part of Problem Facing St. Louis Schools," www.stltoday.com, 27 June 2003.

14. Cheryl Wittenauer, AP Online, 1 September 2003.

15. Doug Moore, "Holden Orders Audit of Schools After Report of $90 Million Deficit," *St. Louis Post-Dispatch*, 10 September 2003. Mayor Francis Slay reported that a recent audit, different from the Governor's audit, conducted by a Clayton firm revealed that a $40 million budget surplus at the end of June 2002 had shrunk to a deficit of $12.3 million by the end of 2003. He added, "the previous administration [Superintendent Cleveland Hammonds] spent $51 million more than they took in in revenue." Evans, Tavia, "More Cuts Planned for St. Louis Schools," *St. Louis American*, 15–21 January 2004.

16. Editorial, "St. Louis Public Schools: Unkind Cuts," *St. Louis Post-Dispatch*, 4 February 2004.

17. According to an article in the *St. Louis American* on June 12, 2003, the state aid that was cut probably accounted for 10 percent or more of the district's $450 million budget. William Purdy, Immediate Past President of the St. Louis Board of Education, "Time for a Hard Look at St. Louis Schools' Prospects for Coming Year," *St. Louis American*, 12 June 2003. Glynn Young, the spokesperson for the St. Louis public schools, has blamed the school district's "drastic cuts," at least in part, on the gap in state aid. Jo Mannies,

"Holden Releases $83 Million in Aid to Schools," *St. Louis Post-Dispatch*, 3 December 2003.

An action was brought by the St. Louis School board against the state to require it to make the state aid payments pursuant to the settlement agreement. The Missouri Circuit Court held the state was required to follow the settlement agreement and to make up the payments it withheld from the school district. This matter is currently under reconsideration by the Circuit Court and is on appeal to the Missouri Court of Appeals. Order and Judgment, *Board of Education v. State of Missouri*, No. 034-00284 (Mo. Cir. Ct. July 7, 2003). According to the district's audited financial report, state aid was reduced by $18 million as a result of the state's action to reduce funding to education statewide. This $18 million is in addition to the $7 million reduction in state aid agreed to in the settlement agreement. *See* infra, pp. 199–200.

18. William Purdy, "Time for a Hard Look at St. Louis Schools' Prospects for Coming Year."

19. "St. Louis School Board Plans to Borrow Special Funds," www.kmov.com, 2 July 2003. The need to repay the loan has already affected the ability of the school district to meet current budgetary needs. Jake Wagman, "City School Board May Trim Budget By Another $23 Million; Roberti Issues Warning," *St. Louis Post-Dispatch*, 14 January 2004.

20. "Judge Allows Schools to Borrow From Deseg Fund,"www.ksdk.com, 8 July 2003.

21. "School Closing List Expected Monday," www.ksdk.com, 14 July 2003.

22. Bob Moore, "Yes Vote By St. Louis School Board Meets a Strong No By Parents and Teachers," www.slfp.com, 16 July 2003.

23. Some custodians were able to remain employees of the school district, but many school maintenance jobs were privatized. Jake Wagman, "Custodians at City Schools Ratify Contract; District Will Cut 40 Jobs; Remaining Workers Will Be Paid Up to 76 percent Less," *St. Louis Post-Dispatch*, 17 October 2003.

24. Jake Wagman, "Schools Plan Would Fire 1,400; But No Teacher Would Lose Job, Managers Say," *St. Louis Post-Dispatch*, 3 August 2003.

25. Charles Bean, telephone conversation with author, 22 January 2004. In response to these school closings and personnel cuts, several black community leaders and parents, dismayed with the school closings and personnel layoffs, organized to encourage black students to refuse to attend the opening day of school. The boycott was largely unsuccessful, and most students attended school on the first day. Jake Wagman, "City Schools Face Day One Showdown; Officials Push Attendance, Union, Parents Talk Boycott," *St. Louis Post-Dispatch*, 8 August 2003.

26. Tavia Evans, "More Cuts Planned for St. Louis Schools," *St. Louis American*, 15–21 January 2004.

27. "'Turnaround' for City Schools Seems to Mean in a Circle," *St. Louis Post-Dispatch*, 13 June 2004.

28. No Child Left Behind Act of 2001, Pub. L. No. 107-110, 115 Stat. 1425.

29. Title I funding, the best estimate of federal funding to St. Louis schools, has increased only slightly since 2001. In 2002, the St. Louis schools were given $18,118,826 in Title I money; in 2003, that amount rose by $127,994. For fiscal year 2004,a more significant increase–$3.265 million–is scheduled. In President Bush's proposed 2004–2005 budget, he has allotted for further increases in Title I funds.

30. But in the first year of this program, only a small number of students actually transferred. The reasons are many and varied. Some parents want their children close to home in schools they know; space is not available in the "better" schools, and the districts do not have the resources to increase the space. Moreover, the "good" schools drawing the most applicants have the least space available. The school districts are obliged to provide transportation for transferring students, but again, budgetary concerns make this extremely difficult. Diana Jean Schemo, "Few Exercise New Right to Leave Failing Schools," *New York Times*, 28 August 2002.

31. As of 2003, there were eight charter schools operating in St. Louis. There is evidence that students attending these schools perform at a lower level that those who attend traditional public schools. Jerry Berger, "Memo to Slay Says Charter Schools Aren't Making the Grade Locally," *St. Louis Post-Dispatch*, 17 December 2003. A recent Rand Corporation study of charter schools in California found that students generally have comparable or slightly lower test scores than those in public schools. Editorial, Robert Joiner Column, "Charter Schools Are Failing to Measure Up," *St. Louis Post-Dispatch*, 11 August 2003. In Kansas City, a few charter schools have seen their students score as well or better than average Kansas City School District students, but many have not. Lynn Franey, "Sponsors Choose to Postpone Key Decisions on Charter Schools, "*Kansas City Star*, 16 October 2003. In Minneapolis, students in regular public schools are fairing better academically than students in charter schools sponsored by the school district. Allie Shah, "Charter

Schools Get Lower Marks," *Minneapolis Star-Tribune*, 12 November 2003.

32. *See* www.whitehouse.gov/news/reports/no-child-left-behind.html.

33. According to a recent newspaper article, the availability of teachers is closely related to the salaries paid by the school districts: Education analysts often say the nation faces a looming teacher shortage. . . . But this year in New York City, the shortage mostly disappeared, despite the difficult conditions in many urban schools. Qualified teachers flocked to New York for starting salaries of $39,000 a year, up from $32,000 in 2001. Those with experience elsewhere started as high as $61,000. Certified teachers left parochial schools, the suburbs and other professions to work for the city. . . . Teachers in middle-class areas will move to disadvantaged schools if salaries in poor neighborhoods rise above suburban rates. The differential has to be big enough to compensate for the greater skill and dedication required. . . . New York City teachers can get a 15 percent bonus for work at the most difficult schools. The state has a program that provides an added $3,400 a year for such assignments. Richard Rothstein, "Teacher Shortages Vanish When the Price Is Right," *New York Times*, 25 September 2002.

34. In 1999, the school district was 200 teachers short at the beginning of the school year, and in 1998, it was 270 teachers short. This shortage was due to a nationwide shortage of teachers, the salary schedule, the difficulty in teaching in an urban school district with a high percentage of poor students of color, and poor planning. "City School Officials Are Trying to Persuade Some Retired Teachers to Return to Classrooms. District is Struggling to Fill 200 Faculty Vacancies," *St. Louis Post-*

Dispatch, 17 August 1999.

35. Charles Bean, telephone conversation.

36. Very early on in the *Liddell* litigation, Chief Judge Meredith suggested that a remedy for past discrimination should include a college scholarship program for black students. This program would have certainly raised the hope of black students. Unfortunately, it never became a part of the court-ordered desegregation plan.

37. A recent editorial in the *St. Louis Post-Dispatch* conveyed a similar message: "[T]here's the equally compelling argument that we'll never truly help low-achieving children until we begin to address social conditions that extend well beyond the schoolhouse," Robert Joiner, "Schools' Social Conditions, Learning Environment Need Our Attention," *St. Louis Post-Dispatch*, 29 December 2003.

38. The federal government has recognized the importance of school continuity. In 1987, the McKinley-Vento Homeless Assistance Act was signed into law. The act mandates that a district pay for transportation costs if a child is displaced from his or her school. The child must meet the definition of homeless in order to be eligible for the transportation. In St. Louis, 12,500 students are eligible. Jake Wagman, "Taxi Bills Are Too High, District Says; Cabs Are Used to Transport Some Homeless Students," *St. Louis Post-Dispatch*, 5 January 2004.

39. In Mt. Vernon, New York, two schools have closed the achievement gap. The principal at one of the schools, Longfellow, involves parents in the learning process. At the beginning of the fourth-grade school year, parents are invited to the school to not only learn about the test their child will be taking that year, but also to take the exam themselves. Of the program, the Longfellow

Principal said, "Some of [the parents] struggle, and that creates empathy," providing them "with a sense of how much their child has to know." David McKay Wilson, "Mt. Vernon Shows How to Close Learning Gap," *The Journal News*, 7 November 2003.

40. Rudolph F. Crew, the former Chancellor of the New York City public schools, who has been retained by the City Board to advise it on education matters, stated:
The organizational sophistication of urban school systems requires focus, focus, and more focus. Having spent years trying to hit instructional moving targets prescribed by politicians, and revolving door superin tendents and principals, most teachers are frankly confused about what's important to the system. Is it test scores? Is it attendance? Is it safety? And on, and on. Whichever road is taken, it must lead to a student being able to read fluently, with comprehension, and to write and make meaning from language. The question facing urban schools is a human resource issue: that is, how to support the development of teachers and their principals in order to organize around the purpose of literacy, expressed in achievable performance goals.
www.c-b-e.org/be/iss0112/a2crew.htm.

41. Beginning in June 2001, the school district undertook a program to install air conditioning in school buildings. As of the end of the 2002–03 school year, 25 schools had been air conditioned. *See Comprehensive Annual Financial Report for the Fiscal Year Ended June 30, 2003*, 10.

42. Charles Bean, telephone conversation.

43. *Zelman v. Simmons-Harris*, 536 U.S. 639, 122 S. Ct. 2460 (2002).

44. Ohio Rev. Code Ann. §§ 3313.974-3313.979 (Anderson 1999 and Supp. 2000).

Index

{About the Authors}

Senior Judge Gerald W. Heaney has served on the United States Court of Appeals for the Eighth Circuit for more than thirty-five years. During these years, he has participated in school desegregation cases involving St. Louis, Missouri; Kansas City, Missouri; Little Rock, Arkansas; North Little Rock, Arkansas; Texarkana, Arkansas; Morrilton, Arkansas; Altheimer, Arkansas; Willsville, Arkansas; and Omaha, Nebraska. He authored thirty-eight opinions in these cases. Judge Heaney graduated from the University of Minnesota Law School in 1941. After serving with the distinguished 2nd Ranger Battalion in World War II, he practiced law in Duluth, Minnesota, until December 1, 1966, when he was appointed to the Court of Appeals by President Lyndon B. Johnson. His extraordinary bravery during the D-Day landing at Normandy earned him a Silver Star. He was decorated with the Bronze Star and five battle stars before he was honorably discharged with the rank of captain on January 19, 1946.

While in private practice, Judge Heaney served as liaison to the Minnesota Legislature for Governor Orville Freeman in education matters and as a regent for the University of Minnesota. He is the author of several law review articles, including "The Political Assault on Affirmative Action: Undermining Forty Years of Progress Toward Equality," 22 *William Mitchell L. Rev.* 119 (1996), and "Busing, Timetables, Goals, and Ratios: Touchstones of Equal Opportunity," 69 *Minnesota L. Rev.* 735 (1985). Judge Heaney was awarded an Honorary Doctor of Law in May 2001 by the University of Minnesota.

Dr. Susan Uchitelle is a long-time educator and community leader. She has a Ph.D. in education policy from Washington University, a Master's in education from Harvard, and an undergraduate degree from the University of Michigan. Dr. Uchitelle directed the Voluntary Interdistrict Coordinating Council, which was responsible for implementing the interdistrict aspect of the St. Louis desegregation plan. Prior to being the executive director of VICC, she worked in all phases of education, including teaching, administration, program development, and the supervisor of instruction for the Missouri State Department of Elementary and Secondary Education. She also served as president of the Clayton School Board. Her publications include "A School Choice Approach to Desegregation: Lessons from the Field," *New Schools, New Communities,* 12, no. 3 (Spring 1996): 53–59, Corwin Press, Inc.; and "When School Desegregation Fuels Education Reform: Lessons from Suburban St. Louis," *Educational Policy,* 8, no. 1 (March 1994), which she co-authored with Amy Stuart Wells and Robert L. Crain. For her work in education, she received the Community Leadership Award, Leadership St. Louis, 1996; Educator of the Year, St. Louis University Chapter of Phi Delta Kappa, 1982; Liberty Bell Award, Bar Association of Metropolitan St. Louis, 1984; and Woman of Achievement, 1991.